FREE VIDEO   FREE   FREE VIDEO

Essential Test Tips Video from Trivium Test Prep

Dear Customer,

Thank you for purchasing from Trivium Test Prep! We're honored to help you prepare for your GACE exam.

To show our appreciation, we're offering a **FREE *GACE Essential Test Tips* Video by Trivium Test Prep.*** Our video includes 35 test preparation strategies that will make you successful on the GACE. All we ask is that you email us your feedback and describe your experience with our product. Amazing, awful, or just so-so: we want to hear what you have to say!

To receive your **FREE *GACE Essential Test Tips* Video**, please email us at 5star@ triviumtestprep.com. Include "Free 5 Star" in the subject line and the following information in your email:

1. The title of the product you purchased.
2. Your rating from 1 – 5 (with 5 being the best).
3. Your feedback about the product, including how our materials helped you meet your goals and ways in which we can improve our products.
4. Your full name and shipping address so we can send your **FREE *GACE Essential Test Tips* Video**.

If you have any questions or concerns please feel free to contact us directly at 5star@triviumtestprep.com.

Thank you!

- Trivium Test Prep Team

*To get access to the free video please email us at 5star@triviumtestprep.com, and please follow the instructions above.

GACE Early Childhood Education (001, 002; 501) Exam Study Guide

COMPREHENSIVE REVIEW WITH PRACTICE TEST QUESTIONS FOR THE GEORGIA ASSESSMENTS FOR THE CERTIFICATION OF EDUCATORS

Table of Contents

Online Resources

To help you fully prepare for your GACE Early Childhood exam, Cirrus includes online resources with the purchase of this study guide.

Practice Test

In addition to the practice test included in this book, we also offer an online exam. Since many exams today are computer based, getting to practice your test-taking skills on the computer is a great way to prepare.

Flash Cards

A convenient supplement to this study guide, Cirrus's flash cards enable you to review important terms easily on your computer or smartphone.

From Stress to Success

Watch From Stress to Success, a brief but insightful YouTube video that offers the tips, tricks, and secrets experts use to score higher on the exam.

Reviews

Leave a review, send us helpful feedback, or sign up for Cirrus promotions—including free books!

Access these materials at:

www.cirrustestprep.com/gace-early-childhood-education-online-resources

Introduction

Congratulations on choosing to take the Georgia Assessments for the Certification of Educators (GACE) Early Childhood Education Assessment (001, 002; 501)! By purchasing this book, you've taken the first step toward becoming an early childhood educator.

This guide will provide you with a detailed overview of the GACE, so you know exactly what to expect on test day. We'll take you through all the concepts covered on the test and give you the opportunity to test your knowledge with practice questions. Even if it's been a while since you last took a major test, don't worry; we'll make sure you're more than ready!

WHAT IS THE GACE?

The GACE Early Childhood Education Assessment is a part of teaching licensure in Georgia. GACE scores are used to complete a state application for teacher certification. The exam ensures that the examinee has the skills and knowledge necessary to become an early childhood educator in Georgia public schools.

WHAT'S ON THE GACE?

The GACE Early Childhood Education Assessment consists of two multiple-choice tests designed to assess whether you possess the knowledge and skills necessary to become an early childhood educator in Georgia. Each test consists of seventy-five questions, and you have a maximum of two hours to complete each test. You may complete both tests in one session or elect to take them individually.

What's on the GACE Early Childhood Assessment?

Concepts	Percentage of Test
Test 1 (001)	
75 multiple-choice questions and 2 constructed response questions	
2 hours	

Subarea I: Reading and Language Arts	
▶ reading for literature and reading for information	
▶ literacy development, fluency, and comprehension	50%
▶ the writing process; tools and resource materials	
▶ speaking, listening, and presenting	
▶ English-language grammar and vocabulary development	

Subarea II: Social Studies	
▶ information processing skills	
▶ historical understanding; history processes	25%
▶ geography concepts and processes	
▶ government, civics, and economics concepts and processes	

Subarea III: Analysis	
▶ appropriate English language arts teaching approaches	25%
▶ appropriate social studies teaching approaches	

Test II (002)	
75 multiple-choice questions	
2 hours	

Subarea I: Mathematics	
▶ counting and cardinality	
▶ operations and algebraic thinking	
▶ numbers and operations in base 10	53%
▶ numbers and fractions	
▶ measurement concepts and data	
▶ geometry	

Subarea II: Science	
▶ characteristics of science	
▶ Earth science	30%
▶ physical science	
▶ life science	

Concepts	Percentage of Test
Test II (002)	
75 multiple-choice questions	
2 hours	
Subarea III: Health Education, Physical Education, and the Arts	17%
▶ health and physical education concepts and influences	
▶ knowledge of the arts, including dance, music, visual arts, and theatre arts	

Note: The combined Test I (001) and Test II (002) has the test code 501.

How is the GACE Scored?

On the GACE, the number of correctly answered questions are used to create your scaled score. Scores are scaled to a number in the range 100 – 300, a passing score being 250. The score shows your performance on the test as a whole and is scaled to allow comparison across various versions of the tests.

There is no penalty for guessing on the GACE, so be sure to eliminate answer choices and answer every question. If you still do not know the answer, guess; you may get it right! Keep in mind that some multiple-choice questions are experimental questions for the purpose of the GACE test makers and will not count toward your overall score. However, since those questions are not indicated on the test, you must respond to every question.

Upon completing your test, you will immediately receive your score. Your score report will be available on your online account. Score reports contain the overall scaled score, the passing status, and subarea scores that indicate your performance on each content area of the test. You can use these subarea scores to better understand your strengths and weaknesses in the material. Scores are automatically submitted to the Georgia Professional Standards Commission and added to your licensure application.

How is the GACE Administered?

The GACE is a computer-administered test. The GACE website allows you to take practice tests and tutorials to acclimate yourself to the computerized format. The GACE is available at testing centers across the nation.

On the day of your test, be sure to bring your admission ticket (which is provided when you register) and photo ID. You are allowed no other personal items in the testing area. Pens, pencils, scratch paper, and headphones (for the listening portion) are provided for you by the testing center. For details on what to expect at your testing center, refer to the GACE website.

ABOUT CIRRUS TEST PREP

Cirrus Test Prep study guides are designed by current and former educators and are tailored to meet your needs as an incoming educator. Our guides offer all of the resources necessary to help you pass teacher certification tests across the nation.

Cirrus clouds are graceful, wispy clouds characterized by their high altitude. Just like cirrus clouds, Cirrus Test Prep's goal is to help educators "aim high" when it comes to obtaining their teacher certification and entering the classroom.

ABOUT THIS GUIDE

This guide will help you master the most important test topics and also develop critical test-taking skills. We have built features into our books to prepare you for your tests and increase your score. Along with a detailed summary of the test's format, content, and scoring, we offer an in-depth overview of the content knowledge required to pass the test. Our sidebars provide interesting information, highlight key concepts, and review content so that you can solidify your understanding of the exam's concepts. Test your knowledge with sample questions and detailed answer explanations in the text that help you think through the problems on the exam and two full-length practice tests that reflect the content and format of the GACE. We're pleased you've chosen Cirrus to be a part of your professional journey!

Reading and Language Arts

EMERGENT LITERACY

LANGUAGE ACQUISITION

Language acquisition is the process through which humans develop the ability to understand and create words and sentences to communicate. Many experts believe that children have an innate ability to acquire **oral language** from their environment. Even before babies can speak, they cry and coo in reaction to environmental stimuli or to communicate their needs. They recognize basic variants in the speech patterns of those around them, such as articulation; they can also identify contrasts when exposed to new languages. This awareness, cooing, and crying quickly turn into **babbling**, the first stage of language acquisition. This stage generally lasts from six months to around twelve months. In this stage, infants make a variety of sounds but may begin to focus on sounds for which they receive positive reinforcement. For example, babbles such as *baba* and *yaya* tend to garner praise and excitement from parents, so these may be repeated until the coveted *mama* or *dada* is produced.

> **DID YOU KNOW?**
>
> Ninety-five percent of all babbling by babies throughout the world is composed of only twelve consonants: p, b, t, d, k, g, m, n, s, h, w, j.

At around one year old, but varying from child to child, children start using first words, generally nouns. During this single-word stage, or **holophrastic stage**, these solitary words are generally used to express entire ideas. For example, "Toy!" may mean "Give me the toy." After a few months, this shifts to two-word utterances such as "Mommy go" or "David bad." The **two-word stage** may last through early toddlerhood but generally gives rise to the **telegraphic phase** of oral language development at around **age two and a half**. In this stage, speech patterns become more advanced, though sometimes prepositions, articles, and other short words are missing. Telegraphic speech includes phrases such as "See plane go!" and "There go teacher." This stage persists until children are mostly fluent in the home language, generally at age three or four.

Like language, a child's journey to writing happens in phases and is heavily influenced by encouragement from parents, teachers, and caretakers. Writing development generally involves three areas:

1. conceptual knowledge (understanding the purpose of writing)
2. procedural knowledge (understanding how to form letters and words)
3. generative knowledge (using words to communicate a meaning)

Even children as young as two begin to draw pictures they use to communicate ideas—their first written representations. This develops into scribbling, which takes on a form more similar to letters. Wavy scribbling or mock handwriting may soon appear as children are exposed to print-rich home environments and classrooms. This emerges into forms that look like individual letters and then forms with actual letters that have some likeness to individual words strung together.

In the **transitional writing stage**, children begin writing letters with spaces in between, although real words are generally not yet being formed. Even in the transitional writing stage, however, many children can make successful attempts at copying letters and words from environmental sources. Writing a child's name or the name of a common classroom object on a card for a child to copy is a way to encourage transitional writing. Be mindful, however, that writing is still emergent, and children may invert letters or fail to make accurate copies of letters.

Table 1.1. Stages of Emergent Writing

Stage	Example
Drawing	
Scribbling	
Wavy scribbles	
Letter-like forms	

Stage	Example
Letter strings	MpLiToHg
Transitional writing	Jio Mpite
Invented and phonetic spelling	My NAM IS HaNa
Word and phrase writing	DOG PIG
Conventional spelling and sentences	HaNNah

As children gain knowledge of sounds, they begin a phase of invented **spelling**. They start communicating words and ideas more clearly, though many words may be represented by only a beginning and ending sound. It is vital to understand this stage as a natural part of the process of emergent writing and allow children to express ideas and practice writing without an overemphasis on spelling errors. As children gain more knowledge of sounds and words, they will begin writing whole words, first with simple single-letter sound constructions such as *dog, hat,* and *fun*. This progresses to the correct spelling of more words and eventually the stringing together of words to make phrases and even short sentences.

Supporting a young child's oral language development is crucial in the classroom. Teachers can help build vocabulary through conversation, songs, and reading aloud to students. Songs and developmentally appropriate books can help reinforce new vocabulary through cadence and repetition. Teachers narrating their own actions ("Now, I am getting the lunch ready") and introducing students to new vocabulary ("This is a drum") through pictures or objects paired with language can help young students as they look to adults for exposure to new words and phrases.

Above all, early childhood educators must ensure their classrooms are rich in conversation and questions. The more adults speak to and ask open-ended questions of young students, the greater students' opportunities to grow in oral language skills.

Print-rich classrooms, full of labeled objects and centers, will help students grasp conceptual knowledge as they see writing used to convey meaning behind objects in their surroundings as well as generative knowledge if students are asked to help in the labeling of such objects. Having a writing center full of different writing implements and other artistic media will encourage students' procedural knowledge as they practice writing letters and words and build fine motor skills. Teachers modeling their own use of writing and providing many opportunities for writing practice throughout the day will aid in students' understanding of the communicative purpose of writing.

It is also vital to encourage frequent writing practice, even outside of explicit instruction. Students at a dramatic play center, for example, might be encouraged to use a notepad to write down a customer's order or a chalkboard to model a teacher giving a lesson. Above all, teachers should ensure that they are scaffolding children's learning to accommodate multiple stages of development happening in a single classroom.

SAMPLE QUESTION

1) During free-choice center time, a kindergarten teacher notices that one of her students has gone to the writing center, taken a piece of lined paper, and written several misspelled phrases. What should the teacher do?

   A. explain the correct spelling of each word

   B. praise the student for the attempt and choosing to practice writing

   C. provide hand-over-hand guidance for the student to erase and rewrite the words

   D. target the student for more explicit spelling instruction

   Answers:

   A. Incorrect. The student will likely not retain this information, and the purpose of the writing center is practice and not perfection since the student is in the invented spelling stage.

   B. Correct. Practice is essential to developing writing and spelling skills, so praise is in order because the student chose this activity. Further, the student is likely in the normal and necessary invented spelling stage.

   C. Incorrect. While hand-over-hand guidance may be appropriate in some cases where motor skills are still developing and students are reticent to write, this student has already written the words. Erasing and rewriting the invented spelling is unnecessary and may be discouraging.

   D. Incorrect. This invented spelling is a normal stage, as students develop more accurate spelling skills through practice.

PRINT AWARENESS

Print awareness involves a basic understanding of the nature of reading: that we read from left to right and top to bottom, and that we are reading words on a page. Very young children without solid print awareness may believe that meaning is gleaned from pictures on a page rather than words. Some younger children may understand that books convey meaning but may not quite know how. Teachers may see these children modeling reading a book upside down.

Key to print awareness are many **concepts of print**. These are the many underlying principles that must be mastered before learning to read. They include things such as knowledge and identification of a word, letter, and sentence; knowledge of the many uses of print; and knowledge of the overarching structure of a book or story (title, beginning, middle, end).

Many students have some print awareness through **environmental print**, or the words printed throughout their everyday environment. Environmental print includes product names, street signs, business names, menus at restaurants, and any other print that students encounter in the normal course of their lives. Teachers can use popular environmental print such as the names and logos of popular children's products, stores, and restaurants to encourage pre-readers to "read" these names. Teachers should also consider using environmental print in the classroom in each of the home languages of their students. For example, a teacher may label the door in English, Spanish, Thai, and Vietnamese. This builds confidence and familiarity and reinforces the idea that these words in languages other than English also have meaning.

Figure 1.1. Concepts of Print Classroom Strategies

When working with young students, teachers should have students point to words on a page and also point to words (versus pictures) themselves during storybook reading since this will reinforce concepts of print and help students develop print awareness. This will help even very young students begin to understand that while both the pictures and words on the page contribute to the overall meaning, the part being read is the words, not the pictures.

SAMPLE QUESTION

2) Which of the following will help gauge a student's print awareness?

    A. asking a student to recount story events

    B. asking a student to point to a sentence

    C. asking a student to write the letter P

    D. asking a student what sound P makes

Answers:

A. Incorrect. This is a recall and comprehension gauging question. It is not related to print awareness.

B. Correct. Knowing the difference between a letter, word, and sentence is an important component of print awareness.

C. Incorrect. This is a motor skills and alphabet knowledge question.

D. Incorrect. This is a letter-sound correspondence question.

PHONOLOGICAL DEVELOPMENT

Phonological awareness is the general ability to understand that within the structure of oral language, there are subparts. These parts include individual words; **syllables**, or units (typically containing a single vowel sound) within words; **onsets**, or the beginning consonant sounds of words (*sw*-im); and **rimes**, or the letters that follow (sw-*im*). Having phonological awareness is a crucial early stage in learning to read and write, and it can be fostered in the initial levels through singing songs and repeating rhyming words and phrases. Any activities or speech that seek to break language into component parts or that help establish an understanding of syllables, onsets, and rimes—"Would *Son*-ya come to circle time?" "Do you want a *c*-at or a *h*-at for your birthday?"—are good choices for helping students begin to recognize the parts within language.

HELPFUL HINT

Remember that onsets are the first part of the word, or the first "button" readers see—the ON button. Rimes are the parts of the word that rhyme such as c-*at*, h-*at*, b-*at*, and so on.

The **alphabetic principle** presumes an understanding that words are made up of written letters that represent spoken sounds. In order to proceed with more advanced reading concepts, children must first have a firm grasp of letter sounds. There is no firm rule on the pace at which the letter sounds should be mastered in their entirety, although most experts agree that those with the greatest frequency and those that will allow children to begin sounding out short words quickly should generally be introduced first. It is also sometimes easiest for children to master simple sounds—/t/ and /s/, for example—over more challenging or confusing sounds such as /b/, /d/, and /i/. Regardless of the way a curriculum breaks up practice with the alphabetic principle (a letter of the week or a teaching of the letters and sounds in rapid succession, etc.), teachers should recognize that repetition is key and students must be given multiple exposures to each letter and sound.

DID YOU KNOW?

The alphabet song was copyrighted in 1835 but is actually an adaptation of a Mozart melody.

Phonemes are distinct units of sound and are the basic units of language. There are twenty-six letters in the alphabet, and there is some agreement among researchers that there are at least forty-four phonemes in English—some letters represent different phonemes and some phonemes are made up of more than one letter. There are eighteen consonant phonemes such as /r/ and /t/, fifteen vowel phonemes such as /Ā/ and /oi/, six r-controlled vowels such as /Ä/, and five digraphs such as /ch/ and /sh/.

Table 1.2. Phoneme Chart

Phoneme	Example	Phoneme	Example	Phoneme	Example
Consonants		**Vowels**		**R-Controlled Vowels**	
/b/	bat	/a/	lap	/ā/	hair
/d/	dog	/ā/	late	/ä/	art
/f/	fish	/e/	bet	/û/	dirt
/g/	goat	/ē/	see	/ô/	draw
/h/	hat	/i/	hit	/ēə/	rear
/j/	jump	/ī/	ride	/üə/	sure
/k/	kick	/o/	hop	**Diagrams/Digraphs**	
/l/	laugh	/ō/	rope	/zh/	measure
/m/	milk	/oo/	look	/ch/	chick
/n/	no	/u/	cut	/sh/	shout
/p/	pot	/ū/	cute	/th/	think
/r/	rat	/y//ü/	you	/ng/	bring
/s/	sit	/oi/	oil		
/t/	toss	/ow/	how		
/v/	vote	/ə/ (schwa)	syringe		
/w/	walk				
/y/	yak				
/z/	zoo				

Phonemic awareness refers to the knowledge of and ability to use these phonemes. This awareness generally does not come naturally, and students will need explicit instruction to master these skills. It is often best to differentiate instruction and work with students in smaller groups when working on phonemic awareness because proficiency levels may vary substantially.

Various activities can aid students in developing phonemic awareness. **Phoneme blending** involves students putting given sounds together to make words. To work on phoneme blending, teachers can say sounds and ask students what word is made: "I like /ch/ /ee/ /z/. What do I like? That's right, I like cheese." Teachers can also ask students to simply repeat or chorally repeat the sounds in words during circle time or storybook reading: "The car went vvvvv-rrrrr-oooo-m!"

HELPFUL HINT

Phoneme blending involves students blending sounds together like putting them in a blender to make a word. Phoneme segmentation involves students unblending, or segmenting, each sound like the segments of a worm.

Phoneme segmentation is generally the inverse of phoneme blending and involves students sounding out a word. Phoneme segmentation is important both for reading and spelling a word. More advanced phonemic awareness activities include **phoneme deletion**, in which a phoneme is removed to make a new word (e.g., ramp – /p/ = ram) and **phoneme substitution**, where one phoneme is changed to make a new word (e.g., fla/t/ to fla/p/).

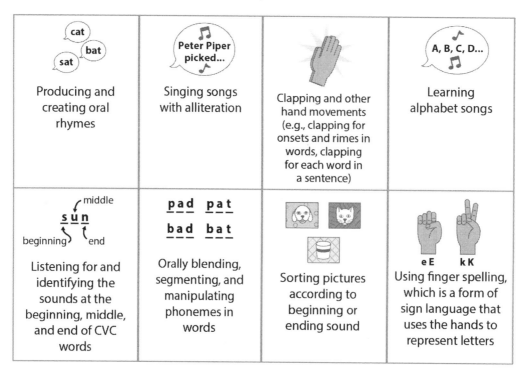

Figure 1.2. Phonological Awareness Classroom Strategies

Early childhood teachers should work on phonemic awareness with students in a variety of contexts. Having students manipulate language orally—"What word could I make if I took away the first letter of cow?"—and encouraging students in high-interest literacy activities in centers with alphabet boards, letter cards, alphabet sorters, and other manipulatives will provide multiple opportunities for students. Educators should also remember students will have varying backgrounds, skill levels, English language proficiencies, and possibly speech and language delays and hearing loss. Some students may need modifications for certain activities; this should be considered in the planning of inclusive activities.

SAMPLE QUESTIONS

3) Which activity would be most appropriate for students to practice onsets and the alphabetic principle?

    A. sorting small animals into tubs based on the initial letter sound of the animal's name

    B. asking students to help clap out the syllables in a student's name

    C. asking students to point to a sentence on a page

    D. having students remove a sound from a word and say the new word

Answers:

    A. **Correct.** This would help students to practice identifying both letter sounds and the initial sounds of words.

    B. Incorrect. This would help students master overall phonological awareness, but not the alphabetic principle or onsets in particular.

    C. Incorrect. This activity is more concerned with concepts of print.

    D. Incorrect. This is phoneme deletion, a strategy to work on phonemic awareness, not onsets and the alphabetic principle.

4) Mark, a kindergartener, has mastered his letter sounds. He is sitting at the oral reading table with Ms. Hayes, who has him practice reading a short sentence. He gets stuck on the word *glad* and looks up at her. Which strategy might Ms. Hayes have Mark use?

    A. phoneme substitution

    B. phoneme blending

    C. phoneme segmentation

    D. thinking of a rhyming word

Answers:

    A. Incorrect. This strategy would make a new word, not the word the student is struggling to read.

    B. Incorrect. In phoneme blending, the student is given the sounds and must then say the word.

C.   **Correct.** This is the strategy of "sounding out."

D.   Incorrect. This will help promote phonological awareness but will not help the student read the word.

Foundational Reading Skills

Phonics

Phonics is an age-old strategy for helping students read by connecting written language to spoken language or by correlating certain sounds with certain letters or groups of letters. Seminal to phonics instruction is a subset of the alphabetic principle—**letter-sound correspondence**. This correspondence is simply the knowledge of a phoneme associated with a given letter. Letter-sound correspondence is a foundational skill for effective phonics instruction, as most phonics strategies will require students to draw rapidly on this memory bank of letter sounds. As previously mentioned, most strategies for introducing students to the letter sounds draw on **high-frequency letter-sound correspondence**, where the most frequent and useful letter sounds are taught first. This will allow students to begin reading as soon as possible without having to wait for mastery of each letter sound.

Phonics instruction draws on the strategy of **decoding**, or the ability to pronounce the sounds of written words orally and glean meaning. Because of its focus on the specific sound structures of words, phonics instruction tends to involve more explicit, direct instruction and is not without critics, who believe it overemphasizes the mechanics of reading while sacrificing the enjoyment. However, most classrooms today employ a combination approach that balances inquiry-based student learning, allowing for the open exploration of high-interest literacy games and activities, with more direct instruction when necessary. Teachers may have any number of mandated or suggested organizational structures for teaching decoding, such as centers balanced with a teacher-directed table or a mandatory computer-based phonics drill segment, but it is highly likely that whatever curriculum a program or school uses, it will contain some phonics component. This approach is proven to work for most students and is adaptable to a variety of student skill levels and special learning needs.

Some words are decodable, meaning they follow basic principles of phonics. These words can typically be sounded out effectively if basic structural deviations, like long vowel sounds with a word ending in –e, and various digraphs, where two letters make a single sound such as /th/ and /ay/, are mastered.

However, there are some words that deviate from basic sound structures and cannot be sounded out. These words must be presented to students with great frequency so they can simply be memorized. These words must become **sight words**, or words that require no decoding because they are instantly recognized and read automatically. It is recommended that some high-frequency decodable words, such as *and* and *get*, also be memorized by sight so as to increase reading rate and fluency.

There are many lists of such words. The most popular is the Dolch Word List, which contains 315 words that are purported to be the most frequently used in English. Early childhood teachers might post some of these high-frequency words around the classroom for maximum exposure or encourage students to play games with sight word flashcards. Repetition will lead to mastery of these words and will help students read more quickly, fluently, and easily.

Figure 1.3. Phonics Classroom Strategies

Helping students practice phonics can involve a variety of strategies and activities, and these should always be developmentally appropriate for grade level and differentiated to accommodate students with varying needs and skills. English language learners will need additional practice with phonemes that are unique to English or simply not part of their home language. Students who come from a background with a language that does not use the Latin alphabet may need more background with the alphabetic principle than native speakers. Additionally, strategies such as visual cuing to indicate certain sounds may be needed to help hearing-impaired students master phonics.

Teachers may also need to provide extension and application activities for gifted students who may become bored with phonics study if they are already reading at a high level of proficiency. Frequently, these students can be accommodated within an existing lesson framework. For example, a teacher may aim for the bulk of her students to master two sight words per week from the Dolch list, but students who already know the whole list might practice spelling these words instead.

SAMPLE QUESTION

5) **The word** *elephant* **is**

    A.   decodable.

    B.   a high-frequency word.

    C.   not composed of phonemes.

    D.   inappropriate for phonics instruction.

Answers:

    A.   **Correct.** The word *elephant* can be decoded using phonics strategies.

    B.   Incorrect. *Elephant* is not one of the most frequently used words in English.

    C.   Incorrect. Phonemes are sounds, so each word has phonemes.

    D.   Incorrect. This word is illustrative of many sound structures.

FLUENCY

Fluency refers to the rate, accuracy, and expression of a piece when read. Fluency is an important measure of a student's reading development; lack of fluency will hamper overall comprehension as well as enjoyment of reading. Reading **rate** is a measure of speed and is generally calculated in words per minute. **Accuracy,** or the correct decoding of words, is generally entwined with rate when measuring fluency, as reading quickly but incorrectly is not desirable.

While fluency is not limited to oral reading, it is virtually impossible to assess fluency during silent reading, and most educators rely on frequent oral reading assessments to help determine student progress. While several standard measures exist, one of the most researched is the Hasbrouck-Tindal oral reading fluency chart. This chart is designed to measure progress over the course of the school year and from grade to grade and compares students in percentiles with their peers on a scale of words read correctly per minute. It is important to remember that all students will develop fluency on a different timeline, and assessments of fluency are most accurate when they are developmentally appropriate and when they are not presented as high-stakes testing situations.

In addition to rate and accuracy, **prosody**, or the overall liveliness and expressiveness of reading, is also a skill to nurture in students. Prosody may involve appropriate pauses and various changes in pitch and intonation based on punctuation and the overall meaning of the piece. Developing prosody in students should involve a combination of modeling by teachers—as they read stories, passages, and even directions aloud—and giving students plenty of opportunities for oral reading practice.

Educators may find it challenging to find time for oral reading assessment in the classroom as they balance multiple priorities. However, teachers must make time to listen to all students, regardless of grade level, read aloud with regularity. While examining written work and performance on independent or group practice activities may give some indication of a student's overall development, to get the fullest picture teachers must gather as much data as possible. Assessing student fluency through oral reading is seminal to an overall understanding of a particular student's learning situation.

> **HELPFUL HINT**
>
> There are various software applications that allow teachers to record and track students' oral reading progress. While this technology cannot replace frequent live listening to students reading, it can augment it and speaks to the importance of oral reading in gauging students' overall literacy development.

Fluency is highly correlated with comprehension because students who struggle to read and decode individual words will have difficulty comprehending entire sentences and paragraphs. Additionally, students who read at a very slow rate may have trouble recalling what they have read. It is well worth the time investment to listen to students read aloud as much as possible.

SAMPLE QUESTION

6) A second-grade teacher notices that his students often read in monotone during oral reading practice. Which strategy would best help his students develop prosody?

    A. setting aside timed oral reading each day

    B. modeling an appropriate reading rate

    C. using ability grouping for silent reading

    (D) having students act out a play from a script

    Answers:

    A. Incorrect. Timed reading does not necessarily develop expression.

    B. Incorrect. Prosody refers to expression, not reading rate.

    C. Incorrect. Prosody is part of oral reading.

    D. **Correct.** This would give students practice reading expressively.

LITERATURE AND INFORMATIONAL TEXTS

GENRES

It is important that students of all ages be exposed to a wide variety of texts. **Informational texts**, or **nonfiction texts**, are texts about the world around us and generally do not use characters to convey information. Science and social studies texts fall into this category. These informational texts are often structured in such a way to organize information in a format that is accessible and meaningful to students.

As part of an introduction to different types of texts, a teacher might ask elementary-aged students to analyze elements of their textbooks or workbooks. Do they have bold headings to help the reader understand when new ideas are being introduced? Do they have **sidebars** to give readers additional information alongside the main body of text?

In contrast, **literary texts**, or **fiction texts**, are usually stories made up by the author. While they may contain true elements or be based on actual events, they usually include plenty of elements designed to keep and capture the reader's interest. They generally have **characters**, which may be real or imagined people, animals, or creatures, and a **plot**, or sequence of story events. The **setting** of fiction texts may be any time or place past, present, future, real, or imagined. While teachers may put a lot of focus on short stories that are highly accessible for young students, it is also important to expose children to other genres so that students get comprehension practice with texts that are unfamiliar at first.

In **drama**, most of the story is centered around dialogue between characters. They are usually separated into segments like chapters known as **acts** and smaller subsegments (generally with a consistent setting) known as **scenes**. Using drama in the classroom is a great way to get students interested in different types of texts. Consider setting up a simple **stage** in a kindergarten or elementary classroom as a natural outgrowth of a dramatic play center sometimes found in preschool classrooms. Building on students' innate curiosity and imagination, the possibilities are endless. Acting out dramas not only helps students work on expressive reading (prosody), but it also reinforces social and emotional learning as students analyze the emotions and actions of characters.

While poetry may be associated with older children, even young students can appreciate and recognize **rhyme**. Poetry with rhyme can help reinforce phonological awareness and is a natural outgrowth of many young children's love of song. **Meter**—or the rhythm, or beat, of the poem—can also be used to engage young students with different texts as a beat can be clapped to, stomped to, or even danced to! Many timeless books for children—such as *One Fish, Two Fish, Red Fish, Blue Fish* and *Each Peach Pear Plum*—have both rhyme and meter and give young children exposure to poetry. Young writers may even begin to write simple poems with one or two **stanzas**, or groups of **lines** similar to paragraphs. Students should be encouraged to recognize and create their own rhyming words as an additional outgrowth of phonological awareness. Asking students to name all the words they can think of that rhyme with dog, for example, will allow for continued practice with rhymes.

The structural elements of literature such as characters, setting, conflict, plot, resolution, point of view, and theme can be introduced alongside other literacy activities, even with students who are pre-readers. Consider bringing these elements into guided storybook sessions while asking questions such as:

- ▶ "Who are the characters on this page?" (characters)
- ▶ "Where does this story happen?" (setting)

- "Why was _____mad/happy/worried, etc.?" (conflict/plot)
- "What happened after_____?" and "How was (problem) fixed?" (conflict/plot/resolution)

Although **point of view**, or the perspective from which the story is told (first person, *I, we*; third person, *he, she, it,* or *they*; sometimes second person, *you*), may be harder for very young students to grasp, teachers can begin introducing the basic concept of differing points of view by reading the **narrator's** part in one voice and each different character in a different voice and encouraging students to do the same. For older students, second-person point of view can be practiced by reading and writing letters: to other students, the teacher, or administrators or other school personnel.

SAMPLE QUESTIONS

7) **Which of the following is an example of an activity that might be used with students to introduce informational texts?**

   A.   having students locate fiction books at the school library

   B.   having students examine the way their social studies textbook is organized

   C.   having students answer questions from different points of view

   D.   asking students questions about different characters in a story

   Answers:

   A.   Incorrect. This pertains to fiction texts, not informational texts.

   B.   Correct. This activity would help students see the structure of an informational text with which they are familiar.

   C.   Incorrect. This would pertain to fiction texts, not informational texts.

   D.   Incorrect. This would pertain to fiction texts, not informational texts.

8) **Which sentence is written in the third-person point of view?**

   A.   Harriet likes to go fishing on the weekends, though she has never caught anything.

   B.   I generally enjoy reading a variety of literature types, but I like historical fiction the best.

   C.   We need to determine the type of problem before we can think about solving it.

   D.   You really must stop calling me at all hours of the night; you are not being considerate.

   Answers:

   A.   Correct. This is a sentence written in third person with the appropriate third-person pronoun *she*.

B.   Incorrect. The pronoun *I* indicates that this sentence is written in first-person point of view.

C.   Incorrect. *We* is a first-person plural pronoun, so this sentence is written in the first person.

D.   Incorrect. The second-person pronoun *you* indicates that this sentence is written in the second person.

KEY IDEAS AND DETAILS

As students progress in their literacy and are able to decode longer passages with some consistency, by the second and third grade the focus will shift to the **comprehension** of many different types of passages. However, even students still practicing decoding and very young pre-readers can be given ample opportunities to explore the **central**, or main, **idea** of a story and make predictions about what might happen next. Questions such as "What was this book about?" and "What do you think character X will do next?" will help students make predictions and **summarize** or condense the main elements of a story.

As the stories read to students become more complex and as students begin reading their own stories, other literary elements can be introduced. Students of all ages generally enjoy stories with **themes**, or topics, to which they can relate or are already exploring. Integrated curriculums, or those that structure several cross-curricular units around a central theme, are popular in many early childhood and some lower elementary settings.

Even without a formal daily or weekly theme in the classroom, teachers can help students make connections by integrating texts from other domains such as science and social studies into literacy activities. For example, a unit on conservation might feature a story that includes a **moral**, or lesson, about the importance of conserving natural resources. Teachers might even encourage students to further explore their own interests and create their own integrated literary experiences by selecting and reading multiple works centered on a theme of their choosing.

Teachers may have students recall important **details** from a text or **analyze** the structure of a piece. Is it a narrative that tells a story, a description of something, or an essay designed to persuade? Can students make **inferences**, or logical conclusions, based on the text? Making inferences is an important skill in developing overall comprehension as it allows students to go deeper than the literal meaning and make conclusions based on previously obtained knowledge and experiences. Whenever teachers ask students to make an inference based on a text, they should be sure to ask them to support their inference with evidence. "How do you know this?" "What made you think this?" "Which part of the story/passage made you think this?" are all good follow-up questions for inferring activities.

As students advance in their comprehension skills, it is also important to ensure that students know that sometimes we all make faulty inferences and that we must constantly evaluate whether we are projecting our own beliefs and experiences onto a text that lacks support for a conclusion we drew. This foundational skill of making sound conclusions from texts will be the base upon which several future higher-level skills, such as identifying bias and providing counterpoints to an argument, will rest.

It is also highly worthwhile that students comprehend images embedded in texts. This helps students get the most from informational texts like textbooks and informational websites or educational software. Pointing out and helping students understand how visual elements promote a greater understanding of concepts or ideas that the author is trying to convey will help students be cognizant of these important elements that exist alongside text. Images can also aid struggling readers to decode. While students should not be reliant on pictures, most texts for young readers include ample images to aid in students' overall understanding and enjoyment, and these should be pointed out and discussed when appropriate.

SAMPLE QUESTION

9) John, a second-grade student, has an assignment to read a paragraph from his social studies textbook and write a sentence that states the central idea. What can John's teacher do to help him with this task?

   A.   ask John what he liked about what he read

   B.   ask John to list all the details

   C.   go over key vocabulary with John

   D.   ask John what he thought was most important

Answers:

   A.   Incorrect. This will not necessarily aid John in identifying the central idea.

   B.   Incorrect. This might be a start, but if the assignment is to identify the central idea, the teacher will want John to limit himself to only the most important or overall idea.

   C.   Incorrect. This will not necessarily help John generate the main idea.

   D.   **Correct.** This will help lead John to the central idea of the paragraph.

ORGANIZATIONAL STRUCTURES OF TEXT

Authors organize information in such a way as to get their point across as clearly as possible. They tend to use a text structure that suits their purpose. This structure may be a **sequence** of events, such as a news story recounting the days leading up to an important event, or a thorough **description** of something, as in the opening pages of a novel, which might describe the main character in finite detail.

Many historical texts are written in a **cause-and-effect** pattern where the cause is presented first and the result is discussed next. A chapter in a social studies text about the Industrial Revolution, for example, may follow this pattern as the Industrial Revolution is cited as the cause for a change in working and living conditions in many cities.

Other works may be organized in a **problem-solution structure**. This might be taught through a collaborative activity where students identify a problem in the classroom, school, or community and then write a letter to a decision maker outlining both the nature of the issue and a possible solution.

Students could also be challenged to **compare and contrast** or explain how two things from their everyday experience are similar and different. Charts and other visual/graphic organizers can help students organize their thoughts. A teacher may ask students, for example, what the differences and similarities are between first and second grade. This might even lead to a persuasive writing assignment about this topic.

While reading nonfiction texts is important, inciting a love of reading is often best accomplished through multiple exposures to high-interest fiction, both classic and contemporary. In order to facilitate deep comprehension of these narratives, teachers can help students understand key elements through a **plot diagram**. This graphic organizer helps students identify the **exposition**, or beginning, of the story, which sets up the reader for what is to come by describing the time, place, and main characters. The plot organizer will then help students move into the primary problem driving the story, or the **conflict**, and the **rising action**, or sequence of events leading to the eventual **climax**, or turning point, which is the apex of the diagram. The curve slopes sharply downward as the **falling action**, or results of the climax, unfolds. The diagram closes with the final **resolution**, or ending of the story. It is important to impart to students that the resolution might not always be happy, but all stories do have one.

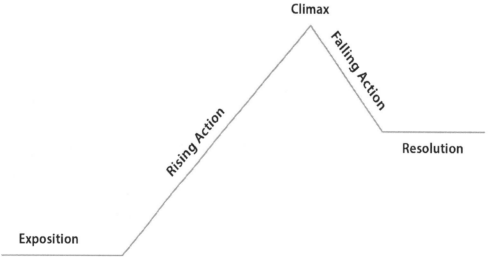

Figure 1.4. Plot Diagram

Introducing the plot diagram is easiest when students already have some background with a story. Teachers may draw on a popular children's movie or fairy tale to introduce these elements. If students are not struggling to comprehend a new text while being introduced to these elements, the understanding will likely come more quickly. Timeless stories with plots that students know by heart are ideal for an initial exploration of the plot diagram.

SAMPLE QUESTION

10) Ms. Jones wants to introduce her first-grade students to new types of text structures they have not seen before. Which activity would best meet her goal?

A. ask students to go to the library and explain the different sections

B. bring in magazines, pamphlets, newspapers, and other items for students to explore

C. have students compare and contrast two different storybook characters they have read about

D. divide students into groups and have them create a plot diagram about their favorite movie

Answers:

A. Incorrect. This activity might expose students to different books but not necessarily different text structures.

B. Correct. This allows for hands-on learning and will help Ms. Jones explain how these different texts are structured for their intended purpose.

C. Incorrect. This will help students compare and contrast characters, not text structures.

D. Incorrect. This will not expose students to different text structures.

POINT OF VIEW

A teacher may refer students to an evil character in a story they have just read or that the class has read together. "Why don't you like this character?" the teacher might query. The initial answers will generally be limited to the actions of said character and what he or she did or did not do that led to the story's conflict. The teacher might then remind students that the character is a creation of the author, so the real reason they like or dislike a character has to do with **point of view**, the perspective the author takes toward a character or subject. It is most likely the author's description, or point of view toward given characters, that makes students like or dislike them.

A discussion of point of view may begin to extend to the structural elements such as first person (author as narrator and generally protagonist), second person (author speaking directly to the reader), and third person (author uses third-person pronouns such as he, she, it, etc.). Teachers might help students associate certain pronouns with certain points of view but should keep in mind the developmental appropriateness of such exercises per the specific student population. It may be more appropriate to ask very young students questions like "Who told the story?" and "What was (character name) like?" to begin to introduce these concepts.

Point of view may also impact the reader's perspective of a text in its conveyance or non-conveyance of information. With first-person point of view, for example, the reader may empathize heavily with the protagonist's perspective because the reader feels that he or she knows the narrator well. Above all, the perspective the reader holds toward a character, setting, topic, or situation will heavily impact the way he or she perceives a work. Because of this, it is vital that students begin to differentiate between their own point of view, colored by their unique perspective, and that which is explicitly stated in the text. This is especially important in integrating literacy with socioemotional learning because we want students to be able to appreciate the myriad perspectives on a given issue or subject and understand that their own point of view may be one of many. Teachers can facilitate a discussion of this by asking students who their favorite or least favorite character in a piece was. Ideally, there will be divergent opinions, and this is an excellent opportunity to explain the ways in which many people can read the same story and have a different point of view.

SAMPLE QUESTION

11) Some students in a kindergarten class are having trouble sharing classroom supplies. Which literacy activity might help students appreciate others' point of view?

   A. reading a story about a character who has to go without what he needs and asking students how they felt about the character

   B. having students write a paragraph on how they can do a better job in sharing classroom supplies

   C. asking students to distinguish between their flawed point of view and the point of view of the classroom rules, which are always correct

   D. reading a fairy tale to students and asking them if they identify more with the evil or good characters

Answers:

   A. **Correct.** This might help students look outside their own point of view to that of someone else and integrate socioemotional and literacy learning.

   B. Incorrect. This is not developmentally appropriate for a kindergarten class.

   C. Incorrect. This is not a literacy activity and might be a challenge for egocentric kindergarteners.

   D. Incorrect. This does not help students see things from a different point of view.

INTEGRATING WRITTEN, VISUAL, AND ORAL INFORMATION

Most children's earliest experiences with reading are with **picture books**. Timeless titles such as *Have You Seen My Duckling?* and *Pancakes for Breakfast* can be appreciated by young children and their parents alike, and being read to from a young age is positively associated with future interest in reading. Picture books help young children engage in "pretend reading" by recounting a story from memory or using a picture book to "read" to a sibling or parent. It is important that educators avoid relegating picture books to the discard pile too early or chide children for their enjoyment of **graphic novels**. Graphics have a place in enhancing interest and comprehension of texts and are prevalent in much of the written media that is consumed in daily life. In fact **visual** literacy, or the ability to comprehend visual texts, is an important predecessor to being able to comprehend more sophisticated written works.

> **DID YOU KNOW?**
>
> Reading to children has a strong correlation to future achievement. According to PISA (Program for International Student Assessment) results from fourteen countries, students whose parents read books to them during the first year of school averaged fourteen points higher on a reading assessment taken at age fifteen.

Teachers may use many types of **multimedia presentations** in the classroom, for example, Power Point, a Smartboard, or a simple white board. Adding visuals to aid in student understanding is important and may help students who process information most easily when it is presented visually. While long lectures are certainly not developmentally appropriate in an early childhood classroom, teachers might project images to use as a springboard for a discussion or writing prompt. Teachers may have elementary students create their own multimedia presentations on a story they have read or have preschool students use a tablet to record a scene they create using toy dinosaurs.

Many preschool classrooms have routine recordings of various **staged** productions as a natural outgrowth of the happenings at the dramatic play center. **Oral presentations** can also be excellent additions to the classroom routine and are easiest when students present about something they know; this generally takes the form of show and tell. In this way teachers can help students begin to process information coming from a variety of sources, both auditory and visual.

It is important that teachers help students compare multiple sources of information. They may take students to see a stage play based on a story the class read or show the film version or play an audio recording of a book. This helps students understand that visual and auditory information may not always match what the mind imagines from reading a story. The characters may look or sound different or the setting may be far from what was imagined.

Teachers might also help students compare multiple texts that seek to convey the same information. For example, one great activity might be to bring in a newspaper article in plain black and white font and have students compare it with an elaborately illustrated magazine article on the same topic. This helps reinforce the role of visual aids in understanding and may even prompt a discussion on the appeal of different types of texts to different audiences, as some readers may prefer the brevity and simplicity of the newspaper article.

Teachers will also want to draw students toward a comprehension of various visual elements embedded in their everyday texts, such as charts and tables in textbooks and on websites and even nutritional information on food packaging. It is essential that literacy is viewed as a complete capability to access written information and that activities be tailored to ensure students have multiple opportunities to practice understanding information presented in many different ways.

SAMPLE QUESTION

12) **Mr. Johnson has a class of kindergarteners who are learning about using visual information to convey ideas. Which literacy activity might he integrate into a science unit on bugs?**

   A.   have students read multiple books on this topic and give oral reports to the class

   B.   have students go outside and find as many bugs as they can

   C.   split the students into groups and have them write a story in which a bug is the main character

   D.   have students create a bug picture book and present it to the class

Answers:

   A.   Incorrect. This does not help students understand visual information.

   B.   Incorrect. This might help students understand more about bugs but is not literacy related.

   C.   Incorrect. This does not help students understand visual information.

   D.   Correct. This helps students understand how the visual representations of bugs in their picture book aid in an understanding of bugs.

TEXT COMPLEXITY

Finding a balance between the complexity of a text and an individual student's current level of literacy development can be challenging. Many programs recognize this challenge and structure goal setting and student assessments in a growth-over-time approach. Regardless of the milestones laid out by a school or district, teachers should always aim for students to tackle ever more sophisticated texts as they develop the foundational skills they need to take on new challenges. However, this does not mean to push students beyond what they can decode. Giving students developmentally inappropriate texts may lead to a denigration of confidence and a lack of interest and enthusiasm for reading.

Many factors contribute to a text's complexity. Before determining appropriateness, texts should be evaluated qualitatively, quantitatively, and per their match to the reader. Quantitative measurements include anything for which a number can be calculated, such as **word frequency**, length of words and **sentence length**, average syllables per word, and so on. These quantitative calculations may result in a range or score being allotted to a text. The most popular of these is that calculated by MetaMetrics, a company that uses word frequency and sentence length in an equation that yields a score. MetaMetrics assigns scores to both readers and texts. Those assigned to readers typically come from standardized tests and measure a student's current level of reading ability; these are called reader measures.

MetaMetrics also assigns **Lexile ranges** to texts called Lexile test measures. While these ranges do not have a direct correlation to grade level in the strictest sense, charts can be used to glean the typical ranges for a given grade. The company purports that the best results come when the reader measure falls within a "sweet spot" range per the text measure.

More than likely, much of what students read (textbooks, passages in software programs, published children's literature) has already been assigned a Lexile text measure. Teachers can raise students' chances of enjoyment and comprehension of texts by ensuring that the Lexile text measure fits within the average range for the grade level and, more importantly, for the individual student's reader measure.

Table 1.3. Lexile Reader and Text Measures for Early Childhood

Grade	Reader Measures, Midyear *25th to 75th Percentile* This is the typical range of reading ability for students in each grade. These measures are designed to help compare a student's level to a typical range; they are not intended to be standards. There are no reader measures for kindergarten students. Rather, text measures are descriptive of what is most appropriate for most kindergarten readers.	Text Measures These text measures have been revised from previous measures to better align with the Common Core State Standards for English Language Arts to ensure that students will meet these standards and be "college and career ready" by the end of high school.
K	---	BR40L to 230L
1	BR120L to 295L	190L to 530L
2	170L to 545L	420L to 650L
3	415L to 760L	520L to 820L

There are, of course, other metrics for measuring the readability of a text. Scales such as the Flesch-Kincaid Grade Level, the Gunning-Fog Index, and the SMOG index may also provide text analytics. A specific program or school may also use another proprietary tool such as Accelerated Reader Book Finder or Scholastic Book Levels.

Beyond the quantitative measures determined by Lexile and others are qualitative measures such as the layout of the text (illustrations, text size), the overall text **structure** (simple narrative chronology, more advanced argumentative essay), **sentence structure** (prevalence of simple or more complex sentences), **levels of meaning** (whether ideas are explicitly or implicitly communicated), and **knowledge demand** (the cultural knowledge or other ideas that the reader must already know). The overall language and **vocabulary** of the text also generally fall under qualitative measures, although some quantitative scales measure the frequency of vocabulary with which students of a particular age or grade are unlikely to be familiar.

No singular measure of any text is sufficient to determine appropriateness for all students. Consider, for example, that Lexile ranges do not take into account the prevalence of mature subject matter and that overall appropriateness must always be considered. Teachers should also always keep in mind the need to differentiate literacy instruction in the classroom. The early childhood years present students with a wide range of previous pre-reading experiences, and educators often find themselves in classrooms of students with a vast array of reading abilities. While literacy development requires the reading of more and more complex texts, it does students little good to be constantly presented with inaccessible reading material. In fact, this can lead to the development of bad habits such as guessing at or skipping unfamiliar words instead of making a conscious effort to decode and waiting for the help of a teacher before confidently trying an unfamiliar word or text.

Whatever strategy a given program employs to address individualization of reading instruction (pull-out, push-in, small groups, intervention teacher, etc.), teachers must strive to find a just-right level of text complexity where students are challenged but not frustrated. Teachers must also rely on their own judgment and knowledge of their students alongside any formal tools used to help measure text complexity.

SAMPLE QUESTION

13) **Which of the following is the best way to differentiate instruction in a first-grade reading classroom?**

A.   practice oral reading only with the more advanced students so those struggling will not feel uncomfortable

B.   use only texts on the lower end of the first-grade Lexile range to ensure they are accessible to all students

C.   set aside time for students to engage in silent reading with a teacher-selected book based on student ability and interests

D.   conduct additional phonics drills with the students who need help with decoding while the other students do a science experiment

Answers:

A.   Incorrect. All students need oral reading practice to develop fluency, rate, and prosody.

B.   Incorrect. This will fail to challenge more advanced students and may be too challenging for others.

C.   **Correct.** This method ensures each student is reading a text appropriate for his or her current skill level.

D.   Incorrect. This might be seen as a punishment and might decrease student confidence.

WRITING

DEVELOPMENTAL STAGES OF WRITING

In their overall plan for developing literacy in students, teachers should give students plenty of opportunities to practice writing alongside reading and analyzing texts. It is important to ensure conscious writing instruction and practice as research suggests that this is sometimes an overlooked component of early childhood literacy curriculum. Some studies even suggest that many pre-kindergarten and kindergarten students spend less than three minutes a day on writing practice.

Learning to write involves three distinct and previously mentioned components: conceptual knowledge, procedural knowledge, and generative knowledge. In helping young students develop conceptual knowledge of writing, teachers should focus on activities that show students the link between print and its intended purpose. Environmental print is a great resource for helping students develop this knowledge as teachers point out classroom signs and posters or those in the school building and on the playground. They can further build early conceptual knowledge by having students **draw** or **scribble** to communicate their own feelings and ideas.

> **QUICK REVIEW**
>
> What are concepts of print? How can teachers encourage print awareness in their classrooms?

Procedural knowledge involves the nuts and bolts of writing. Procedural knowledge–building activities are those that build awareness of basic letter formation, the knowledge that words are made up of letters, the knowledge that words have spaces between them, and the overall mechanics of writing. Procedural knowledge and the alphabetic principle are entwined, and the letter sounds and names should be reinforced when consciously instructing correct letter formation.

Additionally, procedural knowledge of writing will coincide with the development of fine motor skills. Fine motor skills development in the classroom cannot be overemphasized, particularly in a preschool or kindergarten setting. As in any part of emergent literacy, teachers will have students with widely divergent levels of fine motor proficiency. It is essential the classroom provides a variety of opportunities for students to build these skills through the use of manipulatives such as alphabet boards and puzzles and a variety of writing implements such as crayons, markers, and pencils.

The mechanics of writing will generally involve explicit spelling instruction, and this will likely be part of a program's curriculum. It is important to view spelling as part of a developmental continuum and not overemphasize correct spelling too early when preschool students are still forming mock letters or letter strings. However, a standard **continuum of spelling** can be referenced to tailor spelling instruction appropriate to grade level while always keeping in mind the differing developmental levels within the classroom.

Table 1.4. Continuum of Spelling

By the end of first grade, most students should be able to correctly spell short words with . . .	short vowel sounds with a consonant-verb-consonant (cat, dog, pin) pattern [CVC]
	vowel-consonant pattern (up, egg) and [VC]
	simple consonant-vowel pattern (go, no) [CV]
	consonant blends and digraphs in simple and high-frequency words (chat, that) [CCVC]
By the end of second grade, most students should be spelling words with . . .	final consonant blends (rant, fast, bend, link) [CVCC]
	regular long vowel patterns (ride, tube) [CVC]
	double consonant endings (lick, fuss)
	more complex long vowel patterns (suit, fail)
	r-controlled vowels (near, bear, hair, are)
By the end of third grade, most students should be able to spell words with . . .	diphthongs (coil, soon, enjoy, wow)
	soft g's and c's (dice, hedge)
	short vowel patterns (head, sought)
	silent consonants (tomb, known, gnaw, wrote)
	advanced digraphs and blends (phase, character, whose)
	contractions
	soft g's and c's (dice, hedge)
	short vowel patterns (head, sought)
	silent consonants (tomb, known, gnaw, wrote)
	advanced digraphs and blends (phase, character, whose)
	contractions
	two-syllable words
	compound words
	words with suffixes that show number or degree (fastest, foxes)
	special spelling rules such as doubling the final letter on CVC words when adding certain suffixes (napping, saddest)

Explicit spelling instruction will generally begin with simple consonant-vowel-consonant (CVC) patterns and progress as students learn new phonics structures. Practice with homophones, or words that have the same pronunciation but a different spelling and meaning, should begin in third grade, or sooner for some students. Common homophones include there/their/they're, *to/two/too*, and so on. It is important to point out to students that software applications that might detect spelling errors in other words often fail to pick up on spelling errors with homophones, so students should be extra vigilant when editing and revising writing containing these words.

> **DID YOU KNOW?**
>
> Diphthongs are sounds created by two vowels together.

It is also important to balance more explicit spelling practice with time to allow students to practice the third part of emergent writing, generative knowledge. In this domain students learn to write for a purpose that goes beyond simply forming a word and other mechanical concerns. While preschool students may not be able to write their own stories, teachers at this level can still give students practice by having them dictate a story that the teacher writes for them and perhaps even reads back to the class.

As students master more of the procedural knowledge of writing, they can begin generating more pieces on their own. Students generally progress from writing letter strings and word-like structures under a picture they have drawn to writing and spelling simple words to constructing sentences to constructing stories. It is important that the communicative purpose of each be emphasized to help students construct the generative knowledge of writing. A teacher might ask, for example, a student to talk about his or her picture and include an explanation of the letter strings underneath. The student has likely included them to describe or name the picture.

SAMPLE QUESTION

14) **Which word has a CVC pattern?**

   A. gap

   B. onto

   C. drink

   D. and

   Answers:

   A. **Correct.** The pattern is *g* (consonant), *a* (vowel), *p* (consonant).

   B. Incorrect. This word has a vowel-consonant-vowel pattern.

   C. Incorrect. This word has a consonant-vowel-consonant-consonant pattern.

   D. Incorrect. This is a vowel-consonant-consonant pattern.

Types of Writing

Once students are generating their own written pieces, it is prudent to expose them to different types of writing both as readers and writers. **Expository** writing is usually used to inform readers or give a description and may be anything from a recipe in a cookbook to a paragraph in a science or social studies textbook. Expository writing may also be highly **descriptive**, using many rhetorical techniques to describe a person, place, societal problem, or any topic of interest. **Persuasive** writing usually presents an argument and attempts to convince the reader of a certain perspective on the issue. In contrast to expository writing, **narrative** writing tells a story.

Students are primarily exposed to narrative texts in the preschool and early elementary years, and they may be somewhat unfamiliar with other rhetorical techniques. Teachers might introduce descriptive writing by reading a few sentences in a product advertisement and having students imagine what the item is like before showing them the ad. They might then have students write their own description of something they find on the playground or the school cafeteria. Practice with persuasive writing can be particularly engaging. Students might write about a subject of personal interest, for instance a letter to the principal to convince her to allow pets at school, or even a letter to a teacher to persuade him to stop assigning homework!

Students should also practice identifying the rhetorical conventions used in types of literature they encounter. Is a sidebar on a science worksheet attempting to persuade students to recycle? Is a paragraph in a story giving a detailed description of a place? Pointing these things out and engaging students in analyzing the intended purpose of everything they read and write will help them appreciate the need for multiple types of writing.

SAMPLE QUESTION

15) Mr. Dale's third-grade student Sarah is working on a short descriptive paragraph describing her physical appearance. Sarah is having trouble generating ideas for her writing. Which of the following questions could Mr. Dale propose to help Sarah?

A.   What do you want to write about?

B.   What color is your hair?

C.   How many red shirts do you have?

D.   What do you want to persuade readers about?

Answers:

A.   Incorrect. This will not help Sarah as she has already been assigned a topic.

B.   Correct. This question will help Sarah understand the type of things she needs to describe.

C.   Incorrect. This question will not help Sarah describe her appearance.

D.   Incorrect. This is a descriptive and not persuasive writing assignment.

THE AUTHORING CYCLE

Students should understand that writing is a process and that even professional writers go through several phases before their finished product is released. This **authoring cycle** generally includes several phases in which ideas are transformed into written form to effectively communicate meaning. Students first need to **brainstorm** ideas. This can take many forms, and teachers might have the entire class generate ideas for writing topics and record them on the board or screen as an initial step.

Students can then create their own webs or **outlines** to organize their ideas. This initial planning can help students organize their overall point and supporting details. These activities can be based on a book they have read, where they take a stance on the work (e.g., "I liked the book," "I did not like the book," "My favorite/least favorite part was…") and then list the reasons why or why not. Students might also write a simple expository piece in which they introduce an overall topic and then use supporting details to inform the reader. Brainstorming activities can also help students organize the events they wish to recount when writing narratives.

After the brainstorming is complete, students draft their piece and link their ideas together with an introductory statement, support, and concluding section or statement. With scaffolding, students must then go through a **revision** and **editing** process in which they strengthen their piece through the addition of more supporting details and connecting words (because, also, then) and proofread for capitalization, end marks, and spelling.

Teachers may aid students in the revision process by providing a simple checklist to help students ensure they have met certain criteria. One simple revision checklist is the **COPS** mnemonic. This stands for **C**apitalization, **O**rganization, **P**unctuation, and **S**pelling and is used with success in many early elementary classrooms. Teachers may also employ peer and/or teacher feedback as part of the overall revision process. Receiving feedback helps reinforce that the overarching purpose of writing is to communicate ideas, so the perceptions and suggestions of multiple readers must be taken into account when revising a piece.

Students should also **publish** their work after the final copy is created, particularly if the writing project was significant in scope. Having students read their work aloud is one simple and immediate way to publish a piece, as is posting it on a classroom or school bulletin board. Teachers may have students organize and bind their work into a simple book with string or brads or collect student work into a class-wide literary sampler.

If a teacher uses student portfolios in the classroom, he or she may have students prepare their piece for inclusion into a digital or physical folder. This may involve transcribing the piece digitally, adding illustrations, or matting it on construction paper. Teachers should also emphasize to students that seminal to the idea of publishing is sharing the work with others. This is a great way to build a home–school connection while encouraging students to share their work with parents. Teachers should also show student work samples or portfolios at parent conferences to further build the home–school connection.

16) **Which option is NOT a way to publish student writing?**

   A.   hosting a poetry night where students read their work aloud

   B.   submitting a student-authored essay to a writing contest

   C.   asking students to type their piece on the computer

   D.   having students trade a bound book they have created with a friend to read and enjoy

Answers:

   A.   Incorrect. This is a way to publish student writing as publishing implies sharing the work with others.

   B.   Incorrect. This is a way to share the work with others.

   C.   Correct. This does not necessarily share the piece with others; it merely formats it in a different way.

   D.   Incorrect. This allows others to read the piece.

CHARACTERISTICS OF EFFECTIVE WRITING

As students revise and examine their own writing and that of others, they should be mindful of what makes written communication effective. Above all, successful writing that communicates well has a central **focus**, or main idea. Brainstorming and other prewriting activities can help students maintain focus as they plan a piece. While much of the professional writing to which students are exposed will already be thoroughly edited to ensure a consistent focus, asking students to identify the author's focus across a broad range of texts is a solid strategy that spans capacity building in both reading and writing capability. Additionally, students should identify how the author uses details, examples, and other support as part of overall **concept development**. Students should be critical of how authors support their arguments and whether the evidence is sufficient. This can then be parlayed toward a critical reflection of their own writing and whether they have adequately proven a point.

QUICK REVIEW

What are the steps in the authoring cycle?

A knowledge of basic text **organization** will also help students become critical readers and effective writers. While there are many text organizational structures, most effective writing has an introduction, several supporting details organized in a logical sequence, and a conclusion that wraps up the focus of the piece. Having students practice labeling these parts in various texts is an effective strategy, but simply pointing out the beginning, middle, and end of a story can introduce even very young children to the idea of text organization. As students edit and revise their own work, they should pay heed to their own organization of ideas to ensure that the reader will be able to follow a logical pattern in which the information is presented.

Each piece of writing also has a unique **style**, or approach. Style can describe the author's choice of words. Style also includes sentence and paragraph structure. Both word choice and structure can make a piece formal, informal, or somewhere in between. One part of selecting a style is the intended **purpose** and **audience**. Teachers should always draw students' attention toward the reader of their piece. A more formal style, for example, would be called for in writing a letter to the principal advocating for a longer recess than would be necessary when writing a note to a friend. Students should also consider the style of pieces they read to determine why the author might have chosen a particular style convention: Did the writer intend to argue a point to a hostile audience? Inform a group of third graders about the difference between income and expenses? Was the style formal or informal?

Mechanics are the structural elements of writing and include punctuation, capitalization, spelling, grammar, and general conventions of usage. Like most procedural knowledge of writing, this proficiency may vary significantly from student to student and grade level to grade level. A kindergarten class, in particular, may be focused on a unit about capitalizing the first word in a sentence, whereas a second-grade class may be working on forming the past tense of verbs.

Teachers must also ensure they do not presume knowledge of Standard English conventions among students for whom English is not a first language. Correct use of prepositions, irregular verbs, and pronouns may be particularly challenging for these students until they become more experienced in common usage patterns. Teachers should always aim for growth versus perfection when helping students develop skills in editing their writing for errors in mechanics, as these skills continue to build throughout a student's schooling.

SAMPLE QUESTION

17) **Which of the following would most likely employ a highly formal writing style?**

   A.   a cookbook

   B.   a romance novel

   C.   a legal document

   D.   a short story

Answers:

A. Incorrect. Cookbooks are written for a broad audience and are not highly formal as they need to be accessible by multiple readers.

B. Incorrect. Romance novels are generally written in a unique style, but it is not highly formal.

C. **Correct.** Because legal documents must be very specific and not leave room for interpretation, a highly formal and precise style would be used.

D. Incorrect. While some short stories are written more formally than others, this is not a consistent style choice for the genre as a whole.

DIGITAL TOOLS

Increasingly, early childhood programs and schools are incorporating digital learning tools into their curriculum. Many schools have one or more subscriptions to various educational technology platforms that may enhance student learning and **digital literacy**, which is defined as the ability to find, use, and create digital information. **Media literacy**, a key part of digital literacy, is the ability of students to access, analyze, evaluate, and communicate information in both digital and physical form.

Some students may have extensive experiences with accessing digital information at home through previous use of computers, tablets, or phones. However, a similar level of digital literacy among students cannot be assumed, and teachers should explicitly direct students in strategies for gathering and assessing the usefulness of digital information. While the internet has created an unlimited platform for disseminating information, students must be taught early not to trust all sources equally and how to determine the validity and usefulness of a given source.

> **DID YOU KNOW?**
>
> There are many intentionally fake sites on the internet designed to help students practice determining whether online information is legitimate. One example is found at https://zapatopi.net/treeoctopus, where students can learn about the Pacific Northwest Tree Octopus.

Digital tools also provide an excellent way to differentiate literacy instruction through the use of adaptive software programs that target practice for each student's current skill level. Technological tools can also aid students with special needs or limited English proficiency as they navigate the day-to-day activities in the classroom. Devices and applications such as those that allow nonverbal children to communicate and those that help English language learners quickly translate new words may become indispensable learning aids.

Teachers should also incorporate **digital tools** into the writing process as appropriate. This may include the use of word processing or presentation software to aid in student drafting and revising and even perhaps the use of digital storytelling sites, which help students create and publish visual stories. The classroom or school may even have a website or social media page for publishing student-created content. Before publishing any student work online, however, always check with administration and secure necessary parental consent.

SAMPLE QUESTION

18) A first-grade teacher is trying to convince Mr. Walker, her co-teacher, to incorporate more technology into his lessons to meet new district standards. Mr. Walker did not grow up with technology and does not think his students need it. What is one argument that the teacher might propose to Mr. Walker to help him see its value?

- A. Students play video and computer games at home, so they should use technology at school, too.
- B. Technology may help him to differentiate instruction for struggling readers.
- C. The district standards are always based on what is best for students, so he should heed them.
- D. Technology is not bad as long as it is strictly controlled by the teacher.

Answers:

- A. Incorrect. This reasoning probably will not be convincing.
- **B. Correct.** This is one benefit that may help his students and that he might have a hard time arguing against.
- C. Incorrect. He likely already disagrees with these standards as he does not want to implement them.
- D. Incorrect. This is a general statement and does not directly reference how technology might help his students.

THE RESEARCH PROCESS

Research and library skills are an important part of developing overall student literacy. Generally, there are seven steps in the research process:

1. **Identifying and focusing on the topic**. This might be as simple as having students pick a topic they want to learn more about or develop a research question they wish to answer—before searching online.

2. **Finding background information and conducting a preliminary search**. This involves getting a general overview of a topic and possible subtopics. During this stage students may Google a topic or read the Wikipedia page devoted to a particular topic.

3. **Locating materials**. This could involve work at the library and online. Teachers should encourage students to explore a wide variety of possible resources. As appropriate per the research topic, students should also be

encouraged to seek out **primary sources**, or firsthand accounts. Primary sources may be speeches or diaries, surveys or census data, photographs of an event, and several other media that give eyewitness accounts of an event. Many primary sources are available online, and many sites organize these sources into an accessible format for students. Of course, many materials that students find will also be **secondary sources**, or non-firsthand accounts. These include the majority of books, articles, and web pages devoted to a topic.

4. **Evaluating sources**. Students need to determine if certain sources are useful and accessible to them. For example, a library database may generate results for articles in publications to which the library does not have a subscription. Some resources may be inaccessible to students as they may be overly technical or written for an older audience. Students should also make sure they have **credible sources** written by experts. This stage in the research process might be a good time to introduce the different types of information available on the internet and the qualities that help increase reliability (listed author, .edu or .org domain, publication date, etc.).

5. **Note taking**. Note taking may involve the use of formal note cards or simply jotting down main ideas. As developmentally appropriate per student age, teachers should ensure students understand the idea of **paraphrasing**, or changing the author's words into their own, as they take notes. Paraphrasing can help students prevent **plagiarizing**, or presenting someone else's words as their own work.

6. **Writing**. This includes organizing all the notes into sentences and paragraphs. Students need to be cognizant of the overall organization of their work as they introduce a focused topic, provide support, and write a conclusion. Depending on the age group with which teachers work, they may have students make a poster or use another outlet to present their research instead of a formal paper.

7. **Citing sources**. This may include in-text **citations** and preparing a bibliography. To simplify these elements for young students, teachers might use a simpler works cited/bibliography page where students simply list titles of books and authors. Students in the upper elementary grades may work to develop more sophisticated bibliographies in MLA style, as it is generally regarded as the simplest citation style and the one to which students are first introduced.

Of course, these steps may be greatly simplified for very young students and per the scope of the research project. However, even kindergarteners can gather information from sources to answer a simple research question, and first-grade students can contribute to a simple class-wide research project with teacher support. The key is introducing students to the various parts of the research process while providing scaffolding as needed to support students as they explore new outlets for their developing literacy.

SAMPLE QUESTION

19) Mrs. Burns has an inquisitive kindergarten class. During a unit on flags, her students asked many questions about flags from other states and countries. Which research activity might be most appropriate for Mrs. Burns to plan for her students to further explore flags?

    A.   direct them to conduct an online search for three primary sources on flags

    B.   take them to the library and have them use the database to find flag-related articles

    C.   have them write a paper on state flags citing two secondary sources

    D.   help students find pictures of different flags online and then talk about what they like about each one

Answer:

D. Correct. This activity scaffolds students learning and helps them begin to develop research skills. The other activities are not developmentally appropriate for a kindergarten class.

SPEAKING AND LISTENING

Some students may be introverted and others more extroverted. However, all children need help to develop basic skills in speaking and listening to enable them to become effective communicators. There will be times when students must employ **passive listening** where they listen to a speaker or presentation without conversing. These occasions might be at school assemblies, when watching a movie, or when listening to a storyteller. Passive listening, so long as it is done intently, is not necessarily bad; it just implies a lack of two-way communication. In fact, some occasions, such as being a respectful audience member, will require students to employ passive listening skills.

Active listening, on the other hand, should be employed whenever there is two-way communication. Active listening is used in many positive behavioral support programs, so if a school or program employs one of these, active listening may become a skill about which teachers are daily reminding students. The goal of active listening is to ensure that the listener has correctly understood the speaker. This is often extended to include an understanding of and empathy with this speaker. Generally, active listening involves making appropriate **eye contact** with the speaker, waiting for the speaker to finish, and then responding in a way that shows understanding.

Not only should teachers be active listeners to ensure they understand what students are thinking and feeling, but they should also encourage students to employ these techniques whenever they are listening to directions or holding conversations. Active listening can also help students avoid conflict with each other as they refrain from interrupting and practice valuing the thoughts and opinions of others.

Part of listening and responding may involve different **types of questioning** as listeners check for understanding. Speakers generally employ either open-ended questions ("What does your house look like?"), which require a significant response, or closed-ended questions ("Do you like fried chicken?"), which generally require only a simple one-word answer. Speakers may even ask rhetorical questions, which do not require a response but are designed to make the listener think.

An even deeper type of questioning comes from **metacognition**, or an awareness of one's own thinking. Teachers can help students think from a metacognitive per-spective by teaching them to ask themselves questions both about their content knowledge ("Have I seen this before?" "Do I know this or need more practice?") and from a socioemotional perspective ("Am I feeling cranky because I am tired or hungry?" "How would I feel if that happened to me?").

During more formal speaking situations, especially those in which the audience is primarily involved in passive listening, several other measures must also be considered. **Audience awareness** involves being aware of those to whom one is speaking and their level of engagement and interest. One way to increase engagement both in formal and informal speaking situations is through appropriate volume and **articulation**, or clarity of speech. It may help teachers to periodically self-assess their own classroom speaking and listening by asking themselves questions such as "Am I keeping an appropriate volume or raising my voice frequently?" and "Am I asking students enough open-ended questions and using active-listening techniques?" Modeling effective communication for students is an important way to help teach these skills.

SAMPLE QUESTION

20) **Which of the following is an active listening strategy that can be taught to pre-kindergarten students?**

   A.   emphasizing proper articulation

   B.   maintaining eye contact

   C.   using open-ended questioning

   D.   practicing oral presentations

   Answer:

   B.   **Correct.** This is a core part of active listening and can help pre-K students focus on a speaker. The other activities are not a part of active listening.

LANGUAGE

PARTS OF SPEECH

Understanding the structure of language is an important part of effective oral and written communication. Students may not consistently use parts of speech correctly in their writing and speaking until well into their elementary years. Recall that within oral language development are phases in which children leave out needed articles, prepositions, and other linking words. Once speech becomes fully developed and students are generating their own sentences and paragraphs, basic rules of grammar can be introduced. Many structured language arts curriculum resources begin with a study of the eight parts of speech and their function within a sentence.

Nouns are words that indicate a person, place, thing, or idea. They may be either common (*student, teacher, room, school*) or proper (*Blanca, Ms. Robinson, Idaho, Frederick Douglass Elementary School*). **Common nouns** are not capitalized, but **proper nouns** must be capitalized. Nouns may also be singular or plural, and students will need practice in forming the plural form of nouns by adding either −*s* or −*es*.

Pronouns are words that take the place of nouns. They may either serve as subjects (*I, you, he, she, it, we, they*) or as objects (*me, you, her, him, it, us, them*) and are known as **subject pronouns** or **object pronouns**, respectively. Pronouns should always have an **antecedent**, or noun to which they refer. Pronouns must agree in number, person, and gender with their antecedents. Pronoun errors are frequent in developmental writers, and ambiguous pronoun references, lack of pronoun-antecedent agreement, and incorrect use of subject and object pronouns are all common mistakes.

As discussed above, pronouns generally also indicate the perspective or person in which a piece is written. First-person writing generally uses pronouns such as *I*, *me*, *we*, and *our*, and second-person writing uses the pronoun *you*. Third-person texts use a variety of pronouns such as *he*, *she*, *it*, and *them*. Shifts in pronoun person are common in student writing, and teachers need to provide help to students who unnecessarily change point of view in a writing assignment.

Verbs describe an action or state of being or occurrence. They can be action verbs, which like their name implies, describe actions such as *walk, eat,* and *speak,* or linking verbs, which describe states of being or link a subject to additional information (*is, become, seem*). Some verbs may be action verbs or linking verbs depending upon their specific use. If verbs are merely linking a subject to further information, they are considered linking verbs, but if they are expressing an action, they are considered action verbs.

This soup tastes bad.

In this sentence, the verb *tastes* links the subject *soup* to its predicate adjective *bad*, so *tastes* is being used as a linking verb.

> I taste the soup.

In this sentence, *taste* is describing an action, so it is an action verb.

Helping verbs always appear alongside another main verb and show the tense (*will* be, *had* eaten) or possibility (*may* be, *could* last, *might* enjoy) of another verb. Helping verbs are used to **conjugate**, or change, many verbs to different **tenses**. Unnecessary shifts in tense from present to past or future are prevalent in student writing, and English language learners and native speakers alike will need lots of practice with forming challenging tenses such as the present and past perfect and challenging irregular past tenses with verbs such as *to lie*.

Adjectives modify and describe nouns, and their use is essential to descriptive writing. Student errors with adjectives generally include using an incorrect comparative or superlative form ("He is tallest than me!") or confusing adjectives and adverbs ("She eats hungry/She eats hungrily.").

QUICK REVIEW

What are the major phases of oral language development?

Adverbs modify adjectives, verbs, or other adverbs and frequently end in –*ly*. Student errors with adverbs are similar to those with adjectives and generally involve incorrect use of comparatives and superlatives or using adjectives and adverbs interchangeably.

A **preposition** is a word that expresses a relationship between words, and it usually comes before a noun or pronoun. Prepositions help form links in speech and writing, and student errors most frequently involve their omission. Additionally, English language learners may find using prepositions challenging, particularly when they are part of colloquial expressions (e.g., driving me *up* the wall, a pig *in* a poke, etc.).

A **conjunction** joins words or sentence parts together. There are both coordinating conjunctions (*and, but, or, nor, for, yet, so*), which join two independent clauses to form compound sentences, and subordinate conjunctions (*before, while, because, as*, etc.), which join dependent clauses to independent clauses to form complex and compound-complex sentences.

Table 1.5. Subordinating Conjunctions

Time	after, as, as long as, as soon as, before, since, until, when, whenever, while
Manner	as, as if, as though
Cause	because
Condition	although, as long as, even if, even though, if, provided that, though, unless, while

Purpose	in order that, so that, that
Comparison	as, than

An **interjection** expresses a spontaneous feeling and is usually followed by a comma or exclamation point. *Oops, whoa,* and *hmm* are examples of common interjections.

Determiners are not parts of speech in themselves but have a similar function: explaining what a noun refers to. They may be adjectives that are used as articles such as *a, an,* and *the*; possessive adjectives and pronouns (*my, his, ours, your*); demonstrative pronouns such as *this, that, these,* and *those*; or any other words that quantify, distribute, or show a difference (*a little, half, other, such, quite*).

> **HELPFUL HINT**
>
> Students can use the mnemonic PAPA N VIC to remember the eight parts of speech.

Like prepositions, determiners are challenging for English language learners. In some languages, determiners are used in only some situations and not others, and some languages lack certain types of English determiners entirely. English language learners who struggle with determiners might benefit from being paired with a native speaker for peer review to help insert needed articles into a piece.

Additionally, variations exist across all parts of speech in different languages. American Sign Language, as just one example, does not use what we might think of as conjugated verbs to show tense; rather, a sign indicating now, next, before, and so on is inserted into the beginning of the sentence to show the intended meaning. It is important for teachers to understand that grammatical knowledge will be more challenging for some students, and they should strive to ensure the classroom is a place where all students are being supported in their learning.

SAMPLE QUESTIONS

21) **Which of the following is a preposition?**

A. our

B. from

C. has

D. so

Answers:

A. Incorrect. *Our* is a pronoun.

B. Correct. *From* is a preposition.

C. Incorrect. *Has* is a verb.

D. Incorrect. *So* is a coordinating conjunction.

22) **Which of the following skills do students need to master before they can determine whether an adjective or adverb is most appropriate to use in a sentence?**

    A. understanding the difference between a noun and a verb

    B. understanding the difference between a noun and a pronoun

    C. understanding the function of prepositions

    D. being able to form compound sentences

Answers:

    A. **Correct.** Because adjectives modify nouns and adverbs modify verbs, adjectives, or other adverbs, this is a foundational understanding that must precede a discussion of when an adjective or adverb is most appropriate. The other choices are not relevant to adjective versus adverb use.

Constructing Sentences

Good writers use a variety of sentence structures to convey their meaning. While young students will generally start with **simple sentences** consisting of a single, independent clause, students should be encouraged to write more advanced sentences as appropriate. **Compound sentences** are made when two independent clauses are joined together using a comma and coordinating conjunction; a semicolon, either alone or with a transitional expression such as however or moreover; or a colon. Generally, a semicolon alone is only used to join two closely related independent clauses ("My mother likes chocolate; she is a chocoholic."). A colon is generally only used to introduce a second independent clause which is an example or elaboration upon the first ("I have only one thing to say to you: I am very disappointed.").

Complex sentences are formed when a dependent clause is joined to an independent clause with a subordinating conjunction, relative pronoun, or other word. A **dependent clause** is so called because it cannot stand on its own as a sentence, unlike an **independent clause**. The dependent clause may be added anywhere: the beginning, the middle, or the end of the sentence.

> My mother, *who is a gardener*, likes to spend most of her time outdoors.

In this sentence, the dependent clause is "who is a gardener," beginning with the relative pronoun *who*.

> *Because she likes to spend most of her time outdoors*, my mother is a gardener.

Here, the dependent clause is "[b]ecause she likes to spend most of her time outdoors," beginning with the subordinating conjunction *because*.

> My mother is a gardener *as she likes to spend most of her time outdoors.*

In the sentence above, the dependent clause is "as she likes to spend most of her time outdoors," beginning with the subordinating conjunction *as.*

Compound-complex sentences are merely compound sentences with one or more dependent clauses ("My mother is a gardener, but she does not like to spend time outdoors because she has allergies.").

SAMPLE QUESTION

23) **Which of the following is a compound sentence?**

   A.   Jeremy likes to fish by the ocean because he finds it peaceful and relaxing.

   B.   I wish I could buy a new car, but I do not have enough money right now.

   C.   Jenny is a writer, and she writes for thirty minutes every day because she has to keep motivated.

   D.   While the train slowly chugged along the tracks, my little dog stared curiously out the window.

Answers:

   A.   Incorrect. This is a complex sentence, with the dependent clause "because he finds it peaceful and relaxing."

   B.   Correct. Two independent clauses are joined with a comma and the coordinating conjunction *but.*

   C.   Incorrect. This is a compound-complex sentence, with the dependent clause "because she has to keep motivated."

   D.   Incorrect. This is a complex sentence, with the dependent clause "while the train slowly chugged along the tracks."

VARIETIES OF ENGLISH

Early childhood teachers will likely have students whose home language is not English. It is important to preserve and respect multiple languages within the classroom while helping all students understand the nuances that exist within the English language. A **dialect** is a special way that a given group speaks, and having characters speak in different dialects is an important literary device that authors use to convey meaning. Characters may speak in a Southern dialect or in a Boston or Midwestern style. It might be challenging for students to read dialogue written in dialects with which they are unfamiliar, and teachers may need to scaffold learning with these texts.

An **accent** differs from a dialect in that vocabulary and grammar are the same, but pronunciation is different. There may be families at school, for example, who speak English in a British or Southern accent.

A **register** is a speech pattern that is affiliated with a certain social group or situation. Registers may be associated with an age group or ethnic group, and while they have no intrinsic level of correctness or incorrectness, social constructs may cause some people to associate certain registers with being formal or less formal or even from a lower social strata. Many people, and likely many students, will engage in a practice known as code switching, where they will switch between a home language or register and more formal or standard language in different situations. It is important that teachers avoid responding in a negative or judgmental way to the different dialects, accents, and registers that may be used in the everyday oral communications within the classroom.

Texts that students read, particularly narrative ones such as dramas and stories, will often feature a variety of dialects, accents, and registers to aid in the author's development of characters and setting. Poetry may use certain conventions with which students are unfamiliar. Rather than focusing on a thorough explication of poetry, a better strategy is helping students understand how certain language contributes to the overall purpose of the piece through creation of rhythm, rhyme, or visual imagery. Writers of academic work and other formal published pieces tend to employ a more formal usage of language than that found in everyday conversation. Teachers should strive to help students distinguish the differences between written and spoken language in a variety of contexts and situations.

Students will be exposed to a wide variety of vocabulary in a literacy-rich classroom, and teachers can further aid vocabulary acquisition through incorporating new words and new meanings into the daily routine. Some vocabulary acquisition will involve learning **content-specific words** that require students to first understand the vocabulary of the subject before applying the knowledge. Consider that even a kindergarten student must master dozens of basic math terms before applying them. For example, *triangle*, *hexagon*, and *rectangle* must all be learned intrinsically before a student can separate or sort items by shape. Additionally, third graders must learn terms like *habitat*, *natural resource*, *metric system*, and *variable* to apply them to science and math assignments.

Student vocabulary must also grow to include the various homonyms, or **multiple-meaning words**, that exist in the English language. The word *interest*, for example, might mean one thing as it applies to a math unit on saving money and another when used in a freewriting assignment on a topic of *interest*.

SAMPLE QUESTION

24) **Which of the following is an example of code switching that a student might employ to switch between registers?**

   A.   speaking Creole at home and English at school

   B.   using less formal language with friends than with teachers

   C.   speaking Spanish with friends and English in the classroom

   D.   turning off a French accent when in less formal situations

   Answers:

   A.   Incorrect. While switching between languages is code switching, it is not switching registers.

   B.   **Correct.** This is switching between two different social situations—changing registers.

   C.   Incorrect. This is code switching with a language, not a register.

   D.   Incorrect. One usually cannot turn off an accent.

MEANING OF WORDS AND PHRASES

One helpful way to help students learn new vocabulary is through etymology. Many **root words** in English come from Latin or Greek. For example, the Greek root *chrono*, meaning time, makes many common words: *chronology, chronic, chronicle*, and so on. Many English words are made by adding an **affix** to a basic root word. If this affix is added at the beginning, it is known as a **prefix** (*anti–, un–*, etc.), and if it is added to the end of the word, it is known as a **suffix** (*–less, –able*, etc.).

Using this decoding strategy, when students encounter a new or challenging word, they can look for familiar prefixes, suffixes, or roots and ask themselves if the new word is like others they know. This can help students determine meaning from likening a new word to a previously learned word. For example, a student who knows the meaning of the affix *mid–* as in *middle* and *midway* can then apply this knowledge to a history passage with the word *midcentury*. Prefixes and suffixes can also help students identify parts of speech. For example, words ending in *–er* and *–est* are generally adjectives.

Teachers can further challenge students by exposing them to words that go beyond a **literal meaning** to a more figurative description. **Figurative language** includes simile, metaphor, hyperbole, and personification.

Similes compare two unlike things using the words *like* or *as*:

> His throat was as dry as the Sahara Desert.

Metaphors are constructed by comparing two unlike things:

> The carpet was sandpaper beneath my feet.

Hyperbole is an extreme exaggeration:

> My feet are the worst smelling things in the entire school.

Personification involves giving a humanlike quality to a nonhuman:

> The sea speaks and sings its mystery.

Figurative language may be challenging for students to understand at first, so they will need plenty of teacher support when first introducing this concept.

QUICK REVIEW

What is the difference between a prefix and a suffix?

Above all, teachers should emphasize to students that there are multiple ways to glean the meaning of new words in context, and teachers should encourage students to try multiple strategies. Are there pictures on the page that might help? What context clues can be used? What point do students think the author is trying to make? Do students see any prefixes or parts of the word that they know? These are all guiding questions that will help students deepen their ability to learn new words from reading a variety of texts.

SAMPLE QUESTION

25) **Which of the following uses hyperbole?**

    A.   The grass was as green as a crayon.

    B.   The ocean was as vast as the line at the DMV.

    C.   He was the best dancer in the entire world.

    D.   My mother is the best cook I know.

Answers:

    A.   Incorrect. This is a simile.

    B.   Incorrect. This is a simile.

    C.   **Correct.** This is an exaggeration.

    D.   Incorrect. This is a literal statement, not an exaggeration.

TONE

Tone refers to the overall attitude of a piece of literature. It may be influenced by the author's feelings toward the subject matter or audience. The tone of a book on financial independence may be enthusiastic and positive as the author is trying to instill confidence and positivity into the mind of the reader. The tone might be formal, as in a paper a teacher writes to present at a literacy conference, or less formal, as in a note written to a colleague to thank her for help with lunch duty. Students should be encouraged to determine the tone of different pieces they read.

The **word choice**, or author's choice of specific vocabulary to impart meaning, will likely influence tone. A highly formal essay written for a sophisticated technical audience may include lots of vocabulary that students will not understand and contribute to an overall tone of seriousness. A book designed to entertain a young audience may have more simple vocabulary and an overall humorous tone.

Teachers might further ask students to consider why the author chose certain words or presented them in a certain order. **Syntax**, or the arrangement of words into sentences, can have a tremendous impact on a text. Several short, simple sentences might create anticipation: "It was dark. It was raining. My friend drove up." Longer and more complex sentences may create a more formal and sophisticated feel to a piece.

QUICK REVIEW

Consider the venerated character of Yoda in *Star Wars*. What impact is his inverted speech pattern ("Find them I will") intended to have on the audience? Does it make him sound more wise or experienced, for instance?

SAMPLE QUESTION

26) Which of the following does NOT contribute to the tone of a piece?

   A. the author's attitude toward the subject
   B. the inclusion of highly sophisticated vocabulary
   C. the use of highly complex sentence structures
   D. correct capitalization for proper nouns

Answers:

   A. Incorrect. The author's attitude contributes to tone.
   B. Incorrect. Word choice contributes to tone.
   C. Incorrect. Syntax contributes to tone.
   D. Correct. Capitalization does not necessarily contribute to tone and should be relatively standard.

Social Studies

IDENTITY, SOCIAL, AND EMOTIONAL DEVELOPMENT

DEVELOPMENT OF THE SELF

Children are born with amazing social and emotional skills. Even infants have basic emotional regulation skills in their ability to soothe themselves in uncomfortable situations. Emotional development in infants is often strongly linked to attachment theory, whereby securely attached infants form bonds with caregivers and use these secure relationships as a base upon which to explore the world around them.

Attachment theory was developed by researcher Mary Ainsworth. She observed infants and their mothers in a procedure she called the "Strange Situation." An infant was placed in a room with a stranger, both with and without the primary caregiver. After observation of the different scenarios and the infant's behavior, she classified three different attachment styles: secure, resistant, and avoidant.

A securely attached infant uses their primary caregiver as a base upon which to explore their environment and has a normal, healthy attachment to him or her. Infants with resistant attachment cry frequently both at the presence of strangers and the absence of the primary caregiver. They also explore their environment far less. Infants exhibiting avoidant attachment show no emotion when the primary caregiver leaves and can be comforted equally by a caregiver or a stranger. Later, a fourth category, disorganized attachment, was added. Infants in this category have mixed or no reactions in the scenario.

Infants are social beings and generally begin to smile at around two or three months and laugh at around four months. Babies as young as nine months old can express happiness, sadness, and even anger. By one year of age, most children understand the emotional state of others outside of themselves. There are many theories surrounding this period of **primary socialization**, in which young children learn about themselves, their world, and how they fit into it. This initial socialization into the world is generally undertaken by the child's immediate family and close friends.

Erik Erikson's **psychosocial development theory** is one such theory and, as its name suggests, is based heavily on psychology and the idea that children learn through observation and imitation of others. Erickson posited that people go through eight stages of development throughout their lives. The first four stages apply to early childhood.

In the **trust versus mistrust** phase from birth to age two, children are reliant on caregivers to meet most of their needs and develop either a trusting relationship with others if they are cared for appropriately, or a mistrust of others if they are abused or neglected. Erikson proposed that such an experience at this early stage could impact a person's entire life as he or she struggles building trust with people.

In the **autonomy versus shame and doubt** stage, children aged two to three begin to gain a sense of independence and **self-awareness** of their own feelings and desires. This second stage is one of great exploration and attempts at independent thoughts and actions. According to Erikson, children who move beyond this stage develop the autonomy needed to function somewhat independently, while those who do not successfully develop this autonomy are left with constant self-doubt.

Between the ages of three and six, children go through a stage in which their initiative to try new things through experimental play, making new relationships, and increased decision-making is further explored. Those who do not gain these skills may feel guilt and lack confidence. Erikson called this stage **initiative versus guilt**. From ages six to eleven, children go through a stage of **industry versus inferiority**, in which they begin to develop a healthy **self-concept**, or positive idea of self, generated from praise given by others. During this phase, having the approval and acceptance of both adults and peers is very important to children in avoiding feelings of inferiority.

Table 2.1. Erik Erikson's Psychosocial Development Theory

Age	Birth – Age 2	Ages 2 – 3	Ages 3 – 6	Ages 6 – 11
Stage	**trust v. mistrust**	**autonomy v. shame and doubt**	**initiative v. guilt**	**industry v. inferiority**
Virtue	trust	will	purpose	competence
Children learn…	Can people be trusted?	Am I allowed to be myself?	Am I allowed to do the things I want to do?	Can I be successful?

Another foundational theory of early childhood development is that proposed by **Jean Piaget**. Unlike Erikson, who focused on the overall development of the child, Piaget focused more on cognitive development and believed that young children are naturally curious and construct information from their own interactions with their environment. He is one of the great fathers of what is known as **constructivist educational theory**.

Like Erikson, Piaget believed that children develop in stages. In the first stage of development from birth to two years old, young children are in the **sensorimotor stage**. During this stage, knowledge is constructed through the senses. Children may explore through touch, taste, smell, and sight, and they learn the concept of **object permanence**, whereby objects continue to exist even when out of sight.

Next, children enter the **preoperational stage** from ages two to seven, in which they begin to develop some symbolic thought, though some thoughts may still be illogical. However, children develop the concept of **conservation** during this phase, beginning to understand that the characteristics of objects remain unchanged even when they appear to be different. An example of this concept is understanding that two containers hold an equal amount of water even if they are shaped or sized differently.

In the **concrete operational stage**, lasting from ages seven to eleven, children develop more logical reasoning capabilities. In the **formal operational stage**, beginning at age eleven, children begin to develop abstract thinking. Piaget's influence can be seen in many preschool classrooms around the world in which centers are placed in the classroom such that children can freely explore and learn or "construct" knowledge from their environment.

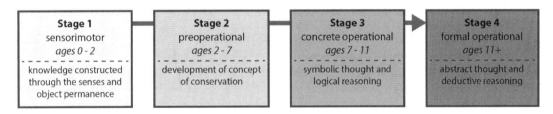

Figure 2.1. Jean Piaget's Stages of Development

Lev Vygotsky also believed that children construct knowledge from their environment. His sociocultural theory provides a framework for understanding a young child's primary socialization into a culture. Vygotsky held that learning happens through social interactions in which children work in the **zone of proximal development**, or the range of tasks that a child cannot perform alone but can complete with assistance from a more proficient peer or teacher. The concept of **scaffolding** learning, in which the teacher assists students to complete tasks until they can do so independently, is based upon this theory. Vygotsky also believed strongly that children learn through play, particularly play that encourages imagination and fosters learning through interaction with others.

Most early childhood programs draw, at least in part, from these three theories, but the role of the teacher/caregiver cannot be overstated. As children begin to develop their **self-identity**, their understanding how they fit into society and what they can contribute, it is essential that teachers help develop positive social skills in their students. Teachers and schools are agents of **secondary socialization**, imparting to children how to behave as a member of a classroom, school, and peer group. Unlike primary socialization, which is strongly influenced by a child's parents, secondary socialization happens outside the home.

Self-awareness, or the knowledge of one's feelings, wants, and thoughts, is also developed in part in the early childhood years. Developing self-awareness and one subset of self-awareness, **metacognition**—thinking about thinking—is a large part of early childhood education and education in general. Students often need to be directed in their development of an understanding of what they know and do not know. Teachers can aid in this development by frequently checking for understanding and encouraging students to make self-assessments of what they do not understand.

One recent topic in early childhood circles is the development of **gender identity**. Research suggests that some teachers unconsciously guide students into gendered play and activities, such as encouraging young boys to play with trucks and young girls to play with dolls. Many schools are encouraging teachers to think beyond traditional gender roles and to support students in exploring their interests, even if they do not align with traditional societal beliefs about the nature of men and women.

SAMPLE QUESTIONS

1) **Mrs. Brown asks Jimmy, a very advanced reader, to work on a literacy project with Hannah, a lower-level reader. Her hope is that Hannah might learn from Jimmy. Which developmental theorist is Mrs. Brown basing this strategy on?**

   A. Erik Erikson

   B. Lev Vygotsky

   C. Jean Piaget

   D. Mary Ainsworth

   Answers:

   A. Incorrect. Erik Erikson's theory of psychosocial development involves children going through distinct stages, but it does not strongly emphasize learning through social interaction.

   B. **Correct.** This teacher is addressing Hannah's zone of proximal development by providing a more proficient peer to assist her.

   C. Incorrect. Piaget believed that children learn through the environment itself, not necessarily through interaction with peers.

   D. Incorrect. Mary Ainsworth developed attachment theory, and this strategy of peer assistance is not based on attachment theory.

2) An infant left crying for several hours by an absent parent may develop problems in reliance on others. At which stage of Erikson's psychosocial theory would this occur?

   A.   trust versus mistrust

   B.   autonomy versus shame and doubt

   C.   initiative versus guilt

   D.   industry versus inferiority

Answers:

   A.   Correct. This child is in the initial stage of Erikson's psychosocial development theory—trust versus mistrust—from birth to age two.

   B.   Incorrect. Autonomy versus shame and doubt is the second stage of Erikson's theory from ages two to three.

   C.   Incorrect. Initiative versus guilt is the third stage of Erikson's theory from ages three to six.

   D.   Incorrect. Industry versus inferiority is the fourth stage of Erikson's theory from ages six to eleven.

SOCIAL BEHAVIOR

One of the biggest roles of the early childhood educator is being a developer of a young child's **social and emotional competence**, or the ability to successfully navigate social situations and exercise **self-regulation** of inappropriate emotional expression. Much research suggests that the social and emotional competence developed in the preschool years in particular is a key predictor of future overall success in school and in the development of a child's overall self-concept. Part of developing this competence is helping students understand the **norms of social behavior** both in the classroom and school community and in society at large. These norms in the United States include saying "please" and "thank you" and using eye contact when speaking, as well as more subtle norms such as keeping appropriate space when sitting next to another person on public transportation. As Figure 4.2 illustrates, these norms vary from culture to culture.

Establishing trusting teacher-student relationships lays a secure foundation for a child's socio-emotional development, and this is the first step in creating a classroom rooted in social skills development. Young children will need teachers to scaffold their learning while developing socio-emotional competencies. However, in order to successfully do this, teachers must first develop strong social and emotional competencies themselves. This includes the ability to

▸   recognize and respond appropriately to the emotions of others.

▸   model appropriate behavior.

▸   understand and recognize emotions in themselves.

▸   form trusting partnerships and appropriate social relationships with colleagues and members of the school community.

Figure 2.2. Greetings from Different Parts of the World

In order to regulate emotions, young children must first learn about them. Unlike actions, emotions are neither intrinsically good nor bad, and children must understand this to recognize the emotions they are feeling and respond appropriately. Teachers can support this through validation of negative emotions—without validating negative actions based on these emotions—and through helping children understand how they are feeling. Questions such as "How did that make you feel?" and affirmations such as "I bet that made you angry" can go a long way toward helping young students think about feelings and develop emotional competence. For children to learn to regulate emotions, they must first learn to recognize them within. Then, children can begin to develop the skills to recognize and respond to the emotions of others.

Many popular school-wide behavioral programs such as **positive behavior intervention and support** (PBIS) include components specifically geared toward recognizing emotions and validating the feelings of others. These programs often specify a continuum of three tiers wherein social competence is taught through both school-wide expectations and more targeted interventions and strategies on the classroom and individual student level.

While teachers may think of emotional learning as being the domain of the preschool and kindergarten classroom, more and more curricular resources and state

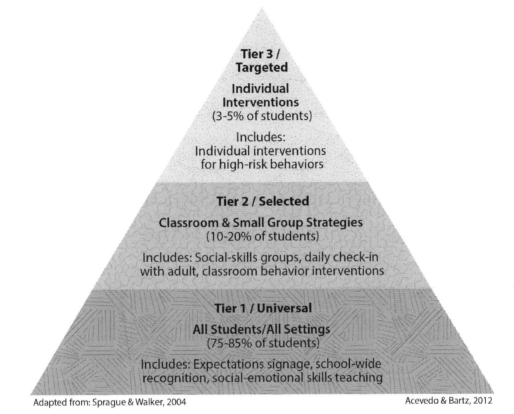

Figure 2.3. Positive Behavior Intervention and Support

and national standards emphasize appropriate emotional regulation throughout the elementary years. These objectives are often integrated with other domains, such as the listening and speaking strands within the Common Core State Standards.

Early childhood teachers also help children in their earliest attempts at socialization, or developing **interpersonal relationships** with peers. Many preschool and some kindergarten classrooms are organized in such a way as to initiate social interaction among students through group seating and center-based cooperative learning activities.

While the classroom layout and curriculum can facilitate positive interactions among students through cooperative activities, teachers must also explicitly teach a variety of social skills such as sharing, turn-taking, listening to and following instructions, and **conflict resolution**. These skills can be taught in class-wide activities like reading stories and literary selections that have themes relating to these skills, and in small-group and individual interventions and scaffolding. Teachers have to balance both, allowing for students to develop social relationships on their own and helping more introverted students successfully navigate daily social situations. Teachers should also remember that it is not the number of friends a student has that is important but rather the quality and appropriateness of interactions with his or her peers. Students (and many times parents) will also need to be reminded of this.

Teachers in the early childhood classroom will also likely have frequent interaction with parents regarding their child's socio-emotional development. Parents might enlist the help of teachers to reinforce a newly acquired social skill such as saying "thank you," or parents might simply inquire as to how their child is faring in making friends at school. Teachers must remain open and honest with parents regarding a student's socio-emotional development and provide reassurance to both parents and child when positive behavior is still developing, while maintaining honest dialogue about a child's current developmental level.

The term **child guidance** is generally used to denote the many ways that teachers help develop appropriate behaviors in students. Theories on appropriate methods of student discipline may vary based on the program and may take either a behaviorist or constructivist developmental approach. Behaviorists who follow the teachings of B.F. Skinner believe that all human behavior is the result of conditioning based on environment. They view the best way to establish positive behaviors as being through punishment and reward, and this approach is generally associated with an authoritarian classroom structure.

More common in many programs is a constructivist approach to child guidance, whereby children learn appropriate social behaviors through their own trial and error, along with purposeful scaffolding from adults. These approaches, based on the work of social constructivist theorists like Lev Vygotsky, seek to help students learn appropriate behaviors through modeling and interaction with adults or peers. These approaches typically also emphasize natural consequences for actions, such as cleaning up a mess made or losing dessert privileges if the dessert was thrown at a friend.

Additionally, many parts of constructivist approaches to student guidance emphasize the development of **moral autonomy**, or the desire to behave morally toward others based on one's own desire to do so, not because one is being forced.

Regardless of the particular approach to guidance within a school or program, children must be given explicit instruction in understanding and responding to emotions and interacting socially, as well as ample opportunity to make decisions and learn from mistakes.

SAMPLE QUESTIONS

3) Mrs. Henry has a class of three-year-old preschoolers. She has several pictures on the wall of different facial expressions (happy, tired, hungry, angry, and so on). Why might Mrs. Henry have such pictures in her classroom?

    A.   to model appropriate social behavior

    B.   to show students how they should behave

    C.   to help students understand different emotions

    D.   to provide age-appropriate classroom rules

Answers:

A.   Incorrect. The faces are not necessarily interacting socially, just emoting.

B.   Incorrect. The faces are not necessarily concerned with behavior, only emotion.

C.   **Correct.** The faces show expressions associated with different emotions. This can provide a visual to aid in understanding different emotions.

D.   Incorrect. These faces are not indicative of classroom rules.

4)   **Mrs. Hayes, a first-grade teacher, always greets her students each morning by name and looks them in the eyes while speaking. How is Mrs. Hayes helping her students to develop positive social behavior?**

A.   through modeling

B.   by scaffolding their learning

C.   by providing lots of opportunities for cooperative learning

D.   by helping them to develop friendships with peers

Answers:

A.   **Correct**. Mrs. Hayes is modeling appropriate social behavior to her students.

B.   Incorrect. Mrs. Hayes is not providing assistance to her students as they tackle a challenging task.

C.   Incorrect. This activity is not cooperative learning.

D.   Incorrect. She is not helping them to develop friendships.

SOCIAL INSTITUTIONS

Another development theorist in the field of early childhood is Urie Bronfenbrenner. He developed what came to be known as the **ecological systems theory**. This theory provides an excellent lens through which to view the multiple social systems and interactions that impact a child. The theory defines five systems at work in the lives of children. The **microsystem** is that which is closest to the child, such as the family, school, temple, mosque, church, synagogue, and any other institutions in the community the child has direct contact with.

Next is the **mesosystem**, the network of relationships among different microsystems that also affect the child. The relationships between parents and teachers and the school and families are crucial mesosystem relationships that will either aid or detract from the development of the child.

Exosystems are relationships between a child and others in his or her social orbit that do not involve the child directly. For example, a parent who has an unpleasant relationship with her boss might impact the child by bringing the stress from this relationship into the household.

Next are **macrosystems**, which can be broadly defined as the overall cultural constructs in which a child lives. Macrosystems may include race and ethnicity, socioeconomic status, political systems, and the general larger environment in which the child lives.

Finally, **chronosystems** represent environmental changes and transitions that happen over the course of a child's life. These might impact microsystems, such as when parents divorce, or macrosystems, such as when the family moves to a foreign country.

The ecological systems theory, sometimes called the **bioecological model**, is very important for teachers to consider both when teaching socio-emotional development and when teaching broader social studies concepts. Teachers should consider that multiple systems outside of the classroom are affecting children and can have a significant impact on each child's social and emotional identity.

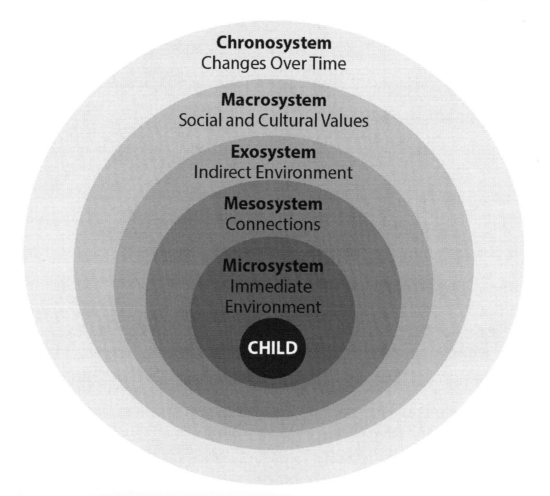

Figure 2.4. Urie Bronfenbrenner's Ecological Systems Theory

In the diverse classrooms of the United States, early childhood teachers will find students who come from a broad range of **social systems and institutions**. Social systems and institutions refer to the networks that create a cohesive whole between individuals, groups, and institutions. Families, cities, schools, and corporations are all types of social systems. These institutions regulate and establish norms for the behavior of individuals across society.

Of course, these norms vary from place to place and from child to child. Teachers should consider that holidays and common religious practices may differ from student to student, and the inclusive classroom environment should recognize and appreciate the many different social, cultural, and religious institutions and systems that might impact students. Even governmental and academic systems might be different in a student's country of origin, so teachers should never presume that certain values or beliefs are held worldwide.

Although social studies instruction begins at birth when families and caregivers help children develop social skills, most formal social studies instruction begins in preschool with themes such as "community helpers," when students learn about the many people and institutions that serve the public. These activities might include study of the **police department**, the **fire department**, **courts of law**, and public **universities**. The emphasis in this introduction to the community is generally on the way these various institutions contribute to the success of the community through education, protection, and conflict resolution.

Classroom activities related to these community helpers might include reading books about various professions, using props in the dramatic play center, and even field trips or special guests. Young children typically enjoy getting to tour a fire truck or receiving a guest presentation from a police officer, and these visits can promote a spirit of understanding and cooperation among various members of the community.

SAMPLE QUESTIONS

5)   Mr. Howard is a second-grade teacher in Houston, and his classroom is full of students from all over the world. He wants to make sure his students are appreciative of many different cultures. Which strategy should he choose?

   A.   not celebrating any holidays to avoid promoting one culture over another

   B.   pointing out that not all students are part of American holidays and traditions

   C.   celebrating many different holidays such as Chinese New Year and Valentine's Day, which sometimes occur in the same week

   D.   having community helpers such as police officers come to visit the class

Answers:

A.   Incorrect. This would not be fun for students, and many schools and programs do still use holidays as thematic units. Students should grow to understand that there are many different holidays, not just one strict set of holidays.

B.   Incorrect. Teachers should not point out differences that might make children feel excluded. Mr. Howard's class will likely be comprised of students whose families choose to celebrate American holidays and those who do not. However, holidays should be seen as inclusive versus exclusionary.

C.   Correct. This exposes children to many different holidays and shows them that there is not one set calendar of holidays for the entire world.

D.   Incorrect. This does not address Mr. Howard's goal to make the classroom culturally inclusive.

6)   **Mrs. Johnson, a third-grade teacher, recently had a conference with Mark's parents that did not go well. The parents were very upset about Mark's scores on his practice test for the end-of-year state test and seemed to blame Mrs. Johnson. Why is it important for Mrs. Johnson to work to repair this relationship?**

A.   She does not want Mark's parents to complain to the principal.

B.   Mark must pass this test to move on to fourth grade.

C.   This may impact Mark as part of his mesosystem.

D.   It sets a bad example for other parents.

Answers:

A.   Incorrect. This is not the primary reason to work to repair this relationship.

B.   Incorrect. While this may be true, this is not directly related to the relationship between Mark's parents and Mrs. Johnson.

C.   Correct. The relationships between teachers and parents are a part of the child's mesosystem and can have an impact on the child's development.

D.   Incorrect. Other parents likely would not know about this rift.

Culture and Cultural Identity

Cultural Perspectives

Students in almost any American classroom will have many different cultural perspectives. While all students will have to adapt to certain parts of the school culture such as behavioral and academic expectations, they will also be part of other **groups** outside of the school community that may have differences and similarities to the **shared experience** within the school. Most state standards provide support for children to learn about and appreciate these similarities and differences.

The school and classroom are unique environments in that students are united in a common goal to grow and learn in a structured setting and are also somewhat separate in their own cultural experiences. All social groups and cultures share basic needs and wants like food, clothing, housing, and security, and they have some method for addressing the concerns of their members. However, what food, clothing, housing, and security look like may vary greatly among groups. A teacher might use the example of a Mongolian reindeer herder to illustrate this. While many Americans may find security in a stable home in one place, nomadic peoples, such as those who pick up their yurts to follow their herds of reindeer, may find security in a portable home that can adapt to the herd's migration.

> **DID YOU KNOW?**
>
> Immigration patterns in the local community are often first observed in the classroom. Hispanic and Asian student enrollment in public schools in particular has grown by over five million students since the 1990s. The states with the most diverse student populations are Nevada, Florida, California, New York, and Texas.

A teacher might also show various examples of food and clothing that, while different from each other, still meet the physical needs of a community. Differences in a group of people's **physical environment** (part of the human environment that includes purely physical factors such as climate and vegetation) may dictate food, clothing, and housing choices, as people tend to use the resources most readily available. A teacher may point out the differences in clothing between those living in different climates and how housing and food may also vary based on a location's proximity to the equator. These discussions are easily integrated into science themes as well, and appreciation for differences while maintaining an understanding of unity in purpose to meet basic needs is essential.

Of course, the way in which different social groups are organized can vary greatly. This may manifest itself on a microlevel within a student's family, whereby certain gender roles are adhered to, or on a macro-level, in which there is a social custom in the community for neighbors to collaborate in providing after-school childcare. Additionally, the **social conditions**, or situation in society based on income, job, or education level, in which one finds oneself may vary across a larger group. For example, all residents of a certain American city may have some shared culture, but this may vary based on socioeconomic status. Higher-income individuals may frequent different stores and restaurants and live in and attend school in different communities.

Teachers will want to model respect for people across a broad social strata and various cultural backgrounds and avoid making direct comparisons that might imply a value judgment. Instead of saying, for example, "Sanya wears a sari, which makes it hard to run, and Jenny wears jeans, which are comfortable," teachers should say things like "Sanya wears a sari, and Jenny wears jeans."

Additionally, every effort should be made to make the classroom environment one in which many different cultural experiences and expressions are valued as part of the shared experience of the classroom. Strategies for this may involve inclusion of diverse cultural artwork in the classroom decor and reading stories from many different cultural and social perspectives. Teachers may also label items in the classroom in different languages representative of the home languages of students or invite families to share traditional food from their culture with the class.

SAMPLE QUESTIONS

7) Which of the following would be most useful for a teacher to show students to help them understand that housing is different in different environments?

A. an image of a New York apartment building and an igloo

B. a drawing of a sprawling suburban home and a simple ranch house

C. a picture of a Native American woman and man

D. a photo of the White House and the Pentagon

Answers:

A. **Correct.** This shows how housing is different based on environmental conditions.

B. Incorrect. This difference is based more on income than environment.

C. Incorrect. This does not pertain to housing.

D. Incorrect. Only one of these is a house, and both are located in similar environments (both within the United States).

8) How might a prekindergarten teacher set up the classroom environment in a way that encourages appreciation for other cultures?

A. having multiple learning centers for subjects like literacy and art

B. including a kimono and sari as part of the dramatic play center

C. labeling all the classroom items with words such as chair, desk, board, and so on

D. clearly posting the classroom rules where all can see

Answers:

A. Incorrect. Learning centers do not necessarily pertain to cultural appreciation.

B. **Correct.** These props help students appreciate the different types of clothing worn in different cultures.

C. Incorrect. This would only help if the labels were in languages other than English.

D. Incorrect. The classroom rules do not directly relate to the appreciation of other cultures.

COMPONENTS OF CULTURE

Every culture has elements of expression that make it unique. Certain **cultural norms**, or attitudes or behaviors that are considered normal, may vary significantly from culture to culture. For instance, typical greetings range from the handshake in the United States to kisses in France. Some cultural norms may be even more subtle. In the United States, where people are often focused on health and thinness, refusing a second helping of dinner might be commonplace; whereas in some cultures, refusing food and drink is considered a very rude practice. Even concepts of physical space and what is appropriate social behavior may vary widely. American travelers to some parts of Asia are often surprised at the size of hotel rooms or how closely people sit together on public transport.

While it is important for students to learn such cultural norms of American society as saying "please" and "thank you" and making eye contact when speaking, teachers should ensure that students are aware that cultural norms may vary considerably. As with any method of instilling appreciation for cultural differences, this lesson is often best taught through hands-on learning. A first-grade teacher might ask a parent to speak to the class about different cultural norms in her country, or a third-grade teacher might assign a class research project on different social customs around the world.

Another part of appreciating culture is an awareness of and respect for that culture's **language**. Since it is easiest for children to learn new languages when they are young, many early childhood programs offer class-wide instruction or language immersion in a second language such as Spanish or Mandarin. This instruction lends itself to a further exploration of the broader culture of Latin America or China and should be pursued to spark students' interest in other cultures.

> **QUICK REVIEW**
>
> What are some cultural norms that have shocked or surprised you while visiting other places?

Early childhood teachers will appreciate the overall differences in language among students and their families and should accommodate these differences. Teachers and schools may translate important information on websites or in newsletters into common home languages of the student population. This shows that the teacher and school respect the different languages spoken and also helps increase communication between schools and families.

The **artistic creations** of any given culture are also a great medium for student exploration. This exploration allows for integration of art and social studies and helps young students

> **DID YOU KNOW?**
>
> Mandarin is the most-spoken language in the world, with 12 percent of the world's population speaking it. It is followed by Spanish (6 percent), English (5 percent), Arabic (5 percent), and Hindi (3.5 percent).

develop fine motor skills as well as an awareness of art in different cultures. Students may study and create any number of pieces specific to a given culture. For example, papier-mâché is a common art activity for young students that is often erroneously associated only with Europe. In fact, the ancient Egyptians and Persians also used the art form to great success. This single art project could be integrated into a broader unit on several different cultures. Similarly, piñatas, typically associated with Mexico, are used in many different cultures, including American birthday celebrations. Because art is enjoyed and appreciated by students of all ages, field trips to art museums and galleries are interesting and effective ways to expose students to art from a variety of cultures, both near and far.

Music is another fun and creative way to introduce students to different cultural, artistic expression. Many classrooms use music to help very young children develop oral language skills and an understanding of sounds and rhyme. Music can be chosen from an international selection geared toward a young audience. Moreover, students might study and even construct instruments from different cultural traditions as they learn about their use. Drums, maracas, castanets, and shakers can easily be made with simple materials. Soothing music from a different cultural tradition can be played in the background of the classroom if appropriate.

Incorporating **literature** from many cultural perspectives into the curriculum is another way to develop cultural awareness. A piece of literature shared with a third-grade class that includes dialogue written in a different dialect and set in a far-off place may spark interest and enthusiasm for further cultural exploration. A storybook read aloud to a kindergarten class followed by guided questions such as "Where did the characters live?" and "What do you know about this place?" may lead to a discussion of different places. There are a great many developmentally appropriate literary titles across a wide range of cultural themes that can easily be matched to a particular social studies unit.

SAMPLE QUESTIONS

9) Mr. Wyatt wants to suggest an activity to the art teacher to use as a springboard for his second-grade class's study of different cultural heritages within the United States. Which activity might be a good suggestion?

   A. students creating a replica of a Civil War cannon

   B. students creating a painting in the cubist style

   C. students making a simple Native American doll

   D. students finger painting a landscape scene

   Answers:

   A. Incorrect. This exposes students to American history, not necessarily a different cultural heritage.

B.   Incorrect. This exposes students to a different style of painting, not necessarily a cultural heritage.

C.   **Correct**. Mr. Wyatt could use this activity as a springboard for a unit about Native Americans and various parts of this cultural heritage.

D.   Incorrect. This exposes students to a different artistic technique and subject matter, not a different culture.

10) **Which is NOT a cultural norm in the United States?**

A.   washing hands after using the bathroom

B.   shaking hands when meeting someone

C.   arriving later than the scheduled time of a meeting

D.   saying "thank you" when receiving a gift

Answers:

A.   Incorrect. This is an important cultural norm that must be taught to students.

B.   Incorrect. This is an American cultural norm.

C.   **Correct**. This is not an American cultural norm, but it is a norm in some countries.

D.   Incorrect. This is an American cultural norm.

CULTURAL RELATIONSHIPS

Few individuals or cultures can provide for all of their needs without help. This leads to **interdependence**, whereby groups or individuals are dependent upon others to meet certain needs. Young children can best grasp this concept by understanding their own dependence on farmers and ranchers to produce the food they eat and on manufacturers to make clothing and products they use.

Elementary-aged students may begin to understand broader ideas of one nation's interdependence upon another. For example, some products not available in one country (like grain in some Middle Eastern countries) must be imported from other countries (like the United States). In exchange, the country with the desired resource receives a payment of cash or a necessary product. This example shows how interdependence leads to the import of grain to some Middle Eastern countries and to the export of grain by the United States. In return, the United States might receive petroleum from a Middle Eastern country.

All parts of the world have different natural resources and thus access to some goods but not others. In some parts of the world and even in some desert regions in the United States, it is impossible to grow food, making these areas dependent on others for their very survival. This makes trade relationships and alliances crucial to meet the most basic needs of a community.

Cultural communities that are **intradependent** are not reliant on outsiders to meet the needs of their members and are able to produce resources within their own communities. This does not mean these communities do not have specialists who provide specific goods and services. For example, the relationship between a farrier (a person who shoes horses) and the Amish community is one of intradependence. The farrier is able to meet the needs of other community members whose horses need shoes. However, he is likely not able to meet all of his own needs. He might rely on a carpenter within his community to make furniture for his home and a roofer to repair his roof. Intradependence is not very common in today's world. It is much more common for even developed countries like the United States to rely on other nations like China to produce certain manufactured goods, even though we have the capability to do so. Labor costs are lower in China, so the goods can be produced at a lower price.

Cultures may experience both **unity** and **diversity** simultaneously. For example, in the United States, people are unified under a common system of government and laws. However, there exists great diversity in ethnicity, religion, and language.

One common idea is that of unity in diversity. That is, certain cultural groups are unified under some common purposes but have a diverse body. Some say that this is the case in the United States.

STUDY TIPS

The prefix *intra–* means "within." The prefix *inter–* means "between or among." Intradependence happens within a group, and interdependence happens among different groups.

Some cultures are more heterogeneous, like many parts of the United States, where people of diverse cultural backgrounds can be found. Others are more homogeneous and have a single and very dominant culture. Since early childhood programs are found in both more and less diverse parts of the nation, and because some schools have a very homogeneous student population, it is vitally important to ensure all students have experiences that allow them to appreciate the different cultures throughout the nation and world.

Teachers in less diverse environments must make a conscious effort to ensure that diversity is appreciated as a construct even where it does not actually exist. Because research suggests that teachers in less diverse environments do not always seek out opportunities to teach about diversity, many state and national standards intentionally include these elements, like requirements relating to the types of literature that are mandated at certain grade levels. Using multicultural literature can be an excellent and authentic way to introduce students to ideas, beliefs, and customs they might be unfamiliar with. This is important to ensure that students will be successful and able to navigate not just their immediate environs but also the ever-shrinking world in which everyone lives.

Globalization, the process by which businesses and organizations operate on an international scale, is rapidly increasing. This increase has led to a **global**

culture, in which certain norms and values are shared across a global scale. The development of a global culture has both negative and positive impacts, as shared understandings lead to more interconnectedness. But sometimes more dominant cultural constructs, such as American consumerism, may spread to the detriment of local culture. While the opening of American fast-food restaurants throughout the world may unite people in their love of french fries or a certain brand of coffee, it might do so at the expense of small local restaurants that preserve traditional cooking methods and foods. It is important for students to understand this dichotomy, as is age appropriate.

SAMPLE QUESTIONS

11) **Which of the following is NOT an example of a downside to a shared global culture?**

    A. Local customs and dress may become extinct.

    B. Local businesses may go out of business.

    C. People may understand each other better.

    D. Local languages may be lost.

    Answers:

    A. Incorrect. This is certainly a downside.

    B. Incorrect. This is also a downside.

    C. Correct. This is a definite advantage to a global culture.

    D. Incorrect. This is a downside.

12) **How might a first-grade teacher introduce the concept of interdependence to her class?**

    A. by discussing trade agreements such as the North American Free Trade Agreement (NAFTA)

    B. by asking students to name the major exports of China

    C. by asking students to list all the items in the classroom not made in America

    D. by asking students where they got their shoes

    Answers:

    A. Incorrect. This is far too advanced a concept for a first-grade class.

    B. Incorrect. This is also too advanced for the grade level.

    C. Incorrect. First-grade students likely would not know this unless every item was labeled.

    D. Correct. This question will help students see that they are dependent on others, since they cannot make their own shoes.

People, Places, and Environments

Spatial Thinking

Humans have long been fascinated with geography and their place on the planet. Today, a person's geographic **location**, or exact position on the earth, is typically defined by latitude and longitude coordinates. However, even before the invention of these systems of measurement, explorers and cartographers made attempts to track location. Early **maps** and **globes** featured known land alongside *terra incognita*, or unknown land, which sparked interest in future maritime exploration. Today's maps and globes, both digital and physical, are far more complex and can help travelers navigate to very exact locations.

This precision is made possible by the geographical reference system of latitude and longitude. Latitude refers to the coordinates that specify the north-south position of a given point on the surface of the earth. These horizontal lines are usually marked and labeled on globes and include the equator—the line representing an angle of 0°—and four other named lines: the Arctic Circle at 66° north,

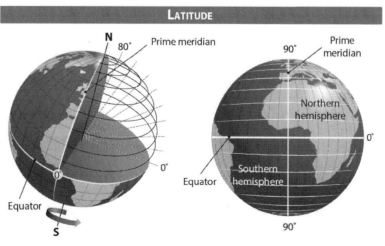

Figure 2.5. Longitude and Latitude

the Antarctic Circle at 66°south, the Tropic of Cancer at 23°north, and the Tropic of Capricorn at 23°south. The climate of locations closer to the equator tends to be hotter because these areas receive more direct sunlight, while the climate of locations farther from it is colder because of the slant of the earth.

Longitude refers to the geographic coordinates that provide an east-west position on the earth's surface. This measurement far postdated the ability to calculate latitude, which could easily be calculated based on the position of the sun and stars. English clockmaker John Harrison invented a device in 1773 that calculated longitude, thereby ushering in a new wave of maritime navigation and exploration. Like latitude, lines of longitude have a central line at 0°, which is known as the **prime meridian**. While there was some initial controversy over where to designate the exact location of this line, it has now been firmly established at the Royal Observatory in Greenwich, United Kingdom. This is the origin of the term Greenwich Mean Time (GMT), or the solar time at this point.

In the past, calculating time on the entirety of the earth's surface was no easy task, as points on Earth seemed to elapse to a new day at different rates. With the establishment of the International Date Line halfway around the world from the prime meridian, however, a standard demarcation was made. This line is roughly based on 180° longitude; however, it deviates slightly to accommodate certain territories. The line shows what day it is based on a concept of Coordinated Universal Time (UTC). Areas can be either ahead of or behind this time, as denoted by UTC+

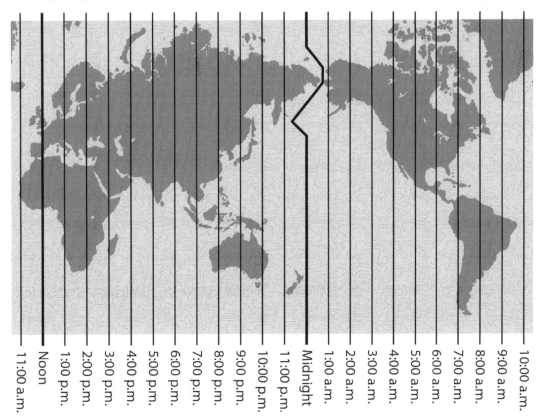

Figure 2.6. Time Zones and the International Date Line

or UTC–. This standard time system allows anyone to know what time and day it is anywhere on the globe.

While a globe is the most accurate representation of the earth's surface, it is not always practical or easy to transport. Unfortunately, no completely accurate flat map exists, though there are several standard map projections that minimize the amount of distortion. The first of these was the **Mercator projection**, developed in 1569 by Flemish geographer Gerardus Mercator. Its strength is its helpfulness in plotting a maritime course (certainly its primary use at the time), and its weakness is its gross distortion of the size of several landmasses, including Greenland, which looks as though it is larger than Africa (which is in fact fourteen times larger).

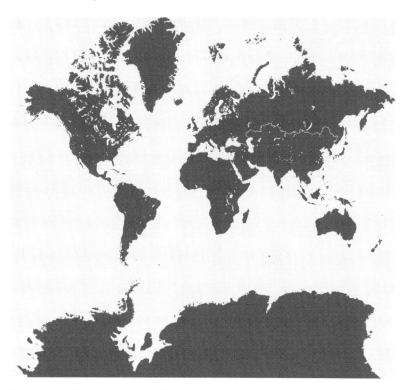

Figure 2.7. Mercator Projection

The **Winkel tripel projection** was proposed in 1921 in hopes of minimizing distortion in area, direction, and distance. This projection does minimize object distortion, but the lines of latitude are not totally parallel and are more curved than in actuality. Still, it is the map of choice for National Geographic, which has used this projection since 1998.

The Robinson projection was devised in 1963 at the behest of the Rand McNally map company. It is a compromise between the Mercator projection and the Winkel tripel projection in that, although there is some distortion, it is mostly near the poles, with some lack of accuracy in the lines of longitude.

Other projections, including new digital map projections, abound. Students should know that no map projection is completely accurate, due to the shape of

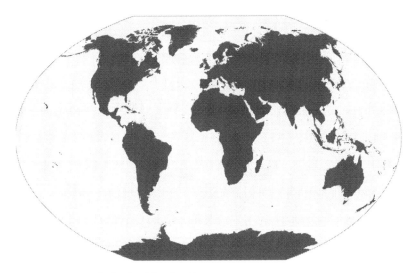

Figure 2.8. Winkel Tripel Projection

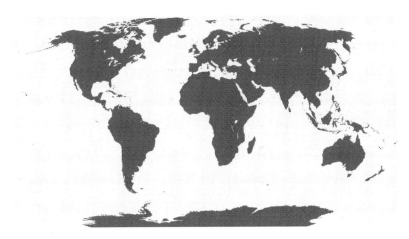

Figure 2.9. Robinson Projection

the planet, and that while flat maps might be good for identifying major regions, landmarks, and streets, globes are still the best tools for measuring precise locations and calculating one's global position. Newer digital maps like Google Earth might be even more accurate because they show changes in a map over time. An interesting activity for students of all ages is comparing the Google Street View of the area around the school with its physical reality. Teachers can spark discussion by asking if the digital map is accurate or what parts of the map may be outdated.

Globes are not practical to use when traveling, so students must be able to read and understand information on maps. In fact, many elementary students report that map-reading questions are the most challenging parts of standardized tests. Perhaps this is because children do not practice this activity much in their daily lives, and turn-by-turn directional technology has now replaced traditional maps in many cases. Map reading is still an essential geographical skill that helps students understand their spatial position in relationship to other locations, as well as how to interpret and understand graphics designed to convey information.

Kindergarten students should be introduced to basic **directional terms** such as left, right, over, and under and should be able to locate basic locations in familiar environments like their school. They should also begin to recognize other major **landmarks**, or easily recognizable places, in their community. By first grade, students should be able to use the cardinal directions as illustrated by the **compass rose** with some fluency to find the location of objects and places. By second grade, students should start to use maps and globes to identify various locations, including being able to identify the map **title**, using the map's **legend** to understand what symbols or colors represent, using the **scale** to measure distances, and using a map's **grid** reference system to identify the coordinates of locations. Students should be afforded plenty of practice with maps and be given opportunities to use and make simple maps. This might take the form of a class-wide project to draw a map of the school in the second or third grade, or even a simple sketch of the classroom layout for kindergarteners and first graders. The key is making the map-focused activities as purposeful and relevant as possible to keep student engagement high and help them recognize and practice using and creating maps with purpose.

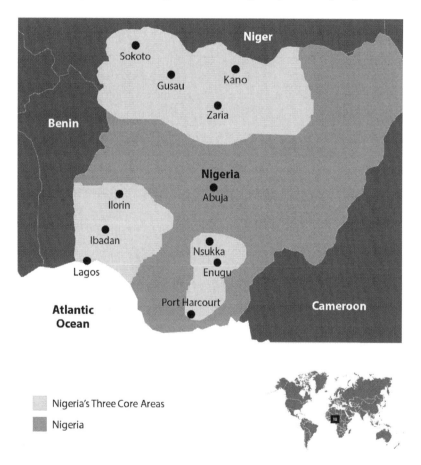

Figure 2.10. Parts of a Map

Maps are not the only type of graphic representations that students need practice with interpreting. Both **graphs** and **charts** are used in many different types of texts, and students need practice in extrapolating information from them. An appropriate chart for a kindergarten student may be a simple pictorial representation, while third-grade students will need significant practice with interpreting various bar and line graphs to meet both social studies and math objectives. The key is providing students

QUICK REVIEW

What types of things might you chart in simple pictorial form in the kindergarten classroom?

with strategies to comprehend graphic information. Teachers can help students develop these skills by asking questions such as "What does _____ mean/represent/ stand for?" and "What information does _____ show?" and "What do you see in the row/column/pie?"

SAMPLE QUESTIONS

13) **Which of the following is a landmark appropriate for a first grader to recognize?**

   A.   the Leaning Tower of Pisa

   B.   London Bridge

   C.   the Statue of Liberty

   D.   the Coliseum

   Answers:

   A.   Incorrect. This is not common enough and would be challenging for a first grader.

   B.   Incorrect. This would also be very challenging for a first grader, especially one who has not traveled.

   C.   Correct. The Statue of Liberty is one of the most widely recognized American landmarks, and it would be appropriate for a first grader to recognize this symbol.

   D.   Incorrect. A first grader would be unlikely to have the background in Roman history to recognize the Coliseum.

14) **Which symbol on a map denotes north, south, east, and west?**

   A.   the compass rose

   B.   the scale

   C.   the grid

   D.   the Mercator projection

   Answers:

   A.   Correct. The compass rose indicates the cardinal directions.

   B.   Incorrect. The scale shows the relative distance as indicated by the map.

C.   Incorrect. The grid is a coordinate system that helps show location by points.

D.   Incorrect. This is one projection used to show the globe on a flat surface.

GEOGRAPHIC PERSPECTIVES

Regions are the basic units of geography and describe areas of land that have common features. Regions can be based on political or cultural similarities but often are defined in terms of climate and vegetation. These regional differences affect human behavior and interaction with the environment. The major climate regions are listed as follows:

- ▶ polar: cold and dry year-round
- ▶ temperate: cold winters, mild summers, some forests and plains/prairies
- ▶ arid: hot and dry year-round and include some deserts (some deserts are found in cold tundra regions as well)
- ▶ tropical: always hot and wet, rain forests
- ▶ Mediterranean: mild winters and hot, dry summers
- ▶ tundra: cold year-round with three subtypes:
  - ▷ Arctic tundra is found in the far Northern Hemisphere and features a very desolate landscape. The ground is frozen in these cold desert regions, making it impossible for most plants to grow.
  - ▷ Antarctic tundra is found in Antarctica and features some desolate landscape and desert. However, some areas support plant life.
  - ▷ Alpine tundra is a mountainous region also without significant plant life.

These environmental conditions impact people in a variety of ways. People living on plains and prairies where there are few trees, for example, often have to build houses out of materials other than lumber. People living in mountain and desert regions may have to import food from other areas since the landscape makes farming difficult. People who live in particularly fragile environments, such as the rain forest, often use the intense biodiversity around them to develop innovative solutions to meet their needs, such as growing small batches of crops in the limited ground space and hunting a wide variety of animals. One challenge facing many of the world's geographic regions is the desire for economic development balanced with the preservation of natural environments. Destroying rain forests, for example, not only displaces animals but also forces their inhabitants to change their very way of life.

QUICK REVIEW

What is the climate of your local community? How does this impact your daily life and the lives of your students?

In addition to the six populated **continents** of North and South America, Asia, Europe, Africa, and Australia, there are two other large formations that account for the solid surface area of the planet. The North Pole is the northernmost point on the globe and is sometimes referred to as the Arctic. It is not a landform in the strictest sense because it is really a large sheet of ice that expands and contracts based on temperature. However, some definitions of "the Arctic" cover the entire region of the Arctic Ocean and inhabited areas such as parts of Canada and Greenland. The South Pole, on the other hand, is located on the continent of Antarctica and represents the southernmost point on the globe. Antarctica boasts no permanent residents, but it is, like the North Pole, an important location for research stations.

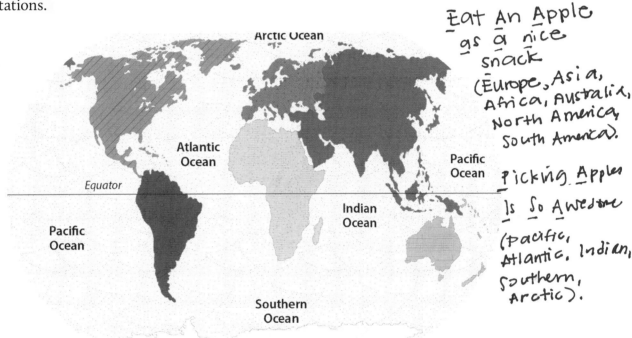

Eat An Apple as a nice snack (Europe, Asia, Africa, Australia, North America, South America).

Picking Apples Is So Awesome (Pacific, Atlantic, Indian, Southern, Arctic).

Figure 2.11. The Continents and Oceans

The surface of the earth is 71 percent water, and its continents are surrounded by five **oceans**: the Atlantic, Pacific, Indian, Arctic, and Antarctic. The Antarctic Ocean is also sometimes referred to as the Southern Ocean or the Antarctic Sea. These saltwater bodies are connected by **seas**, which are generally smaller than oceans, often surrounded partly or wholly by land, saltwater, and usually connect with their larger counterparts.

Rivers and their smaller cousins, **streams**, are flowing bodies of water that empty into seas and oceans and are generally freshwater. **Lakes**, like seas, are large bodies of water that are surrounded by land; though unlike seas,

STUDY TIPS

Ensure that you can identify the Atlantic, Pacific, Indian, Arctic, and Antarctic Oceans on a map or globe without labels. Can you come up with a mnemonic device that would help students remember the names and locations of the oceans?

they are usually freshwater. While some lakes are natural, many are artificial and constructed for recreation. Most other bodies of water are naturally occurring and impact those in their vicinity. People who live near large bodies of water use the water source for food and transportation. Teachers whose programs are located near a body of water can ask students to consider the ways in which the body of water impacts the life of the community. Is fishing a popular local industry? Does the beach or lake promote tourism to the area?

SAMPLE QUESTIONS

15) **What is the main distinction between rivers and lakes?**

A.   Rivers are surrounded by land, and lakes are not.

B.   Lakes are generally saltwater, and rivers are generally freshwater.

C.   Rivers divide continents, while lakes are within continents.

D.   Lakes do not flow, while rivers flow into seas and oceans.

Answers:

A.   Incorrect. Both rivers and lakes are surrounded by land.

B.   Incorrect. Both lakes and rivers are generally freshwater.

C.   Incorrect. Both lakes and rivers are within continents.

D.   Correct. Rivers flow into seas and oceans, but lakes do not.

16) **Mrs. Martin, who teaches first grade in the Arizona desert, wants to help her students understand how climate affects the way humans live in a given area. Which integrated social studies and science activity would help her class understand this concept?**

A.   showing them a video of people shopping for a new house in another state

B.   planting a few different crops in the school garden to see which ones grow

C.   bringing in a guest chef to talk to the students about different flavor profiles

D.   having her students design their "dream house" out of blocks

Answers:

A.   Incorrect. This is not pertinent to climate.

B.   Correct. Because the school is in the desert, some crops will survive and others will not (or all will die), prompting a discussion about how people living in the desert grow only certain crops or must import food.

C.   Incorrect. This activity does not pertain to climate.

D.   Incorrect. Again, this project is not related to climate.

HUMAN–ENVIRONMENTAL INTERACTION

Our planet is divided into political divisions based on governmental jurisdiction. The largest units of these are sovereign states or nation-states that are generally referred to as countries. Within these **countries** are smaller units known as **states**, provinces, counties, parishes, districts, and cities or towns. The United States follows a pattern of states subdivided into counties or parishes and then cities or towns. It is important that, as developmentally appropriate, students understand that **borders** between both countries and states are human constructs. While the lines of demarcation may be based upon physical boundaries such as rivers or mountains, these are political borders created by humans that do not exist organically.

There are two primary types of communities based on population density. **Rural** communities such as farms and villages contain a smaller population of people, and they often participate in an agrarian, or **farming**, lifestyle. Farming is a somewhat general term often used to describe the use of land or water for the production or obtainment of food. This includes **ranching**, which uses land to produce livestock, and **fishing**, which extracts food from bodies of water or raises fish in tanks. **Urban** communities are cities and towns where the economy is driven by business and the **trade**, or exchange, of goods and services.

While both urban and rural areas may be important to the overall economy, or wealth of resources, of a country or region, urban areas tend to be centers of commerce and production. Cities originally developed around markets later grew around factories as industry developed. Factories are large buildings where products are made, originally by humans and increasingly by machines controlled by humans. Some cities are known for a particular type of factory, such as the automotive production factories in Detroit, Michigan. Additionally, most cities have elaborate transportation networks that move people and goods from one place to another. People living in cities often have many public transportation options such as trains, subways, and buses. These options are more limited in rural communities because of remoteness and lack of population density.

Rural areas, however, produce many raw materials and crops that must be transported to manufacturing centers and cities for production and sale to consumers. Since those who rely on ranching and fishing require land to produce or procure their foodstuffs, they, too, tend to be located in areas remote from urban centers. A railroad system that uses trains to ship important commodities, and a **highway** system that uses **trucks** to transport goods are very important to the **transportation** network of rural and remote communities. Without such networks, interdependent relationships between communities would not be possible. This interdependence is often marked by raw goods and commodities such as cotton and soybeans being produced in rural areas and then shipped to urban areas for transformation into processed foods and clothing. These finished goods are then shipped and sold both to urban and rural communities.

Though transporting goods over water does not require the same type of transportation network as transporting goods over land, this method does rely on the construction of ports and canals, which might be highly relevant to the economy of a given community. Although generally more expensive, **airplanes** can be used to transport people and goods. In some very remote areas, such as rural Alaska, airplane travel is the only method of transportation available because road and rail networks do not exist. Even in urban areas, the reliance on **shipping** direct to the consumer has become very popular as more and more people rely on the internet to buy consumer goods.

One trend in the United States has been increasing urbanization, or the shift in population from rural to urban areas. Recent data from the US Census Bureau revealed that over 80 percent of Americans live in urban areas. In some very fast-growing cities, the pace of **construction** of new homes, schools, and roads is often unable to accommodate population growth. This creates many urban problems like traffic, school overcrowding, and lack of affordable housing.

The desire of people to move from a rural area to an urban one (or from any area to a new area) is generally the result of both push and pull factors. **Push factors** are situations that push people from their community. These could include drought, lack of educational or economic opportunity, or the loss of a job or livelihood. **Pull factors** are situations that pull people toward a new community. These factors could be the promise of a new job or the possibility of more educational or social opportunities. Some students may have experienced these factors in their own family's immigration to the United States. An existing network of extended family in the United States might have been a pull factor, for example.

Both urban and rural areas have advantages and disadvantages related to population density. High-population density in urban areas often leads to pollution, traffic, and crowded conditions. Conversely, life in a rural area may bring limited educational and economic opportunities and even less access to technological innovation.

STUDY TIPS

Create a chart comparing the advantages and disadvantages of urban and rural life. Then list the economic contributions that both urban and rural communities make to any society.

In many developed nations, and particularly the United States, people strike a balance between urban and rural in the establishment of suburban communities. These communities, located just on the outskirts of major cities, give residents access to the city's economic resources while allowing them to enjoy some of the positive elements of rural life, such as open green areas and larger living spaces. Teachers with programs located in any of these urban, rural, or suburban communities must strive to help children understand that even within a country or state, humans live in many different types of places.

SAMPLE QUESTIONS

17) Ms. Annie is a pre-kindergarten teacher in a rural community in Iowa. She is reading a story to her students about a girl who is afraid of taking the elevator to her twelfth-floor Manhattan apartment. What question would be most appropriate for her to ask her students to help them understand the different environments people live in as described in the story?

A.   Is the story set in an urban, rural, or suburban environment?

B.   Why is the girl afraid of taking the elevator up?

C.   Is Manhattan an island?

D.   What kind of house does the girl live in?

Answers:

A.   Incorrect. This is too advanced for a prekindergarten class.

B.   Incorrect. This is a question about plot, not about different environments.

C.   Incorrect. Prekindergarten students in rural Iowa likely would not know the answer to this question.

D.   Correct. This will help lead students in a discussion about different types of houses such as apartments in urban areas.

18) Mr. Martin's third-grade student Hector is very interested in trains. Mr. Martin wants to make sure Hector's research project interests him and pertains to the assignment's topic of the American economy. Which topical suggestion might Mr. Martin make to Hector?

A.   trains throughout American history

B.   the role of trains in cattle ranching

C.   the invention of the steam engine

D.   the decline of the American railroad

Answers:

A.   Incorrect. This topic is not specifically about the economy, and Hector might choose to discuss other aspects of trains in American history.

B.   Correct. This topic is pertinent to the role of trains in a subset of the American economy: cattle ranching.

C.   Incorrect. This topic does not necessarily pertain to the economy.

D.   Incorrect. This topic might have something to do with the changing American economy, but it is related more to other transportation options than to the economy.

TIME, CONTINUITY, AND CHANGE

CHRONOLOGICAL THINKING

Humans have long realized that there were others who came before them. **History**, or the study of past events, helps humans situate themselves in time. The strictest definition of history is the study of the past through the examination of written records; however, more contemporary definitions cite many other disciplines as being part of the overall study of history.

- ▸ **archaeology**: the study of human history through artifacts and remains
- ▸ **anthropology**: the study of human cultural development and evolution
- ▸ **sociology**: the study of human society

Many historians have found that an interdisciplinary approach often provides tremendous benefits, particularly when studying past cultures that did not leave any written accounts.

Students should be exposed to textual sources such as books, articles, and stories, as well as to other **historical data** such as timelines, maps, graphs, and tables. These sources should reference the entire expanse of human history, including what is commonly referred to as **prehistory**, or the period before humans left a written record of their experiences.

> **QUICK REVIEW**
>
> What sources can be used to study prehistory?

Children's understanding of history begins in late preschool when they start to understand concepts of time. Students at age four can begin to understand that a day is shorter than a month and a second is shorter than a minute. They can begin to grasp that their birthday is next week or that they went to the park yesterday. Teachers can reinforce this chronological knowledge by encouraging young students to use words that express time relationships, such as before, after, tomorrow, and so on. Teachers can also encourage young students to understand the distant past through concrete pictorial representations like ancient Egyptian artifacts, and they can make predictions about the future after reading stories or examining pictures with futuristic themes.

By kindergarten, most children begin to understand that some events happen at a certain time each day, such as art first, then center time, and finally recess. Calendar-tracking activities are generally very popular in kindergarten classrooms, as these aid in students' understanding of the passage of time. These activities may involve having students track and mark off time each day, week, month, or even year. This will help students in their eventual progression in the elementary years in grasping more advanced concepts of time such as centuries (one-hundred-year periods) and even millennia (one-thousand-year periods).

Many educators once believed that young children should not be exposed to unsettling parts of history, but the latest research indicates that it is far better to present a more balanced view of **key historical events**, even when presenting these events to a preschool audience. While it is not prudent to burden young children with the atrocities of **war** and genocide, it is most certainly not appropriate to present a historical event leaving out key events and concepts. For example, teaching first-grade students that the Pilgrims settled uninhabited land would be historically inaccurate and leave them with a gross oversimplification of a very complex event that sparked a series of interactions and future events. When talking of **natural disasters**, economic crises, or other upsetting events that are part of the elementary curriculum, it is vital to support students in their understanding that studying troubling historical events is part of the overall study of history.

One popular curriculum strategy is using fictional works on various topics of cultural and historical sensitivity as part of social studies. This can allow for troubling or difficult topics to be introduced and handled more readily than in a personal context. For example, a second-grade student might find it upsetting to discuss her own experiences with racism, but reading an age-appropriate book on segregation such as *These Hands* by Margaret H. Mason might allow her to discuss the concept safely in the context of the social studies curriculum.

Social studies teachers should make an effort to discuss current events in the context of students' everyday lives, as is age appropriate. Are their parents going to vote in the upcoming **elections**? Do students know the candidates who are running? These are excellent questions to spark discussion. Helping students maintain an awareness of current events will help them to develop an interest in staying informed and participating in the civic life of the community.

SAMPLE QUESTIONS

19) How can a kindergarten teacher help her students develop an understanding of chronology?

   A. directing students to make timelines showing major events in world history

   B. having a classroom calendar that students use to mark off each day

   C. explaining the concepts of year, century, and millennium

   D. assigning students a project to write about the major events of their lives

Answers:

   A. Incorrect. This is not developmentally appropriate for a kindergartener.

   B. **Correct.** This gives students a visual representation of the passage of time.

   C. Incorrect. Kindergarten students would not understand this.

   D. Incorrect. This would not be developmentally appropriate for a kindergarten class.

20) **Miss Clark wants to incorporate visual/graphic literacy activities into her third-grade class's study of Native Americans. Which activity would be most appropriate?**

   A.   asking a Native American community member to visit the class and speak on her experiences

   B.   reading an age-appropriate story about the Navajo people to the class

   C.   having her students write an essay comparing two Native American tribes

   D.   giving her students a chart that shows the different regions in which certain tribes live

Answers:

   A.   Incorrect. This activity does not promote visual/graphic literacy.

   B.   Incorrect. This activity promotes general literacy but not visual/graphic literacy in particular.

   C.   Incorrect. This activity promotes general literacy in writing ability but not visual/graphic literacy.

   D.   **Correct.** This activity will help her students use and understand social studies information presented graphically and aid in the development of overall visual/graphic literacy.

Social Studies Tools

It is important for students to be exposed to a rich variety of both primary and secondary sources in their study of history and society. Graphic literacy is an important part of a social studies curriculum, and activities must be calibrated for age and grade appropriateness. Kindergarten students, for example, might create their own **map** of the playground, coloring in the locations of trees, play equipment, bathrooms, and so on. This will help them understand not only that the map represents concrete locations and objects but also that it can be used for directional purposes. Older students may create and even use more sophisticated maps. A second- or third-grade class might, with support from the teacher, work to create a map of the school or use a simple map to go on a school or classroom scavenger hunt.

Maps and globes can also be used to help students pinpoint their location in relationship to others. By first grade, most students should be able to identify their city, state, and the United States on a map or globe, though this will likely take explicit teaching. Second-grade students should be able to locate additional places such as the state capital, major cities within the state, the location of various oceans and bodies of water, and the location of Canada and Mexico. By third grade, students should begin practicing with a map grid system and various map symbols to enable them to use maps even when they are referencing unfamiliar locations.

Students of all ages should also be exposed to **timelines**. In a preschool or kindergarten classroom, this might be as simple as the daily schedule posted in the classroom in both written and visual form. Visual schedules are very popular in many programs, and these graphics are the simplest form of a daily timeline. They might illustrate, for example, when different classes, lunch, and recess are set to occur.

Today's Schedule

8:00 a	🕗	Reading
9:00 a	🕘	Writing
10:00 a	🕙	Math
11:00 a	🕚	Social Studies
12:00 p	🕛	Lunch
12:45 p	🕐	Recess
1:30 p	🕜	Science
2:30 p	🕝	Music

Figure 2.12. A Visual Schedule

Teachers might further reinforce the daily timeline by mixing up the elements of the daily schedule and asking students to put them back in the correct order. Older students in first or second grade may even be encouraged to create their own daily schedule or timeline that shows their activities before and after school. By third grade, students should begin creating and understanding historical events on a timeline.

Students will also need to be able to understand and interpret quantitative information in both **graphs** and **tables**. These will range in complexity based on student age and grade level but should be a common part of the social studies curriculum. Graphs showing increases, decreases, or back-and-forth changes over time help students understand changing economic or social conditions as well as basic mathematical concepts. Tables help students organize and compartmental-ize information and details. Using graphs and tables in the social studies classroom will also integrate social studies, math, and science curriculum and help students make connections and use math skills to analyze graphic relationships in a social studies context.

QUICK REVIEW

What are some specific mathematical concepts that can be integrated into social studies units on using graphs and charts?

Another important, though relatively recent, addition to the historical record are **photographs**. Unlike many historical narratives, photographs are often **primary sources**, or historical artifacts in themselves. Photographs can make history far more interesting for young students, and any historical study in the early childhood grade levels should make use of as many photographs as possible. It is important, as part of visual literacy in the social studies context, that students examine photographs carefully for their implicit meaning. Teachers might ask the following questions when helping students evaluate historical photographs:

▶ Why do you think the photographer took this picture?

▶ When do you think this photograph was taken? Why?

▶ Do you think the person wanted his/her photo taken? Why or why not?

▶ What event is this photograph showing/documenting?

Additionally, photography might be a part of the early childhood classroom's own historical documentation. Preschool and kindergarten teachers using student portfolios as part of an overall assessment strategy might take and include photographs of students in these digital or physical records of student progress, if school policy permits. Students might also be encouraged to use photography to document class- or school-wide events. With the simplification of camera technology and the ease of use of most tablet computers, even prekindergarten students can take photos of an important school or class event. These photos can then be organized into a visual timeline (with the aid of the teacher) on a classroom bulletin board or even organized into a scrapbook. Taking and using photographs to document events will help students understand the role of photography in social studies. Teachers should always follow school policy regarding photography at school events.

> **DID YOU KNOW?**
>
> The National Archives (archives.gov) and the Library of Congress (loc.gov) have links to thousands of digital photograph collections in various online archives.

SAMPLE QUESTIONS

21) **Which activity would be most appropriate to introduce a timeline to a prekindergarten classroom?**

A. creating a timeline of all the annual holidays and calculating when each will occur

B. asking students to help place visual images of the day's activities into the proper order

C. directing students to create a timeline of the major events of the Civil War

D. encouraging students to keep a journal documenting their daily activity in order

Answers:

A.   Incorrect. This activity is far too advanced for a prekindergarten class.

B.   Correct. This activity helps students understand the daily chronology.

C.   Incorrect. This activity is not developmentally appropriate for a prekindergarten class.

D.   Incorrect. Again, this activity is far too advanced for this grade level.

22) **Mr. Fuller is in a parent-student-teacher conference with Lisa, his kindergarten student. He opens Lisa's portfolio to the page with pictures of her conducting show-and-tell, which he has arranged in order with the words FIRST, SECOND, NEXT, and LAST. He then asks Lisa to explain this page to her mother. Why is he doing this?**

A.   He wants to ensure that Lisa understands the purpose of the portfolio in documenting her progress.

B.   He thinks Lisa's mother will be impressed with her vocabulary development as she is describing the photos.

C.   This reinforces Lisa's understanding of chronology of events.

D.   This helps Lisa grasp that these photographs are primary sources.

Answers:

A.   Incorrect. It is unlikely that Lisa would understand the concept of the portfolio as assessment/documentation of progress.

B.   Incorrect. Lisa might have the chance to demonstrate her vocabulary skills to her mother, but vocabulary is not Mr. Fuller's primary motivation.

C.   Correct. This activity helps Lisa link the visual photographic representations with what she did first, second, next, and last.

D.   Incorrect. This activity does not clearly demonstrate to Lisa that the photographs are primary soruces.

CIVICS AND GOVERNMENT

CIVICS CONCEPTS

A well-managed early childhood classroom will introduce students to many different civics concepts through explicit teaching and everyday interactions. Basic concepts of **justice**, or fair treatment, will likely come up quite frequently when young children are involved. In the early childhood classroom, this more often involves ensuring each child gets his or her needs met versus treating each child in the exact same way. This often plays out in assessing the reason for or antecedent of a child's behavior. A teacher ignoring a child's inappropriate behavior might be acceptable if the reason for the behavior was desire for attention, but if attention-seeking was not the likely antecedent of the behavior and if there is a social lesson to be taught, ignoring the behavior may not be the best approach.

In helping students to understand the concept of justice, it is important to equate justice, as much as is possible, with a fitting consequence for an action. It might be just, for example, for Stephanie to be selected as the second-grade Pledge of Allegiance leader because of her excellent classroom conduct and high rates of homework completion. It might also be just for third grader Max to clean up the mess he made in the cafeteria after lunch, causing him to miss classwork and have extra homework. These are natural consequences for actions that represent the truest idea of justice.

As a social studies construct, justice generally refers to the justice system, in which people are held accountable for the consequences of their actions within society. This typically involves the role of the courts to ascribe particular penalties for certain illicit actions. Teachers can help students understand the basic tenets of the justice system at many grade levels. Preschool and kindergarten teachers might help students identify the role of community helpers like police officers, lawyers, and judges. First-grade teachers may ask students to declare whether they believe a character in a story is guilty or innocent of a given charge. Second- and third-grade teachers may explore the justice process even more deeply and hold simple mock trials or have students participate in mock criminal investigations. It is also important to point out, as is age appropriate, that in the United States, it is the **rule of law**, or the idea that it is the law itself, that governs, rather than government officials. In this way, the law empowers its agents in government to enforce it. It grants them no powers outside of it.

Equality is another important civics ideology that should be discussed in the classroom and in society. It is not always easy to achieve equality in a classroom with varying student needs and limited resources or in a society with many different people with varying needs and similarly limited resources. While there are differing opinions about whether all Americans truly enjoy equality in terms of the legal system, the justice system is founded upon the principle of equality before the law in which all people should be treated equally both in the creation and implementation of the law.

Unlike the concept of equality, in which all people are treated the same, the concept of **equity** involves giving individuals what they need to be successful. Classrooms are places where equality exists in some cases, and equity exists in others. For example, a teacher might promote equality by giving all her first-grade students ten spelling words each week. She might promote equity by giving her English-Language Learners a list of ten different words that are more appropriate to their current skill level.

There may be other parts of educational equity within a school or classroom as well. Many schools, realizing that hungry children cannot learn at the same rate as children who get enough to eat, offer free lunches to students who cannot afford to bring or purchase their own lunches. Students with Individualized Education Programs (IEPs) may have accommodations within the classroom such as scribes, interpreters, or educational aides to promote equity. Federal programs like Title 1 and the Every Student Succeeds Act (ESSA) are designed to promote equity in educational environments by ensuring that students with special needs or from disadvantaged backgrounds receive the support they need to take full advantage of educational opportunities. It is important that teachers take the tenets of these programs seriously and familiarize themselves with all of the resources available to their students and help students and family obtain the resources they need. This will help promote an equitable educational environment.

Figure 2.13. Equality Versus Equity

Teachers should also promote **tolerance**, or the acceptance of beliefs or behaviors that one does not necessarily agree with, as appropriate in the classroom and help students understand the need for tolerance in pluralistic American society. Freedom of religion is a core tenet of the United States, and many classrooms will have students with different belief systems. Helping students to be understanding and tolerant of the beliefs of others starts with accepting differences. While some students might not understand why certain dietary or dress restrictions are observed by their peers, part of promoting tolerance includes helping students understand that there are many different ways of doing things. The nonprofit organization Teaching Tolerance (tolerance.org) created a list of standards appropriate for each K–12 grade level that can be used as a reference to guide explicit instruction to help students develop tolerance.

SAMPLE QUESTIONS

23) Mrs. Rose has just welcomed a new third grader named Noor into her classroom. Unlike the other students, Noor wears a hijab. Mrs. Rose notices that one of the more vocal students has made some disparaging comments about Noor's "funny hat." What theme might Mrs. Rose consider for her next social studies lesson?

A. tolerance

B. equality

C. equity

D. justice

Answers:

A. **Correct.** Mrs. Rose can help address this issue by promoting tolerance of different religions and styles of dress.

B. Incorrect. Equality does not necessarily pertain to this situation.

C. Incorrect. Equity does not pertain directly to this situation.

D. Incorrect. This situation is about tolerance of difference, not fairness.

24) **Mr. Haskell is always reminding his class that it is the classroom rules that govern the classroom, not the teacher. What concept is he basing this statement upon?**

A. justice

B. tolerance

C. rule of law

D. equity

Answers:

A. Incorrect. This is not a statement about fairness so much as rule of law.

B. Incorrect. This is not a statement about tolerance.

C. **Correct.** Mr. Haskell is likening his classroom rules to laws that apply to everyone, even the teacher.

D. Incorrect. This is not a statement about equity.

CIVIC PARTICIPATION

Civic participation, or participating in issues of public concern, is important, but it is not practiced in many communities. Low turnouts, particularly at local elections, are evidence of this trend. However, this trend can be reversed by educating young people about how individuals in a society can help in the **decision-making** that affects their communities.

To participate in civic life, individuals must first be informed of the **issues**. Teachers can help their students keep up with current events on a local, national, and global scale through social studies lessons on contemporary issues. Teachers can point out that there are often different **points of view** on any given issue and that different groups bring different backgrounds and desires to any issue. A teacher may illustrate this by proposing an increase in social studies time and a decrease in math time. He or she might then ask the class to weigh in on the issue. Is everyone in favor? Why are some groups against this? Students are likely to have different points of view based on their ease with or interest in either subject. Often in civic matters, one must compromise, or meet those with a different point of view in the middle on an issue. This give-and-take is part of what makes democracy work.

In a representative democracy, such as that of the United States, power and authority in decision-making rest with elected officials who have been designated by the people. The process of electing officials and raising issues of public concern to these officials brings many different viewpoints, as illustrated by the example of students weighing in on the issue of more social studies and less math time. In this example, students approach the issue from an individual perspective: those who like social studies and dislike math would be in favor of more social studies time, while those who like math more may not be in favor. This perspective represents the individual needs of students. However, students must consider many perspectives on the issue. Would a decrease in math time leave students ill-prepared for state tests? Would students who need more math practice be at a disadvantage? These considerations might then lead to making a decision based on the overall needs of the group, which must be balanced with individual needs and preferences. This is a key part of the democratic process.

Students should understand their role as members of many different communities. They must be advocates in their local community to ensure their schools, hospitals, roads, and local services are operating smoothly and efficiently. They should also appreciate their role in the larger city, state, and nation regarding their future ability to vote, organize, and have their voices heard.

DID YOU KNOW?

Only around 55 percent of eligible Americans voted in the 2016 national election.

Students should also understand their role as global citizens who must protect the natural resources and biodiversity of the planet. The topic of global **citizenship**, or actions taken to promote social, political, or environmental issues on a global scale, is easily integrated with science topics such as recycling, conservation, and environmental advocacy. Environmental protection is necessary for keeping the plant and animal life on Earth diverse. It is also vital since all living things, their environment, and the economy are interdependent. A teacher might discuss this concept broadly with younger students by explaining that we must protect the earth in order to continue using its resources such as food and water.

Older students might delve more deeply into this issue and examine the cause-and-effect relationship between lack of environmental resource protection and the local economy. For example, a community reliant on the shrimping industry might be severely impacted by pollution in the Gulf of Mexico. This action by humans on the environment impacts the shrimp in the Gulf, whose populations may die out or dwindle. This, in turn,

DID YOU KNOW?

The United Nations Educational, Scientific and Cultural Organization (UNESCO) has created learning tools and objectives for each grade level to promote global citizenship and education.

impacts the local economy, as shrimping may no longer be possible. This can have all sorts of further consequences, as shrimpers may leave the community, forcing the businesses that served the shrimpers (grocery and clothing stores, restaurants, and so on) to also go out of business. In this way, the environment and the economy are interdependent, and an action on one will impact the other.

It is also worthwhile to point out that the American early childhood classroom is an increasingly diverse place. It is unreasonable to assume that all students in any given classroom have the same national identity or even US citizenship. Teachers should respect and encourage the civic growth of all students, regardless of citizenship status or country of origin. Respect for this diversity under a common shared identity as humans is another key component of global citizenship. Globally responsible students will understand that human dignity, or the inherent value and worth of all humans, must be preserved on both a local and global scale.

SAMPLE QUESTIONS

25) **Ms. Sturgis happens upon two of her first-grade students in a heated argument about what game to play at recess. Which strategy might help her students learn to compromise?**

   A.   picking the game herself and telling the students which game to play

   B.   designating one student to decide which game to play

   C.   proposing that they join the kickball game already in progress

   D.   suggesting that they play one game for five minutes and the other game the next five minutes

Answers:

   A.   Incorrect. This solution does not encourage compromise, since Ms. Sturgis solved the problem for the students.

   B.   Incorrect. This suggestion also does not encourage compromise and might be seen as unfair.

   C.   Incorrect. This idea avoids the issue and misses the opportunity to teach compromise.

   D.   Correct. This suggestion is a compromise in which both students give and take something.

26) **Which activity is associated with global citizenship?**

   A.   organizing a clothing drive to help a local shelter

   B.   serving on a jury

   C.   voting in a national election

   D.   recycling

Answers:

   A.   Incorrect. This activity is being a good local citizen.

   B.   Incorrect. This activity is also being a good local citizen.

   C.   Incorrect. This activity is being a good national citizen.

D.   **Correct**. This activity is part of global citizenship since recycling affects the entire planet.

UNITED STATES GOVERNMENT

Understanding the basics of government will help children to grow up to be responsible citizens who select leaders fit for their office. The United States government is composed of three branches: the executive, legislative, and judicial. A system of **checks and balances** keeps each branch from having too much power.

The **executive branch** of government is made up of the **president, vice president**, and fifteen executive departments, including the Departments of Defense, Commerce, State, Justice, Labor, and so on. The executive branch enforces the laws. The president and vice president are elected members of the executive branch, but officials in other executive branch departments and agencies are appointed.

The legislative branch includes both houses of **Congress**: the Senate and the House of Representatives. The legislative branch makes the laws. Members of both the House and the Senate are elected, with each state electing two senators per state, and the number of representatives totaling 435 but varying in number based on state population. California and Texas have the most representatives at fifty-three and thirty-six, respectively, while some less-populous states have only one representative.

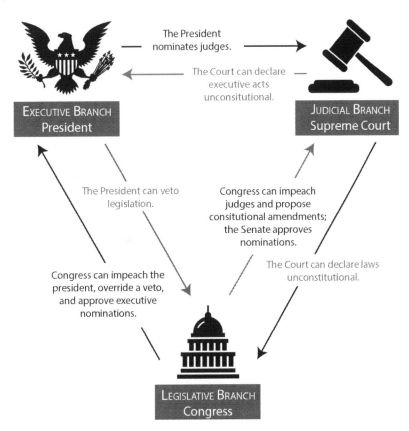

Figure 2.14. Checks and Balances

The judicial branch comprises the federal court system, including the **Supreme Court**. The Supreme Court is made up of nine justices who are nominated by the president and approved by the Senate. The judicial branch interprets the meaning of the laws.

STUDY TIPS

The names of the different branches of government tell what they do. The executive branch is like the executive of a company—it ensures the "execution" of the company's objectives (like laws). The legislative branch "legislates," or deals in making laws. The judicial branch "judges," or interprets the laws.

The federal government was formed by and operates based on the outline set out in the **Constitution**. In its interpretation of the laws made by Congress, the Supreme Court frequently examines whether legislation is in line with this document. While the basic governmental framework has been laid out, the political actors are selected through citizens who **vote** in **elections**.

Early childhood classrooms are excellent places to encourage an understanding of representative democracy. Teachers might have the class vote on classroom issues such as what type of class pet to get. The early childhood classroom is also an appropriate environment for students to learn the role of government officials as servants of the public. Having special "classroom helpers" assigned to complete key housekeeping or administrative tasks can help students understand service to the classroom community. Assigning a student the responsibility of emptying out the pencil sharpener each day or collecting assignments, for example, can help students to appreciate the value in service to community, the foundation upon which all public service should rest.

SAMPLE QUESTIONS

27) Mr. Harrison wants to teach his third-grade class about how a written document, such as the Constitution, can outline the procedures an organization or country must follow. Which activity meets this goal?

   A.   having students research the history of the Constitution

   B.   directing students to draft a "classroom compact"

   C.   asking students to compare their rules at home with the school rules

   D.   organizing a school-wide recycling program

   Answers:

   A.   Incorrect. Researching the Constitution's history does not directly address this goal, as there are many different parts related to the history of the Constitution.

   B.   **Correct.** This activity will help his students make the connection between the Constitution that outlines the rules our government must follow and a "classroom compact" that will outline the rules the classroom must operate within.

C.   Incorrect. Comparing home and school rules is not related to a written document, as it is unlikely that the rules of the home are written.

D.   Incorrect. A school recycling program is more about global citizenship than understanding the Constitution.

28) **Which of the following is NOT an elected position?**

A.   US senator

B.   US representative

C.   vice president

D.   secretary of state

Answers:

A.   Incorrect. US senators are elected.

B.   Incorrect. US representatives are elected.

C.   Incorrect. The vice president is elected.

D.   **Correct.** The secretary of state is appointed by the president.

Mathematics

Emergent Mathematics

Children cultivate math skills from a very young age. **Emergent mathematics** refers to how young children develop math skills over time through intellectual development and interaction with their environment.

Skills such as **counting** and skip counting, which involve rote memorization of numeric words in a proper order, are some of the most important math concepts introduced to young children. **Skip counting** is a form of counting where numbers are not consecutively recited by one. Skip counting can occur in twos, threes, or in any fixed pattern. As children learn counting, they may not quite understand the concept of one-to-one correspondence in **numeration**.

One-to-one correspondence is the ability to say one number for each object pointed to or touched consecutively. For instance, when counting out "one, two, three, four" using **counters** or other objects, children who have not developed the concept of one-to-one correspondence may skip an object or count it more than once. Placing objects in a line and using counting motions like pointing or clapping while saying each number out loud helps correlate each number to an object.

Which group has more counters?

Students who understand 1:1 correspondence will count the objects and say this group has more counters.

Students learning 1:1 correspondence may say this group has more counters because it takes up more space.

Figure 3.1. One-to-One Correspondence

Pattern matching, **grouping**, **sorting**, and **sequencing** are concepts in early math development that aid in understanding numeration. As children begin to categorize objects in their environment by how they are alike or different, a natural sense of order occurs. Since many fundamental math skills cannot be directly taught at a young age, **manipulatives** in the form of toys, puzzles, games, or even general household items provide excellent practice material. Toy blocks can be grouped or sorted by color, shape, or size; clothes can be arranged or sequenced by **pattern**; toys can be put away while counting each one.

Many children love using their fingers to count. In the past, using fingers was not considered an acceptable convention, but research has shown that children who count with fingers are better at quantitative tasks, as it is a natural sensory activity linking movement with brain activity. Counting on fingers is easily accessible, quick, and free.

Children revel in repetition, so the more such chores are undertaken, the better their recognition of crucial skills like number conservation. **Number conservation** refers to the understanding that a number of objects remains the same even when the objects are rearranged. A child putting away five stuffed animals will recognize that the quantity does not change regardless of which animal is put away first.

Over time, a child maturing in age and cognitive development will have the ability to mentally conduct numeration in various ways. One such way is by **subitizing**—the capacity to view a small number of objects and immediately recognize how many there are without counting. Another numeric skill involves mastering one-to-one correspondence, which leads to an understanding of **cardinality**—finding out how many objects are in a group or set.

HELPFUL HINT

Help students connect counting to cardinality: When counting objects in a set, the last word said is the number of objects in that set.

SAMPLE QUESTIONS

1) Chris puts away his ten stuffed animal toys every night. He learns that the quantity does not change regardless of which animal is put away first. Which of the following concepts is the child learning?

   A. skip counting

   B. number conservation

   C. sorting

   D. pattern matching

   Answers:

   A. Incorrect. Skip counting omits numbers in a pattern.

   B. **Correct.** Number conservation refers to the understanding that the number of objects remains the same even when they are rearranged.

C.   Incorrect. Sorting is the process of dividing items into groups based on their characteristics.

D.   Incorrect. Pattern matching requires ordering or sorting by a pattern or design.

2)   **Kelly helped her mother bake chocolate chip cookies. After they were cool and placed on a plate, she immediately exclaimed that there were five cookies. Which of the following skills is Kelly demonstrating?**

A.   sequencing

B.   sorting

C.   skip counting

D.   subitizing

Answers:

A.   Incorrect. Sequencing is putting objects in a certain order.

B.   Incorrect. Sorting is a way to categorize objects by how they are alike or different.

C.   Incorrect. Skip counting omits numbers in a pattern.

D.   **Correct.** Subitizing refers to the capacity to identify a small number of objects and immediately recognize how many there are without counting.

NUMBERS AND OPERATIONS

As children mature, they can gradually perform mental math and use numbers in everyday situations. But if children were to randomly manipulate numbers, they would not comprehend which number is relevant in a circumstance. They need to be introduced to deeper concepts to understand the true relevance of a number.

These deeper concepts include understanding place value, using the four basic mathematical operations with whole numbers, and fractions.

PLACE VALUE

A **digit** (0 to 9) is a symbol used to make numbers. For instance, 5,182 is made up of the digits 5, 1, 8, and 2. The value of the position of each digit in a number is called its **place value**. In the number 5,182, the digit *5* is in the **thousands** place, *1* is in the **hundred**s place, *8* is in the **tens** place, and *2* is in the **ones** place.

A **place value chart** is a good visual aid to show children how to understand the value of digits using pictures or objects like base-ten blocks. The chart has place values listed right to left in the way numbers are typically formed. The chart also aids in reading and writing multi-digit numbers accurately, as each digit is placed in a column that correlates to its value.

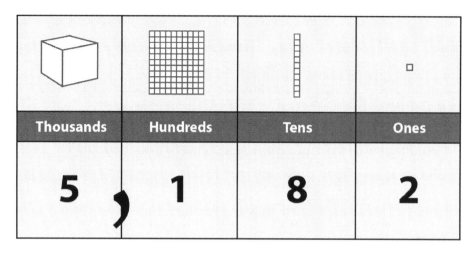

$$5000 + 100 + 80 + 2 = 5,182$$

Figure 3.2. Place Value Chart

Another way to express a number is by decomposing it. **Decomposing** a number breaks it down into individual parts. For instance, 6,417 can be decomposed to 6,000 + 400 + 10 + 7. Similarly, **composing** a number involves adding the individual parts. So, 9,000 + 400 + 30 + 1 can be written as 9,431.

Rounding is a useful skill. When working with large figures, for instance, it is easier to work with values rounded to the nearest ten or hundred; it is not always necessary to work with an exact number. **Rounding** a number makes it simpler to work with.

COMMON STUDENT ERRORS

▸ misunderstanding how to expand numbers (306 = 30 + 6)
▸ decreasing the number in the specified place when rounding down (163 → 150).

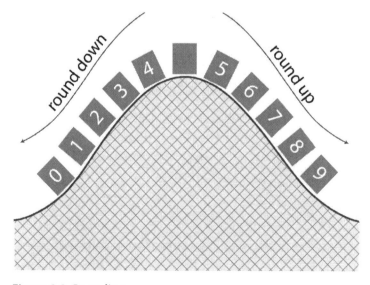

Figure 3.3. Rounding

Using whole numbers makes it easier to explain rounding. **Whole numbers** are numbers 0, 1, 2, 3, 4, and so on. They do not include negative numbers, decimals, or fractions. Rounding a whole number like 83 to the nearest ten gives 80, because 83 is closer to 80 than it is to 90. But 87 will be rounded up to 90. Similarly, rounding the number 345 to the nearest hundred is 300 since 345 is closer to 300 than it is to 400. Rounding the number 5,782 to the nearest hundred will be 5,800, because the hundreds value of 782 is closer to 800 than it is to 700.

SAMPLE QUESTIONS

3)   In which of the following scenarios would it be appropriate to use rounding?

A.   A window repairer measures windows that need glass replacement.

B.   A teacher is ordering pizzas for a school party with one hundred students.

C.   In a marathon, winners take first, second, and third prize.

D.   A man is paying for a shirt at a store and needs to know the amount.

Answers:

A.   Incorrect. If the glass is expected to fit into the window frame, it should be measured exactly.

B.   **Correct.** The teacher can estimate how many pizzas she will need by assuming each person will eat a certain amount and multiplying by 100.

C.   Incorrect. Marathons are timed to the second, so exact timings need to be recorded.

D.   Incorrect. Bills for consumer purchases include the amount of tax, so they are exact.

4)   Two students in a class were asked to round the number 30,409 to the nearest thousand. Sam says it will be rounded to 31,000, and Paul says it will be rounded to 30,400. Which student is correct?

A.   They are both correct.

B.   Sam is correct.

C.   Paul is correct.

D.   They are both incorrect.

Answer:

D)   **Correct.** The number 30,409 rounded to the thousands place is 30,000. Sam rounded up instead of down, and Paul rounded to the hundreds place.

OPERATIONS WITH WHOLE NUMBERS

The four basic operations in math are addition, subtraction, multiplication, and division.

The concept of addition can be explained to children through visuals, such as two groups of blocks. Students can count the number of blocks in the first group and the number of blocks in the second group. After combining the groups together, the students should count all the blocks; they have just **added** the two sets of blocks together.

There are many ways to introduce addition: using counters or manipulatives, a **number line**, or paper and pencil. Counters provide a hands-on approach to counting out amounts, much like using fingers to count. As children learn to count out each amount before adding, they reinforce one-to-one correspondence.

Number lines help children visualize addition in the form of measurement and help them understand what the answers of addition and subtraction mean. For an addition equation like 6 + 3, take the first **addend**, 6, on the number line. Then "jump" three spaces to the right, landing at 9. In a subtraction equation like 10 – 4, mark 10 on the number line. Then "jump" four spaces to the left, landing at 6. Eventually students can use the number line with negative numbers, fractions, and decimals.

Figure 3.4. Number Line

Helping children get the gist of addition involves familiarizing them with common symbols like the addition and equal signs (+ and =) and words such as *addends, plus, all together, in all,* and *sum*. Once they understand these, they can progress to simple paper-and-pencil exercises with addition sentences or equations such as 3 + 4 = 7.

After children have achieved a certain level of familiarity with the above, they will be able to learn different strategies for addition, such as counting forward or backward, skip counting, grouping, and using doubles. **Grouping** refers to viewing numbers in a sequence that makes logical sense. For example, there are many ways to group numbers to add up to 10: 1 and 9, 2 and 8, 3 and 7, 4 and 6 all add up to 10. Using **doubles** is a type of grouping where the two numbers used in an addition equation are the same: 2 + 2, 3 + 3, 4 + 4, and so on. Both these strategies help children strengthen number sense and expand their thinking.

COMMON STUDENT ERRORS

▸ always subtracting the smaller number from the larger number (953 – 27 = 934)

▸ thinking that subtraction is commutative (9 – 4 = 4 – 9)

Subtraction can be explained as the inverse or opposite of addition because the two operations cancel each other out. Terms such as *minuend, minus, take away, left, remaining,* and *difference* should be introduced.

An everyday scenario can help get the concept across: "You have ten blocks and you give me three. How many blocks do you have left?" Children count out ten blocks and then move three blocks away. After they count out the seven remaining blocks, they have **subtracted** 3 from 10. They can understand a simple subtraction equation, 10 – 3 = 7.

An extremely useful technique in relating addition and subtraction is a fact family. Just like people, numbers have relationships with each other under certain circumstances. For example, 5 + 2 is the same as 2 + 5. They both add up to 7. Understanding that can help children deduce that 7 – 2 = 5 and 7 – 5 = 2. The same three numbers have an addition and subtraction relationship. This relationship is called a **fact family**. A fact family like this one always gives two addition equations and two subtraction equations.

Multiplication and division are also inverse operations and are typically introduced at a point when a child can comfortably identify numbers up to 20 and is familiar with addition and subtraction. They can begin to understand terms such as *multiplier, factor, product, multiply,* and *times*.

Multiplication is basically repeated addition, so 5 × 3 is the same as 5 + 5 + 5. A **multiplication chart** can help students learn the multiple of small whole numbers. In the chart, children can just focus on the diagonals (2 × 2, 3 × 3, 4 × 4, etc.) and the section either above or below the diagonal (because of the commutative property of multiplication, which states that 5 × 3 is equivalent to 3 × 5).

X	0	1	2	3	4	5	6	7	8	9	10
0	0	0	0	0	0	0	0	0	0	0	0
1	0	1	2	3	4	5	6	7	8	9	10
2	0	2	4	6	8	10	12	14	16	18	20
3	0	3	6	9	12	15	18	21	24	27	30
4	0	4	8	12	16	20	24	28	32	36	40
5	0	5	10	15	20	25	30	35	40	45	50
6	0	6	12	18	24	30	36	42	48	54	60
7	0	7	14	21	28	35	42	49	56	63	70
8	0	8	16	24	32	40	48	56	64	72	80
9	0	9	18	27	36	45	54	63	72	81	90
10	0	10	20	30	40	50	60	70	80	90	100

Figure 3.5. Multiplication Chart

It is no surprise that children develop concrete understanding with the aid of visual representations, such as cookie dough laid out on a baking tray, seats in a movie theatre, or a dozen donuts in a box. They are commonly arranged in rows and columns, which is called an **array**. Arrays can help explain multiplication using rows and columns: The number of rows and columns each refer to the factors used in a multiplication equation.

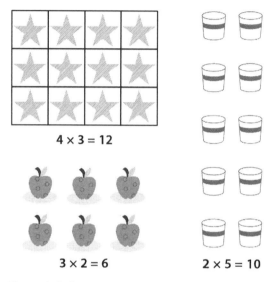

Figure 3.6. Arrays

Just as addition and subtraction are related in fact families, multiplication and division have a relationship too. **Division** is the act of splitting into equal parts or groups. For example, if three friends wish to share a pizza cut into nine slices, how many slices would each friend get? The terms *divisor, dividend, quotient, divided by,* and *remainder* are used in division. In this example, $\frac{9}{3}$ (or $9 \div 3$) equals three wholes. If a number does not completely divide to give a whole number, the division will result in a **remainder**. For example, sharing twelve cupcakes with five friends $\left(\frac{12}{5} \text{ or } 12 \div 5\right)$ will result in two whole cupcakes per friend with two left over, or a remainder of 2.

Arrays can also be used with division problems. In Figure 3.7, seven people are to share fourteen pizza slices. How many slices will each person get? The division equation is written as $14 \div 7 = 2$. The fourteen pizza slices are split into seven equal groups. That results in two slices per person.

Multiplication and division are inverse operations and related through fact families. For instance, 3×6 is the same as 6×3. They both multiply to give 18. Now, using these same numbers, a child can deduce that 18 ÷ 3 = 6 and 18 ÷ 3 = 6. The three numbers have a multiplication and division relationship. A fact family such as this one always includes two multiplication equations and two division equations.

$$14 \div 7 = 2$$

Figure 3.7. Using Arrays for Division

SAMPLE QUESTIONS

5) Selena had seven pencils. She gave two pencils to her friend Amy. How many pencils does she have now?　　7 - 2 = 5

Which of the following problems has the same mathematical structure as the problem above?

A. Selena brought three friends to the end-of-summer party. Amy brought two friends. How many friends did they bring together?

B. Selena brought ten carrot sticks for lunch. How many carrots sticks were left after she ate six?

C. Selena earned two stickers every school day this week, Monday through Friday. How many stickers did she earn?

D. Selena has seven markers. Amy has three more markers than Selena does. How many markers does Amy have?

Answers:

A. Incorrect. This is an addition problem (3 + 2 = 5)

B. Correct. This is a subtraction problem (10 – 6 = 4), as is the scenario in the question (7 – 2 = 5).

C. Incorrect. This is a multiplication problem (2 × 5 = 10).

D. Incorrect. This is an addition problem (7 + 3 = 10).

6) A teacher is passing out candy to a group of students. There are six students in the group, and each student will get two pieces of candy. How many pieces of candy does the teacher need?

Which of the following arrays shows the solution to this problem?

A.

B.

C.

D.

Answer:

A. **Correct.** Array A shows the operations $6 \times 2 = 12$, which is the number of students times the number of pieces of candy each student will receive.

FRACTIONS

A fraction can be described as part of a whole. The top number of a fraction is called the **numerator**, and the bottom number is the **denominator**. The numerator represents how many of the parts are taken, and the denominator represents how many equal parts the object is split into. A fraction is the division of the top number by the bottom number.

For early learners, a **visual fraction model** is a pictorial way of understanding fractions. It could include objects, shapes, or figures divided into fractions.

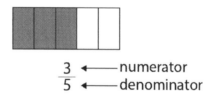

$\dfrac{3}{5}$ ← numerator
denominator

Figure 3.8. Visual Fraction Model

A **unit fraction** is a fraction in which the numerator is 1, such as $\frac{1}{6}$ or $\frac{1}{10}$. While the numerator stays 1, the denominator is the number that determines whether the value of a unit fraction decreases or increases. Consider the following two figures.

Rectangle A is divided into 4 equal parts, and rectangle B is divided in two parts. The unit fraction in A is $\frac{1}{4}$ and the one in B is $\frac{1}{2}$. Visually it is clear that $\frac{1}{4}$ is smaller than $\frac{1}{2}$. Rectangle A has been divided into more equal parts than rectangle B; hence its unit fraction is smaller.

The math operations of addition, subtraction, multiplication, and division can be executed on fractions just as on whole numbers, but with a few modifications.

When adding or subtracting two fractions, the denominator is important. For fractions with like (same) denominators, simply add or subtract the numerator and write the final answer over the same denominator. For example, $\frac{3}{10} + \frac{5}{10} = \frac{8}{10}$ and $\frac{5}{6} - \frac{1}{6} = \frac{4}{6}$.

Figure 3.9. Comparing Unit Fractions

For fractions with unlike (different) denominators, first find a common denominator. When two or more denominators are the same or brought to the same number, that number is called a **common denominator**. A common denominator can be found by finding the smallest whole number that is divisible by both denominators. Another way is to simply multiply denominators together to result in a common number.

After finding the common denominator, the two fractions can be rewritten with the new denominator and added as usual. For instance, when adding $\frac{3}{4}$ to $\frac{1}{8}$, the denominators 4 and 8 have 8 as a common multiple. 4 goes into 8 twice (4 × 2). 8 is the smallest whole number divisible by 4 and 8. So, $\frac{3}{4}$ can be brought to the common denominator of 8 by multiplying both the numerator, 3, and the denominator, 4, by 2. This addition equation can now be expressed as $\frac{6}{8} + \frac{1}{8} = \frac{7}{8}$.

> COMMON STUDENT ERRORS
>
> ▸ thinking that the fraction with the larger denominator is larger $\left(\frac{1}{5} > \frac{1}{3}\right)$
> ▸ adding the numerators and the denominators $\left(\frac{1}{3} + \frac{2}{5} = \frac{3}{8}\right)$
> ▸ misunderstanding the relationship between the fraction bar and the decimal $\left(\frac{3}{5} = 3.5 \text{ or } 0.35\right)$

Similarly, in a subtraction equation like $\frac{3}{5} - \frac{1}{15}$, the denominators 5 and 15 have 15 as a common multiple. 5 goes into 15 three times. So, $\frac{3}{5}$ can be brought to a common denominator of 15 by multiplying the numerator, 3, and the denominator, 5, by 3. This subtraction equation can now be written as $\frac{9}{15} - \frac{1}{15} = \frac{8}{15}$.

The following are examples of adding and subtracting fractions with like and unlike denominators.

Addition:

▸ $\frac{7}{11} + \frac{2}{11} = \frac{9}{11}$ (like denominators)

▶ $\frac{2}{9} + \frac{1}{3} = \frac{2}{9} + \frac{3}{9} = \frac{5}{9}$ (unlike denominators)

Subtraction:

▶ $\frac{9}{12} - \frac{2}{12} = \frac{7}{12}$ (like denominators)

▶ $\frac{5}{6} - \frac{1}{3} = \frac{5}{6} - \frac{2}{6} = \frac{3}{6}$ (unlike denominators)

Multiplying fractions requires the least work. Both numerators are multiplied, and both denominators are multiplied.

Multiplication: $\frac{4}{5} \times \frac{3}{7} = \frac{(4 \times 3)}{(5 \times 7)} = \frac{12}{35}$

In dividing fractions, first find the reciprocal of the second fraction. A **reciprocal** is found by swapping the numerator and denominator. After taking the reciprocal of the second fraction, simply multiply the two fractions as usual to arrive at the final answer.

Division: $\frac{1}{3} \div \frac{2}{5} = \frac{1}{3} \times \frac{5}{2} = \frac{5}{6}$

Multiplication and division can result in large numerators and/or denominators. Fractions should be **simplified**—or **reduced**—for ease of understanding by dividing both the numerator and denominator by their greatest common factor. The greatest common factor—or GCF—is the highest number that can divide exactly into two or more numbers. A **common factor** is a number that can be divided into two or more numbers. The factors of 6 are 1, 2, 3, 6, and the factors of 15 are 1, 3, 5, 15. Both 6 and 15 have common factors of 1 and 3. The largest of those common factors is called the greatest common factor.

In the fraction $\frac{8}{12}$, the numerator 8 and the denominator 12 have 4 as their greatest common factor (that is, 4 is the highest factor common to both numbers). After dividing both numbers, the reduced fraction is now $\frac{2}{3}$. $\frac{8}{12}$ and $\frac{2}{3}$ are called **equivalent** fractions because even though they are expressed differently, they represent the same quantity.

Fractions are not always less than 1. There are fractions where the numerator is larger than the denominator. These are called **improper fractions**. In such cases, decomposing a fraction can be useful. **Decomposing** fractions involves splitting them into smaller pieces. Consider the improper fraction $\frac{7}{5}$. This can be decomposed into a part equal to 1 and a part smaller than 1: $\frac{7}{5} = \frac{5}{5} + \frac{2}{5}$.

$1 \quad + \quad \frac{3}{5} \quad = 1\frac{3}{5} \longleftarrow$ mixed number

or

$\frac{5}{5} \quad + \quad \frac{3}{5} \quad = \frac{8}{5} \longleftarrow$ improper fraction

Figure 3.10. Types of Fractions

There are also fractions that contain whole numbers with a fractional part. These are called **mixed numbers**. For instance, $4\frac{2}{3}$ is a mixed number. This number can be decomposed as:

$$= 1 + 1 + 1 + 1 + \frac{2}{3}$$
$$= \frac{3}{3} + \frac{3}{3} + \frac{3}{3} + \frac{3}{3} + \frac{1}{3} + \frac{1}{3}$$

This results in six fractions with a common denominator of 3. Decomposing fractions can make addition and subtraction of some fractions more straightforward.

Many real-life circumstances involve fractions. For instance:

Mom bought $\frac{5}{12}$ of a pound of chicken. Dad bought $\frac{1}{3}$ of a pound of chicken. Who purchased the larger amount?

First, bring both fractions to a common denominator (12 in this case). So, for Dad's chicken weighing $\frac{1}{3}$ pound (multiply both the numerator and denominator by 4), $\frac{1}{3} = \frac{4}{12}$. Upon comparison, $\frac{5}{12}$ is greater than $\frac{4}{12}$ since the numerator 5 is larger than 4. So, Mom purchased the larger amount.

Comparing fractions can also be done by using grid or **area models**.

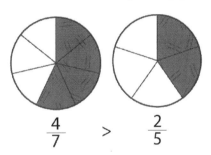

$$\frac{4}{7} > \frac{2}{5}$$

Figure 3.11. Comparing Fractions

SAMPLE QUESTIONS

7) Carla divides her pizza into eight equal slices and takes one slice. If the amount of pizza remaining is written as a fraction, the numerator will be which of the following values?

A. 1
B. 7
C. 8
D. 9

Answer:

B. **Correct.** Seven of eight pizza slices are left after Carla takes one, so $\frac{7}{8}$ of the pizza remains. 7 is the numerator of this fraction.

8) **Which of the following is the best definition of decomposing fractions?**

    A.   separating the numerator and denominator into individual numbers

    B.   finding the reciprocal of a fraction

    C.   splitting a fraction into smaller pieces

    D.   creating equivalent fractions

Answers:

    A.   Incorrect. There is no need to separate the numerator and denominator.

    B.   Incorrect. Finding the reciprocal of a fraction is used when dividing two fractions.

    C.   **Correct.** Decomposing fractions is the process of splitting it into smaller pieces.

    D.   Incorrect. Creating equivalent fractions helps reduce a large fraction into a simpler form.

RATIOS AND PERCENTAGES

Fractions can be expressed in different ways—ratio, percent, and decimal. These different forms can all represent the same number. A **ratio** is a comparison of two numbers. As its definition indicates, a fraction specifies a part of a whole, but a ratio is an indicator of how much of one thing there is compared to another.

For instance, in a pouch containing eight blue and five red marbles, there are eight blue marbles to five red marbles—or a ratio to 8 to 5, also written 8:5. In a recipe that calls for six cups of flour and three cups of milk, the ratio of flour to milk is 6:3. Ratios are similar to fractions and illustrate the relationship between part and whole.

Another example is a classroom full of students. There are ten girls, eleven boys, and two instructors in a classroom. The following shows part-to-part and part-to-whole ratios.

Part to Part	Part to Whole
Ratio of boys to girls: 11:10 or $\frac{11}{10}$	Ratio of boys to all students: 11:21 or $\frac{11}{21}$
Ratio of instructors to girls: 2:10 or $\frac{2}{10}$	Ratio of girls to entire class: 10:23 or $\frac{10}{23}$

A **percent** is a type of fraction where the denominator is always 100, meaning it refers to parts per one hundred. Using 100 makes comparisons simple because the whole is always the same. A percent is easily identifiable by the percent symbol, %, added at the end. Students should first understand that 100% is considered all of everything. 100% of a class with thirty students refers to all thirty students. 50%

refers to half—in this case, half of thirty, which is fifteen students (30 ÷ 2 = 15). Graph paper is a very useful tool in teaching percent to students.

Figure 3.12. Drawing Percents on Graph Paper

A percent can be easily converted into a **decimal** by removing the percent symbol and dividing the number by 100. Also, dividing the numerator of a fraction by its denominator gives a decimal. The following example shows the progression of ratio to fraction to percent to decimal.

$$3:20 \quad = \quad \frac{3}{20} \quad = \quad \frac{3(5)}{20(5)} \quad = \quad \frac{15}{100} \quad = \quad 15\% \quad = \quad 0.15$$

ratio   fraction   *multiply to get a*   percent   decimal
                             common
                       denominator of 100

Figure 3.13. Relationship Between Ratios, Fractions, Percents, and Decimals

SAMPLE QUESTION

9) A teacher is preparing a lesson with the objective of converting fractions to percents. Which of the following skills should students be able to perform before the teacher begins the lesson?

A. comparing unit fractions

B. finding the reciprocal of a fraction

C. decomposing fractions

D. creating a common denominator

Answer:

D. Correct. To convert a fraction to a percent, the student will need to convert fractions so they have a denominator of 100.

ALGEBRAIC THINKING

Algebraic thinking is about simplifying mathematical ideas and developing the ability to express reasoning in age-appropriate ways. It involves the ability to identify, extend, describe, create patterns, manipulate properties, and implement order of math operations.

PATTERNS

A pattern is a series or **sequence** that repeats. People's lives are a series of patterns—they wake up, get ready for work or school, make the drive back home, make dinner, etc. Then the cycle repeats.

Children are known to do well with structure and routine. The predictable nature of what comes next—patterns—in their day-to-day schedule helps them feel secure. Even babies can identify patterns soon after birth. An expectable routine of feeding, playing, and napping is based on patterns of repetition.

Children with a good understanding of patterns are enhancing their problem-solving, number manipulation, and counting skills. Identifying patterns is a vital skill in mathematical reasoning.

In math, patterns are sequences that repeat based on a rule. Common types of patterns in math are number patterns and shape patterns. These involve different numbers or shapes ordered and repeated according to a rule. Here is a game that can help children understand patterns. Using a box of blocks, the teacher lays out these colors in order:

> Red, Blue, Yellow, Green, Red, Blue, Yellow, Green

Children should **predict** or guess the following pattern. For variety, the teacher can use different colors or a different number of blocks, or other items like crayons, beads, and beanbags. Sometimes children follow the pattern for a while and then begin to make up their own. They may feel bored or want to use their favorite color. Rather than correcting them, the teacher should reinforce the concept by encouraging them to try different patterns.

Recognizing patterns is not just a visual matching skill. Songs are full of repetition, and children gravitate toward catchy tunes. Many songs have an appealing hook that children love to repeat. Beating rhythmically on a drum or lid of a container with hands or spoons can give children practice with recurring musical pattern matching.

HELPFUL HINT

Teachers can use paint and paper to teach students about symmetry: Paint a picture on the top half of a piece of paper, then fold the paper in half while the paint is still wet. The image created will be a mirror image of the original painting. The painting as a whole is symmetrical, and the fold line is the line of symmetry.

There are also naturally occurring patterns in nature. Examples include trees, spirals, stripes, waves, and symmetries. **Symmetry** occurs when a shape looks the same when it has been flipped or turned. For example, a sunflower looks the same no matter how it is rotated around its center.

Children can find symmetry outdoors. Many flowers are symmetrical. Teachers should experiment with plucked flowers and encourage the children to find symmetry in them. The following are some symmetrical patterns in nature.

Figure 3.14. Examples of Symmetry in Nature

SAMPLE QUESTIONS

10) Which of the following has more than one line of symmetry?

   A.   heart

   B.   circle

   C.   kite

   D.   the letter M

   Answer:

   B.   Correct. A circle has infinite lines of symmetry. The other shapes have one line of symmetry that cuts the shape vertically through the center.

11) Three-year-old Jess is playing with a box of that contains counters in five different colors. She takes a big handful of counters from the box and lays down a blue counter, followed by a red, then a yellow, then a green, then an orange. After a few minutes, she has five lines of counters, each following the same sequence of colors. What skill is she reinforcing?

   A.   pattern matching

   B.   counting

   C.   sorting

   D.   identifying

   Answer:

   A.   Correct. Jess is matching the color pattern by creating lines of counters that match the original pattern.

PROPERTIES AND ORDER OF OPERATIONS

As children become comfortable with addition, subtraction, multiplication, and division, they initially gain exposure performing these operations between two numbers. But what if an expression requires multiple operations? There are rules that dictate the order in which these operations are to be completed.

A math equation with multiple operations could include a combination of any of the four basic math operations plus parentheses and exponents. **Parentheses**, ( ), are symbols used to group things together. They take precedence in any math expression, and the operation(s) inside them must be performed first.

The next operation that takes precedence is exponents. An **exponent** is a number written as a superscript above a base number that indicates how many times to use that base number in multiplication. For example, $2^4 = 2 \times 2 \times 2 \times 2 = 16$. The exponent is 4 and the base number is 2. Sometimes it is phrased as 2 "to the power of" 4.

The general rule for the order of operations is:

- ▶ Any operation inside **P**arentheses is solved first.
- ▶ Any number with an **E**xponent is solved next.
- ▶ Then **M**ultiply and **D**ivide from left to right.
- ▶ Lastly, **A**dd and **S**ubtract from left to right.

The initials above spell the acronym **PEMDAS**.

At this point, children can be introduced to "tricks" and properties of math operations that will make problem solving easier. There are four basic properties of math operations.

The **commutative property** (for addition and multiplication) maintains that the order of the numbers in a math expression does not matter. For example, in addition, 5 + 4 and 4 + 5 have the same result, 9. In multiplication, 3 × 7 and 7 × 3 both equal 21. Switching the two numbers in an addition or multiplication equation does not change the end value. The commutative property does not apply to subtraction or division.

The **associative property** refers to the order a single operation (for example, addition) is done within a group. These groups are typically contained within parentheses. An addition equation like 3 + (9 + 5) can be written as (3 + 9) + 5 to equal 17. In multiplication, 6 × (2 × 4) can be written as (6 × 2) × 4 to yield 48. This property requires regrouping numbers. The associative property does not apply to subtraction or division.

The **distributive** property refers to distributing through the values within parentheses. For example, 3 × (6 + 2) can be rewritten as 3 × 6 + 3 × 2. (Remember that multiplication and division are performed before addition and subtraction.) Both equations produce the answer 24.

Addition and multiplication have a special property called the identity property. The **additive identity** is zero. This means any number added to zero remains the same and keeps its identity: 6 + 0 = 6 or 0 + 2 = 2. The **multiplicative identity** is one. This means any number multiplied by one remains the same and retains its identity: 130 × 1 = 130 or 1 × 54 = 54.

QUICK REVIEW

Which property is described in the statement 8 + 20 = 20 + 8?

SAMPLE QUESTIONS

12) **Ms. Kyle's fifth-grade students were asked to write an equation depicting the additive identity property. Which of the following students is correct?**

   A.   Anna: 15 × 4 = 4 × 15

   B.   Bob: 20 × 1 = 20

   C.   Michael: 18 + 4 = 4 + 18

   D.   Jen: 27 + 0 = 27

   Answers:

   A.   Incorrect. Anna has written the commutative property of multiplication.

   B.   Incorrect. Bob has written the multiplicative identity property.

   C.   Incorrect. Michael has written the commutative property of addition.

   D.   Correct. Jen has written the additive identity property.

13) **Which of the following skills should students master before learning the associative property?**

   A.   order of operations

   B.   decomposing whole numbers

   C.   multiplication

   D.   adding fractions

   Answers:

   A.   Incorrect. The associative property is a part of the order of operations and must be understood to master it.

   B.   Incorrect. Decomposing whole numbers is not a skill that is needed to understand the associative property.

   C.   Correct. The associative property addresses grouping addition or multiplication problems. To understand the associative property, students should know how to add and multiply.

   D.   Incorrect. While some associative property problems may involve fractions, most will involve whole numbers.

GEOMETRY, MEASUREMENT, AND DATA

A good understanding of counting, basic math operations, and the properties and order of math operations leads to higher levels of algebraic thinking and problem-solving skills. Children can eventually work with problems involving geometry, measurement, and interpretation of data.

MEASUREMENT

Measurement refers to numbers that show size or amount of some characteristic. The numbers can refer to characteristics like length, weight, time, money, or distance and are measured in specific units such as feet, pounds, minutes, dollars, or miles. A **unit of measurement** is the unit or term used to measure a characteristic. These units can be standard or nonstandard.

A **standard unit of measurement** is a defined, universal convention used to quantify the characteristic being measured. Examples include inches, miles, and meters (for distance) or ounces, pounds, and kilograms (for mass). A **nonstandard** unit of measurement refers to items not commonly used for measuring, such as paper clips, popsicle sticks, or an arm length.

Standard units of measurement can be classified into a number of systems. Most countries use the **metric** system, which uses units such as centimeters, kilometers, grams, and kilograms. In the United States, **US customary** units are used, including inches, feet, ounces, and pounds.

Children love measuring, especially **length** or **height**. They gain a degree of satisfaction in knowing the longest or tallest object in a group. They can use a nonstandard unit of measurement like a pencil or a stick to measure various things around the house or classroom. They can use a ruler to measure small items. They can now understand terms such as *length, how long, how short, width, tall, height,* and *inches.*

COMMON STUDENT ERRORS
▸ starting at the wrong end of the ruler or at 1 instead of at 0
▸ counting the lines instead of the spaces on a ruler

Another way to get them to practice math skills through measurement is by introducing them to metric mass, types of currency (money), and telling time.

People generally use the word *weight* to express how heavy or light something is. Weight is actually the measure of gravity pulling on an object, and **mass** is how much matter is packed into an object. Weight can vary depending on gravitational pull. For instance, the weight of an object on the moon is less than that on Earth because the gravitational pull is weaker on the moon. However, the object's mass remains the same. The standard unit of measurement for mass is kilogram.

Older children should be familiar with **money**: the denominations of US currency, skip counting, and converting currency. The four most-used coins and their values (penny = one cent, nickel = five cents, dime = ten cents, quarter = twenty-five cents) can be used to show conversions between values, such as the relationships between nickels and dimes, pennies and nickels, and nickels and quarters. Using play money is a great way to practice these types of calculations, which often involve skip counting.

The comfort of knowing what comes next in their day-to-day schedule has been shown to help children understand and manage **time**. However, teaching the concept of time to children can be a challenging undertaking.

Which type of clock is best to start with—analog or digital? The analog clock has moveable parts and can show elapsed time. It is also visually appealing. It can cover most of the concepts a child is expected to know with regard to time. A digital clock may seem easier, but it is less useful for showing elapsed time or future time (like how many hours till dinner, or when to wake up in the morning, etc.).

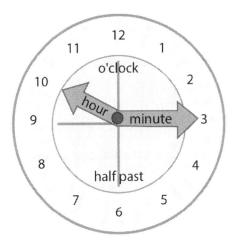

Figure 3.15. Analog Clock Made from a Paper Plate

An analog clock can introduce students to hours and minutes. The ability to count to sixty will benefit them in this exercise. Teachers can slowly introduce skip counting by fives (for the minute hand). Terms such as *hour, minute, o'clock, half past, quarter past,* and *quarter till* can be introduced concurrently. Once children are comfortable with the ins and outs of an analog clock, they can experiment with a digital clock. A fun activity involves matching time on a digital clock to an analog clock.

14) **A kindergarten teacher asks her students to choose a nonstandard unit to measure the length of the classroom. Which of the following is the most appropriate nonstandard unit for the students to use?**

   A.   a carpet square

   B.   paper clips

   C.   a yardstick

   D.   popsicle sticks

   Answers:

   A.   **Correct.** Students can lay carpet squares end-to-end to measure the length of the room.

   B.   Incorrect. Paper clips will be too short, making it difficult for students to get an accurate measurement.

   C.   Incorrect. A yardstick measures a standard unit (inches and feet).

   D.   Incorrect. Popsicle sticks will be too short, making it difficult for students to get an accurate measurement.

TWO-DIMENSIONAL SHAPES

Shapes can be described in various dimensions. A one-dimensional (1-D) object is just a point or points on a line. A common 1-D measurement is distance. A two-dimensional (2-D) object is a closed, flat figure with no depth and can be expressed on a **plane**—for example, a drawing of a triangle, square, or rectangle on a paper. It has length and width. A simple way to describe a three-dimensional (3-D) solid is something that takes up space—a ball, tree, house, or a car. It has height, depth, length, surface area, and volume.

Children's first drawings are probably replications of triangles, circles, rectangles, and squares—standard 2-D shapes. By age five, hand-eye coordination improves and drawings become more recognizable. This is a precursor to basic understanding of geometry. At this point, terms like *base*, *height*, *sides*, and many others become relevant.

An easy way to teach children to compose a 2-D shape is by first placing the corners—or vertices. For example, for a triangle, a student should draw three points on paper and join the points with lines. The triangle now has three corners and three **sides**. In more advanced geometry, children are ready to understand that the measure of the space between two lines that connect is called an **angle**. Another term to introduce is the bottom of a triangle, which is called the **base**. The measurement from the top of a triangle to its base is called the **height**.

Shape	Sides Angles	Looks Like
Circle	no flat side no angles	*clock*
Triangle	3 sides 3 angles	YIELD *yield sign*
Square	4 sides 4 angles	*keyboard keys*
Rectangle	4 sides 4 angles	*TV*
Hexagon	6 sides 6 angles	*white shapes in soccer ball*

Figure 3.16. Two-Dimensional Shapes Anchor Chart

Just like a triangle, a rectangle and a square can be composed by first placing the vertices and then connecting the points. Squares and rectangles are classified as **quadrilaterals**—four-sided figures with four straight sides. A square is a type of rectangle. Both have four right angles, but a **square**'s sides are all the same length, while a **rectangle** has two long sides and two short sides. The **length** of a rectangle is typically its longer side, while the **height** (or width) is its shorter side.

A circle is a 2-D shape with equal height and width (which is called the **diameter**). It is worth mentioning that half of a circle's diameter is called its **radius**. The radius is used to find area and circumference (the length of the circle's outline). However, a circle does not contain any corners or vertices, so a child trying to free draw a circle could very well end up with a misshapen circle. Sketching a circle is a challenge for young children as they do not have points or vertices to connect. One suggestion is to draw circles of different sizes on a paper and let the child trace over them. Another tip is to tie a pencil's end to a thread and secure the other end of the thread

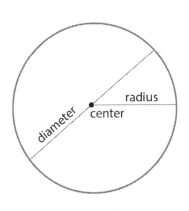

Figure 3.17. Parts of a Circle

to a paper clip pierced into the center of a piece of paper. This will ensure that the thread stays taut as the child attempts to draw the outline of the circle. Advanced tools to draw circles include protractors, compasses, and stencils or templates.

A precursor to very advanced math topics like geometry, algebra, trigonometry, and calculus involves understanding the concept of area and perimeter of 2-D shapes. The **perimeter** is the length of the outline of a 2-D shape. The **area** of a 2-D shape is the amount of space inside it. Perimeter can be taught by letting students use nonstandard units of measurement like paper clips or toothpicks to measure the outline of an object like a book or a piece of paper. Unifix® or math cubes can be used to fill up the insides of a 2-D shape, introducing students to the concept of area.

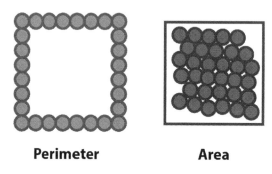

Perimeter   **Area**

Figure 3.18. Using Nonstandard Units to Measure Perimeter and Area

SAMPLE QUESTION

15) A second-grade teacher has completed a lesson on categorizing types of two-dimensional shapes. She draws the figure below on the board and asks her students to give a possible name for the shape.

1.5 in   1.5 in

1.5 in   1.5 in

Ari says it is a rectangle.

Edmundo says it is a square.

Donny says it is a quadrilateral.

Which student(s) correctly named the figure?

A.   Ari and Donny

B.   Edmundo only

C.   Edmundo and Donny

D.   all three students

Answer:

D. **Correct.** The figure is a quadrilateral, a square, and a rectangle: It has four equal, parallel sides and four right angles.

THREE–DIMENSIONAL SHAPES

Three-dimensional (3-D) shapes have distinct attributes and characteristics. The main attribute differentiating 2-D shapes from 3-D shapes is that 2-D shapes are considered "flat," while 3-D shapes take up space—they can be held and are solid.

It is this attribute of 3-D shapes that associates them with objects in everyday life. For example, a beach ball is a **sphere**; sugar cubes are **cubes**; Egyptian pyramids are **pyramids**; a wedge of cheese can be a **prism**. Many of these 3-D solids are human-made. When discussing engineered 3-D solids with students, teachers should ask how students think engineers or designers created them. What types of measurements would they have to know to create these objects?

memorize chart!

Shape	Net	Faces Vertices	Looks Like
Sphere	can't be flattened	1 curved face no vertices	*baseball balloon the moon*
Cube		6 faces 8 vertices	*dice ice cube*
Rectangular Prism		6 faces 8 vertices	*lego book box*
Pyramid		5 faces 5 vertices	*pyramids in Egypt*
Cylinder		2 flat faces 1 curved face	*cup soda can marker*
Cone		1 flat face 1 curved face	*ice cream cone party hat*

Figure 3.19. Three-Dimensional Shapes Anchor Chart

The **volume** of a 3-D shape is the amount of space it occupies. There are mathematical formulas for calculating volume depending on the shape. The **surface area** is the total area of every surface of a 3-D shape. The **face** of a 3-D shape is any flat, visible surface. For instance, a cube has six square faces. Its surface area is the area of all its six faces added together. A visual way for children to find the surface area of a 3-D solid is to flatten it into a 2-D shape (on paper). This flattened version is called a **net**. Figure 3.19 shows shapes and their nets.

SAMPLE QUESTIONS

16) **Which 3-D solid has four triangular faces and one square face?**

    A.   pyramid

    B.   cube

    C.   rectangular prism

    D.   cylinder

Answers:

    A.   **Correct.** A pyramid has four triangular faces and one square face.

    B.   Incorrect. There are no triangular faces on a cube.

    C.   Incorrect. There are no triangular faces on a rectangular prism.

    D.   Incorrect. There are no triangular faces on a cylinder.

17) **Which of the following shapes is produced when the net below is folded to make a 3-D shape?**

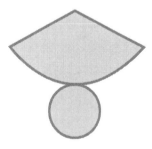

    A.   cylinder

    B.   cone

    C.   cube

    D.   pyramid

Answer:

    B.   **Correct.** A cone has an enclosed slanted curve with a circular base.

COLLECTING, ORGANIZING, AND PRESENTING DATA

The world is filled with numerical information that needs to be collected, organized, and deciphered. Some examples of such numerical information are test scores of students in a classroom, income of people in an organization, or costs of airline tickets. Manipulating information or data is the basis for the science of statistical analysis. Data collection is the process of grouping and measuring information on specific topics. This data can be displayed in the form of pictures, charts, or graphs. A **graph** is an illustration of values or data. Graphs are useful because they are visual and can represent the data better than words and numbers alone. Graphs and charts may be considered compact and concise depictions of data.

A **bar graph** is a display of bars of different colors or sizes. The longer the bar, the larger the number represented. For example, the bar graph in figure 3.20 shows the **comparison** of the number of students who chose dog, elephant, cat, giraffe, or koala as their favorite animal. It shows quantitative data and is best used to compare among different groups.

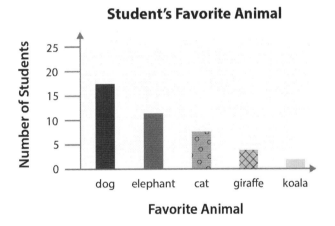

Figure 3.20. Bar Graph

A **line graph** is a type of graph that uses data values as points connected by lines. It is typically used to show how the variable being measured changes in value. The example in figure 3.21 shows the math test scores of a student through middle school and high school years. A math score is marked for each grade and each point is connected by lines. It is a type of chart used to visualize the changes in the value of a variable over time.

Scatter plots are like line graphs, but their purpose is unique. They are used to show how one variable (or set) can be affected by another. In other words, a scatter plot shows the **correlation** between the two variables or sets of data being plotted. In the figure 3.22, student test scores are plotted against the number of hours spent studying. The more hours spent studying, the better the test scores. Both variables are increasing together, indicating a positive correlation.

Math Scores by Grade Level

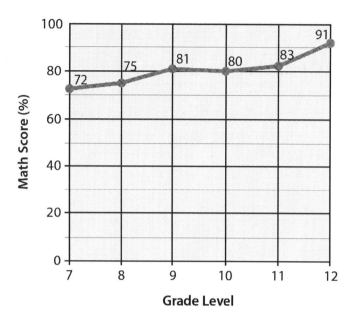

Figure 3.21. Line Graph

Hours of Study vs. Test Scores

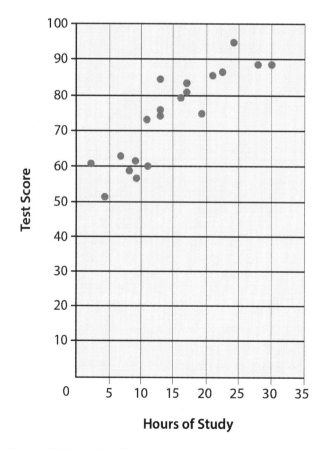

Figure 3.22. Scatter Plot

Pie charts are circular graphs. They look like a pie divided into slices. Pie charts are useful when showing quantities as parts of a whole. They are a common statistical graphic used in the business world. They can also be useful in a school environment. For instance, the pie chart in figure 3.23 shows the number of textbooks classified by genre in a school's library. It shows quantitative data. The largest slice represents the category with the highest number of books. The entire circle represents all books in the library.

Number of Library Books by Topic

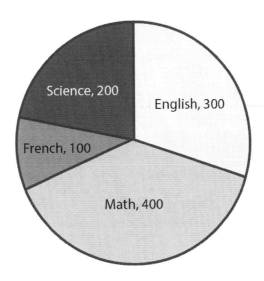

Figure 3.23. Pie Chart

A **line plot** is a type of graph that shows data frequency along a number line. Take an example of student test scores. This is a list of test scores received by twenty students.

86, 84, 87, 81, 84, 89, 81, 87, 92, 91, 92,
88, 81, 86, 85, 84, 88, 82, 83, 86

To make a line plot, establish a range that includes all the data in suitable intervals. Then plot each number using a symbol (such as an X or an *).

Figure 3.24. Line Plot

A **stem-and-leaf** plot shows data frequency among the categories of values that occur. These plots are useful for presenting the same set of data in the shape of a distribution. Using the same example of the twenty student test scores, first sort the data in ascending order.

> 81, 81, 81, 82, 83, 84, 84, 84, 85, 86, 86,
> 86, 87, 87, 88, 88, 89, 91, 92, 92

The *stem* consists of the highest (or first) place value digit of the data numbers (in this case, tens) and the *leaf* consists of all the other digit(s) (in this case, ones).

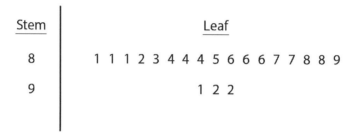

Stem	Leaf
8	1 1 1 2 3 4 4 4 5 6 6 6 7 7 8 8 9
9	1 2 2

Figure 3.25. Stem-and-Leaf Plot

To read a stem-and-leaf plot, simply connect the tens (first column) to the ones (second column).

How is all this data in the form of graphs, charts, and plots meaningful? Statistical tools such as mean, median, and mode give insight into viewing this data in specific forms.

The **average**—or **mean**—of a group of data refers to the sum of all data divided by the total number of data items. This is a way to measure what value best represents a sample of data. Think of the average as the "spokesperson" for the entire data set. For example, Li, Jess, and Antoine get allowances of $14, $20, and $17 respectively. What amount could serve as the "spokesperson" for the students' allowances? Find the average: (14 + 20 + 17)/3 = 51/3 = 17. Take the total amount received ($51), and divide that by the total number of people (3). The average of $17 is one way to describe the data set.

HELPFUL HINT

You can use the following rhyme to teach statistical terms:

Hey diddle diddle,

The median's the middle.

You add and divide the mean.

The mode's the one you find the most,

and the range is the difference between.

Again take the example of the twenty student test scores. If the scores were redistributed to ensure that each student has the same score, that score is referred to as the mean. Just as in calculating the average, first add up all the test scores.

$$86 + 84 + 87 + 81 + 84 + 89 + 81 + 87 + 92 + 91 + 92 + 88 + 81 + 86$$
$$+ 85 + 84 + 88 + 82 + 83 + 86 = 1{,}712$$

Divide this by the number of scores (20). $\frac{1{,}717}{20}$ = 85.9, which is the mean score for each student.

When there are extreme values in a data set and the data is very spread out, the average could be skewed high or low due to the wide range of data. In this case, the mean may actually misrepresent the data. The **median**, which is the middle value of a data group, is a good substitute in this instance. Unlike the average or mean, the median is not affected by a very low or very high data value.

Using the same example of the twenty student test scores, here are the scores in ascending order:

$$81, 81, 81, 82, 83, 84, 84, 84, 85, \mathbf{86}, \mathbf{86},$$
$$86, 87, 87, 88, 88, 89, 91, 92, 92$$

Since this is an even group of data, the median will be the average of the middle two values (in bold). The median here is $\frac{(86 + 86)}{2}$ = 86.

Another statistical tool is called the **mode**, which is the number or numbers that occur most frequently in the data. Here is a conceivable scenario for using the mode instead of the average. Say, for instance, a teacher is measuring the height of each of her fifteen fifth-grade students as part of a math unit on measurement. Most students are of similar height, but she has one exceptionally tall student. Finding the average height of the group of fifteen students will result in a skewed number because of the one tall student. So using the mode can be effective, as it will show where most of the student's heights lie. Unlike the average or the median, the mode is not unique. In a data set, there can be several different data values that occur at the same frequency. This will result in more than one mode. In the example of the twenty student test scores, the modes of the data set are 81, 84, and 86. They all occur three times.

The range is the difference between the smallest and the largest values.

SAMPLE QUESTIONS

18) A second-grade teacher has her students pick which genre of movie they like they best. Which of the following should the students use to present their data?

   A. line plot
   B. scatter plot
   C. stem-and-leaf plot
   D. pie chart

Answers:

A.   Incorrect. A line plot is best used to track the frequency of data points.

B.   Incorrect. A scatter plot is used the show the correlation between two variables.

C.   Incorrect. A stem-and-leaf plot is best used to track the frequency of data points.

D.   **Correct.** A pie chart is best used when comparing part of a whole (in this case genres of movies).

19)   For a school project, Imani contacted an ice-cream store owner to collect data on ice-cream sales. She wanted to know which flavor customers purchase the most. The owner's response was chocolate. Which of the following statistical measures does chocolate represent?

A.   mode

B.   mean

C.   median

D.   range

Answers:

A.   **Correct.** The mode is the most frequently occurring data value, which is chocolate.

B.   Incorrect. The mean is the sum of all data values divided by the total number of data items.

C.   Incorrect. The median is the middle value of a data group.

D.   Incorrect. The range is the difference between the largest and smallest data value.

Science

SCIENTIFIC INQUIRY

Scientific inquiry refers to the methods used to understand the fundamental concepts and processes within the disciplines of physical science, life science, Earth and space science, engineering and technology, and others. Scientific inquiry requires an understanding of basic science skills, including observation, description, and classification. For example, when conducting an experiment, students formulate questions, test hypotheses, and communicate information to help explain the world.

It is very important that early childhood educators make a conscious effort to include evidence-based scientific teaching into their classrooms. Many in the field of early childhood education once believed that these concepts were too abstract for young children

> **DID YOU KNOW?**
>
> STEM jobs are projected to grow at a much higher rate than other occupations through 2020. Introducing scientific concepts in early childhood can help prepare students for this economy.

to grasp and should be saved for higher grades. Current research suggests quite the opposite, and the national push for science education and the creation of the Next Generation Science Standards for grades kindergarten through twelve put science education in the forefront.

UNIFYING SCIENTIFIC CONCEPTS

A major idea behind scientific inquiry is **unifying scientific concepts**. Unifying scientific concepts provide students with themes across scientific disciplines to help them understand the natural world. Some of these concepts are:

- ▶ **Evolution**: Evolution is a theory that explains how living species change over a period of time and how they have come to be the way they are today. While dinosaurs are a favorite topic of interest in many early childhood classrooms, and not all state and national standards reference evolution explicitly, current research indicates that teaching evolution early (kindergarten through second grade) might have strong benefits. Most notable among these is helping students to clear up misconceptions or questions that they may have.

▶ **Systems**: Systems are sets of connected parts that work together to form a whole. The human body, a lake, and a classroom terrarium are all examples of systems that students can easily grasp. Much of early childhood science education revolves around the interrelationship of living things and how they work together. This organization can be observed on a broader level when students take a field trip to a nature conservancy or even in the microcosm of a fish tank in the classroom. Part of a foundational understanding of the concept of systems is the idea that all living things have a role to play. A teacher in a preschool classroom with a class pet might point out, for example, that the pet is entirely dependent upon humans to feed and care for it, just as students are dependent upon their parents to meet their own basic needs.

▶ **Cycles**: Cycles are the sequences of changing states of systems. The life cycle of the butterfly is a very popular and easy way for very young students to be introduced to this concept. The water cycle, the life cycle of a plant, and many others are great ways to increase students' knowledge and interest in the cyclical nature of all living things.

▶ **Organization**: Each part of a system has a purpose, and those parts work together in a specific way. For example, the human body must maintain a state of **equilibrium**, or balance, among component parts and systems. The inner ear is a system that balances opposing actions. If the inner ear does not maintain equilibrium, the balance is off, and the person will feel dizzy or fall. There is also organization among groups of living things in which schools of fish, herds of buffalo, and even families of humans work together to reach common goals.

SAMPLE QUESTION

1) A first-grade teacher wants to help her students understand that living organisms often start off in one form and then grow and change over time to meet their needs. Which class-wide project would be best to help students meet this objective?

   A. planting seeds and then observing plants as they grow

   B. asking students to make a poster for the classroom about the water cycle

   C. taking a field trip to the zoo to observe different animals and their young

   D. picking vegetables from the school garden to make a salad that the whole class enjoys

Answers:

A. **Correct.** This activity will help students understand that plants begin as seeds and then change and grow over their life cycle.

B. Incorrect. This activity is not necessarily about living organisms specifically.

C. Incorrect. This activity, as described, will not aid in student understanding. If the teacher was pointing out along the way that the animals "grow fangs" or "shed feathers" as they mature, then this would be an appropriate activity.

D. Incorrect. The vegetables aren't changing to meet their own needs; humans are meeting their own needs by harvesting the vegetables.

THE SCIENTIFIC PROCESS AND BASIC SCIENCE SKILLS

A major part of scientific inquiry is the scientific process. The scientific process is how science is performed. It includes basic science skills and the scientific method. The first step in the process is for students to think of the **purpose** of the experiment and ask a **question** that defines the problem or issue to be resolved.

Figure 4.1. The Scientific Process

For example, students may want to see what will happen when they put celery in water with food coloring. They might ask: "What will happen to celery when it is placed in a cup of water with blue food coloring?" After creating a question, the students conduct an investigation, or **research**, the topic. The students might check to see if someone else has asked the same question, or they may do further research on the very nature of celery. Then the students form a **hypothesis**, which is a prediction about what will happen during the experiment. The students' hypothesis might be: "Half of the celery stick will turn blue, and the other half will stay green."

The next step in the scientific process is the **experiment**. An experiment tests the hypothesis in controlled conditions. While the students conduct their experiment, they should be **collecting data**, or gathering and measuring information from the experiment. They should also **classify** their data, or sort it into different groups. After the experiment, students will **analyze** the data, draw a **conclusion**, make **inferences**, and create an **analysis**. This means that the students will determine what the data means, explain what happened during the experiment, and show the results of the experiment. In the example above, students might notice that the celery stick completely changed color after a week. They might infer that because the water is blue, and the celery needs water to live, the blue water travels up the celery stick, making it blue.

The last part of the scientific process is **representing findings** from the experiment. In other words, the students must share the results of the experiment—the **evidence**, or the reasoning, that either supports or disproves their hypothesis.

Table 4.1. The Scientific Process

Step	Example
Purpose/question	Which type of soil is the best to use for planting?
Hypothesis	Sandy soil is the best to use for planting.
Experiment	Gather three planters. Put sand in one, dirt soil in one, and clay in the other. Add a plant to each. Observe what happens to the three plants.
Record observations	The plants start to grow. The plant in the sandy soil is shorter than the plant in the dirt soil. The plant in the clay soil is the shortest.
Draw a conclusion	Dirt soil is the best soil to use for planting.

Encouraging students to discover through the scientific method is particularly important and can be integrated into several other parts of the overall curriculum. For example, prekindergarten students at a block center might be encouraged to develop a hypothesis as to what might happen if more and more blocks are stacked in varying configurations and then test their hypothesis by stacking the blocks in different ways. Second-grade students learning a new computer drag-and-drop coding program might first form a hypothesis as to what will happen if they drop pieces into a certain order; then they test this theory.

Integrating inquiry-based learning—allowing children to use their natural curiosity to explore the world around them—throughout the school day can often be done with less effort than it might at first appear. First-grade students observing bugs on the playground at recess, for example, might be encouraged to explore the topic further during library time by checking out books on the subject. Third-grade students learning responsible global citizenship might use scientific inquiry to see how many families they can encourage to begin recycling in a school-wide recycling program through different targeted awareness and outreach campaigns.

QUICK REVIEW

Can you think of a scientific experiment that would be appropriate for students in pre-K, kindergarten, first grade, and second grade?

The opportunities for integration of scientific principles are virtually limitless, and teachers should use them. Research suggests that not only is a child's interest in scientific fields best developed in early childhood but also their language and literacy development often occur best in a scientific context as they hear and use new language used to describe the world around them.

SAMPLE QUESTIONS

2) **What makes a good hypothesis?**

   A. The hypothesis is written clearly.

   B. The hypothesis is written as a question.

   C. The hypothesis is testable.

   D. The hypothesis describes the experiment.

   Answers:

   A. Incorrect. Although the hypothesis should be written clearly, that is not what makes it a good hypothesis.

   B. Incorrect. The hypothesis is not a question; it must be written as a statement.

   C. Correct. The hypothesis must be testable.

   D. Incorrect. The hypothesis does not need to describe the experiment. The hypothesis is a prediction about what will happen during the experiment.

3) **Mr. Martinez wants to integrate more science concepts into his existing second-grade reading curriculum. Which activity would be best?**

   A. using words, like *mammals* and *habitats,* as part of an existing vocabulary lesson

   B. encouraging students to make observations of things that are happening in the classroom

   C. asking students open-ended questions

   D. reading a book to the class about a young man who wants to be a scientist

Answers:

A. **Correct.** Using words is a great way to combine overall vocabulary development as well as new science vocabulary that students will need an understanding of for explicit science instruction.

B. Incorrect. Making observations does not relate to reading.

C. Incorrect. Asking open-ended questions is very important but does not relate directly to integration into a reading curriculum.

D. Incorrect. This activity pertains to reading and somewhat to science, but by second grade, most students should be reading on their own.

PHYSICAL SCIENCE

Physical science is any science that deals with inanimate matter or energy. Physical science investigates the basic phenomena of the physical world. Topics in physical science include:

▸ the properties of objects and materials, such as the states of matter (solid, liquid, gas)

▸ forms of energy, such as light, electricity, heat, and magnetism; forces, such as pushing and pulling; and phenomena, such as the reflection and absorption of light and the production and conduction of heat

▸ motion, or the change of position of objects when a force is applied

MATTER

Matter is a substance that occupies physical space. **Atoms** are the basis of all matter in the universe. Any object or material that contains atoms and takes up space contains matter.

Objects can be measured by mass and volume. **Mass** is the amount of matter an object contains. **Volume** is how much space it takes up. For example, a table tennis ball and a golf ball have about the same volume, but the golf ball has more mass. Problems with mass and volume are explicit parts of the Common Core State Math Standards beginning in third grade, so their underlying conceptual foundations should be well established in science lessons beforehand.

Any number of activities is appropriate even for very young children to help students explore mass and volume with hands-on exploration. A prekindergarten or kindergarten class might, for example, experiment with pouring a set volume of water into containers of different sizes. Even if the experiment gets messy and the containers overflow, students can gain an appreciation for what happens when the volume of the water exceeds the volume of the container.

In most of the early childhood grades (pre-K – second grade), activities involving the measurement of mass are generally combined with activities involving the measurement of weight. Mass and weight activities are associated because the concept of mass independent of gravity is hard for younger children to understand.

These activities usually center around the use of a balance scale or digital scale. Young students might first develop a hypothesis of which item they think might weigh more and then test this hypothesis. Any and all classroom and natural objects can be studied in this way, and older students can be encouraged to record their data into tables for further analysis.

Matter can be found in three states: solid, liquid, and gas. **Solids** have a firm shape that can be measured in length, width, and height. A brick is an example of a solid. **Liquids** flow easily, or move in a smooth way. They take the shape of any container they are poured into. Water is an example of a liquid. **Gases** are neither liquid nor solid. They spread out when warmed and contract when cooled.

One timeless experiment for students of any age is filling three balloons with a solid (ice perhaps), a liquid (usually water), and a gas (usually air or helium). Students can then record their observations of the three balloons. Which is heaviest? Which is the lightest, and which is the most sturdy, easiest to roll/ move, and so on?

Solid   Liquid   Gas

Figure 4.2. States of Matter

Students might also learn by having the different states of matter reinforced as they learn other scientific concepts. The water cycle, for example, gives students an opportunity to understand how water moves through these three states and how it is unique in that it is the only compound in which all three states of matter occur naturally.

Temperature is the measurement of how much energy is contained in the particles in matter. High energy materials have a higher temperature, and low energy materials have a lower temperature. Temperature is measured using a thermometer and can be described in units of Fahrenheit or Celsius.

During calendar and weather lessons for pre-K and kindergarten students, the concept of temperature as it pertains to weather should gradually be built. Young students can also experiment by describing certain objects or foods as hot, warm, cool, and cold; safety should be maintained, of course. Older elementary students in the first, second, and third grades might begin to use a thermometer to take various measurements: a glass of ice water, perhaps, or a cup of warm tea.

Substances will change states of matter when their temperature reaches a certain point, which is unique for every substance. Water, for example, will freeze to form ice at 32°F (0°C) and will boil to form water vapor at 212°F (100°C).

Generally, adding energy (making the material hotter) changes a substance to a higher energy state. Transitions from a higher to lower energy state release energy, making the material colder. Each of these changes has a specific name:

► solid to liquid: melting

► liquid to solid: freezing

► liquid to gas: evaporation

► gas to liquid: condensation

► solid to gas: sublimation

► gas to solid: deposition

These changes of substances can be observed by students in a variety of ways. Different items can be placed in the sun to observe melting and evaporation by measuring and drawing a line on a cup of water each day. Even sublimation can be observed (slowly) if ice is left in the freezer for a great length of time or if a teacher purchases a block of dry ice for a demonstration.

HELPFUL HINT

In both physical and chemical changes, matter is always conserved, meaning it can never be created or destroyed.

Matter can undergo two primary types of changes. An object is still fundamentally the same object after a **physical change**. For example, a pencil is still a pencil after it is broken into two pieces. Other examples of physical changes include melting butter and crushing a can.

QUICK REVIEW

What other safe, controlled, and developmentally appropriate activities involving chemical changes can you think of to use with early childhood students?

On the other hand, an object or material is fundamentally different after a **chemical change**. Baking is a chemical change that converts flour, butter, milk, and sugar into a cake. One interesting activity with chemical changes is having students mix up several versions of the same cake recipe leaving out key ingredients (such as oil, egg, baking powder, or flour) in each version. They can then make observations about the different cakes after they are baked (with scaffolding by the teacher). This will help students see how the chemical changes that happen during baking impact the final product.

4) A first-grade student notices that there is dew on the grass in the morning but not in the afternoon after the sun has come out. What two phenomena is the student noticing?

   A. deposition and sublimation

   B. melting and evaporation

   C. condensation and evaporation

   D. freezing and evaporation

   Answers:

   A. Incorrect. Deposition describes when a substance is transformed from a gas to a solid; sublimation describes a substance's transformation from a solid to a gas. No solids are involved here.

   B. Incorrect. Since dew is not a solid that is transformed into a liquid, this is not the correct answer.

   C. Correct. Dew is water vapor in the air that condenses as liquid on the ground. It then evaporates back into gas as the day heats up.

   D. Incorrect. Dew is not a liquid that has been transformed into a solid.

5) Which of the following states of matter adopt the shape AND size of the container they are placed in?

   A. liquids

   B. solids

   C. liquids and gases

   D. gases

   Answers:

   A. Incorrect. Liquids cannot change their size. They take the shape of their container, but their volume remains the same.

   B. Incorrect. Solids cannot change their shape and size for a container, but they do expand and contract with temperature. Solids have a size and a shape of their own.

   C. Incorrect. Liquids cannot change their size, but gases can.

   D. Correct. Gases adopt the shape and size of the container in which they are placed.

ENERGY

Energy is the capacity of an object to do work—to cause some sort of movement or change. Basic concepts of energy can be related to light, heat, electricity, and magnetism.

Go on →

Light is the form of energy that makes it possible for the eye to see. Colors are the result of objects interacting with light. When light hits an object, it can be **absorbed**—or soaked in. Some objects are **transparent**, meaning that they let all light pass though. Others are **translucent**, meaning they only let some light through. **Opaque** objects let no light pass through.

Light can also be **reflected**. When light is reflected, it bounces off an object or surface. This property of light can be demonstrated by shining a flashlight on a mirror. Light can also be broken into its spectral colors (red, orange, yellow, green, blue, indigo, and violet) by using a prism, or a material that **refracts** or bends light.

There are numerous experiments and explorations that can be undertaken with light, from building a simple kaleidoscope with a paper towel tube to leaving "secret messages" that can only be

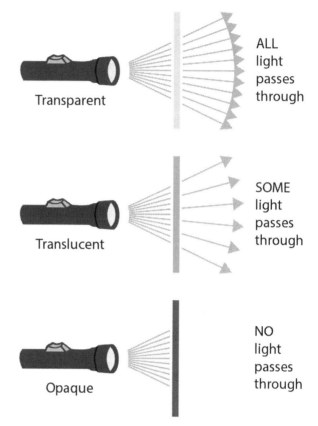

Figure 4.3. Transparent, Translucent, and Opaque Materials

decoded with black lights. Students often really enjoy seeing the full spectrum of visible, and sometimes invisible, light. The Next Generation Science Standards include strands for investigating sunlight in kindergarten, and both sunlight and other types of light in first grade. These elements should be integrated into the curriculum in these grades as much as possible.

Another form of energy is **heat**. Heat is the transfer or flow of energy due to the difference in temperature between two objects. Heat energy is the result of the movement of atoms or molecules and can be transferred from one object to another through **conduction**. This occurs when heat energy is transferred between particles of different temperatures. For example, if you place a warm object and a cold one together, heat will pass from the warm object to the cold one through conduction. Conduction will continue until both objects achieve the same temperature.

> **HELPFUL HINT**
>
> The order of the colors in the spectrum of visible light can be remembered using the mnemonic **ROY G. BIV**: red, orange, yellow, green, blue, indigo, violet.

Figure 4.4. Reflection

Electricity is the movement of negatively charged electrons through matter. The electrical energy available through a wall outlet or stored in batteries is used to do work when it powers devices like light bulbs, televisions, and phones. Many experiments with electricity—conducted at very low voltages, often with holiday lights and 9-volt batteries—can take place in second- and third-grade classrooms with heavy scaffolding from the teacher to ensure student safety.

Magnetism is a force that is closely related to electricity. It arises from the specific alignment of electrons in a material. The magnetic force can attract (pull) or repel (push) objects that contain a magnetic material, like iron, inside them. A magnet has two ends, called poles, where the magnets are the strongest. The **north pole** of one magnet attracts (pulls) the **south pole** of a second magnet, but the like poles repel each other.

Opposite poles attract

Like poles repel

Figure 4.5. Magnets

Students of all ages love magnets, and unlike some other hands-on science activities, allowing students to experiment freely with magnets is generally quite safe. Giving individual or groups of students a variety of objects to test as being either magnetic or non-magnetic is an appropriate activity for learners in kindergarten and beyond. The activity can be expanded in the elementary grades to include the recording of the magnetic properties (or lack thereof) of different objects in a table, chart, or graph.

SAMPLE QUESTIONS

6)   A first-grade teacher sets up a table with various materials, such as clear plastic, colored plastic, white paper, transparency film, cardboard, and flashlights. She encourages her students to make a hypothesis about what will happen when each material is placed in the beam of light from the flashlight. What topic is the teacher most likely going to introduce with the experiment?

   A.   conduction

   B.   refraction

   C.   translucency

   D.   spectral light

   Answers:

   A.   Incorrect. Conduction refers to the process by which heat or electricity moves from one object to another.

   B.   Incorrect. While some refraction might happen during this experiment, the various objects indicate the teacher is likely focusing more on how light passes though objects.

   C.   Correct. The teacher is likely helping students grasp that some objects are translucent, and others transparent or opaque.

   D.   Incorrect. The experiment does not involve breaking light into its spectral colors.

7)   A second-grade teacher puts three spoons in her morning cup of very hot coffee: one plastic, one metal, and one wooden. She then invites students to come up and carefully feel the end of each spoon. What concept is the teacher introducing to the students?

   A.   She is teaching them about heat-conductive materials.

   B.   She is teaching them to properly use laboratory equipment.

   C.   She is teaching them about electrical conductors and insulators.

   D.   She is encouraging students to make and test a hypothesis.

   Answers:

   A.   Correct. The spoons will feel warm to varying degrees based on how heat conductive they are.

   B.   Incorrect. This is not necessarily laboratory equipment, just everyday items.

   C.   Incorrect. While the different spoon materials also have varying degrees of electrical conduction/insulation, this experiment is about heat conduction, not electrical conduction.

   D.   Incorrect. The teacher did not ask her students to form a hypothesis first.

MOTION

Physics, or the science of motion, can be simplified for young students, but it should be taught starting in kindergarten when students begin to explore motion and the speed and position of an object. Students might experiment, for example, with pushing matchbox cars down an incline. They might notice that the steeper the incline, the higher the speed of the car as it races down the track.

Speed is the measurement of how fast something moves relative to a certain point. It is often measured in miles per hour in the United States, though a common measure in many scientific labs is meters per second. **Velocity** is different from speed in that it is the rate of change in an object's position, accounting for both speed and direction.

The Next Generation Science Standards call for explicit instruction of **force**, or the push or pull on an object, in kindergarten. By experimenting with various objects, students can see that the harder one pushes or pulls, the further the object in question will travel. Students can also see force in action with magnets and springs.

By third grade, students should be predicting a pattern of motion based on force and other factors, such as **gravity**—the force that attracts everything toward Earth's center or another body having mass—and **friction**, the resistance in motion when objects rub against each other. Friction causes moving objects to slow down as kinetic (or moving) energy changes to heat energy. Students can test this simply by going outside on a cold day and rubbing their hands together. The friction will create heat and make one's hands somewhat warmer.

Students can also experiment with force and friction with the use of wheeled cars or other toy vehicles. Students might hypothesize, for example, which type of surface (carpet, grass, dirt, concrete, tile, etc.) will make the car go the fastest and then test their hypothesis through experimentation. Students can further make and test predictions about gravity by dropping objects of different sizes and weight from a given point and timing how long they take to fall.

SAMPLE QUESTIONS

8) **How is velocity different from speed?**

   A. Velocity applies only to objects in motion.

   B. Speed accounts for an object's direction.

   C. Velocity applies only to objects in an environment free of gravity.

   D. Velocity accounts for both speed and direction.

   Answers:

   A. Incorrect. Both speed and velocity apply to objects in motion.

   B. Incorrect. Speed does not account for an object's direction.

C.   Incorrect. Velocity applies to all objects in motion.

D.   Correct. Unlike speed, velocity also accounts for an object's direction.

9)   **A kindergarten student scoots around the classroom carpet on his knees and then notices red marks on his knee caps. What caused this?**

A.   high velocity

B.   rapid acceleration

C.   friction

D.   gravity

Answers:

A.   Incorrect. Velocity without contact with another object would not cause the rug burns.

B.   Incorrect. Acceleration without contact with another object would not cause the rug burns.

C.   Correct. Friction is the force of two objects (the knees and the carpet) rubbing against each other to produce heat (a rug burn).

D.   Incorrect. While gravity keeps the student on the rug, it does not directly cause the red marks.

EARTH AND SPACE SCIENCE

Earth and space science explores the relationships among the ocean, land, and atmosphere of our planet, as well as the properties of celestial objects and how they affect Earth. It includes understanding the movements and cycles that occur on Earth and in space: weather, seasons, daylight, water, carbon, tectonic plates, and more. It also includes studying the physical and chemical makeup of our planet and others.

THE SOLAR SYSTEM

A **solar system** includes a **star** and all the matter that orbits that star, including asteroids, comets, meteoroids, planets, and their moons. Stars are giant balls of extremely hot gas made up of hydrogen and helium, held together by gravity. The core of a star produces energy. Some of that energy is released as light, which makes the star glow.

An **asteroid** is a small, rocky, planet-like body that circles the sun. The size of an asteroid can range from about three feet to more than five hundred miles across. A **comet** is a chunk of dust and ice that orbits the sun. There are billions of comets in our solar system. Most comets never pass close to Earth.

Meteoroids are very small, rocky bodies in our solar system; they range in size from a speck to several feet across. Meteoroids travel through space and occasionally enter Earth's atmosphere, where they become known as **meteors**—or shooting stars. If they do not burn up, the piece that ends up on Earth's surface is known as a **meteorite**.

A **moon** is a natural satellite that revolves around a planet. Planets vary in the number of moons they have. Moons do not give off their own light but reflect light from the sun, making them appear to shine.

Planets are an important part of the solar system, too. Planets are large, natural objects that orbit—or circle around—stars. Eight planets orbit our sun. From closest to the sun to farthest, these planets are **Mercury**, **Venus**, **Earth**, **Mars**, **Jupiter**, **Saturn**, **Uranus**, and **Neptune**.

> **HELPFUL HINT**
>
> The phrase *My Very Educated Mother Just Served Us Noodles* can help students remember the order of the planets: Mercury, Venus, Earth, Mars, Jupiter, Saturn, Uranus, Neptune.

- Mercury is the smallest planet and is only a little bit larger than Earth's moon. Mercury rotates very slowly and has no moon.

- Venus is the sixth-largest planet in the solar system and has a dense, cloudy atmosphere. The clouds that cover Venus reflect light and make it the brightest planet as seen from Earth. It is also the closest planet to Earth and only a little smaller in size by comparison.

- Earth is the fifth-largest planet in our solar system. Life, as we know it, has only been found on Earth.

- Mars is the seventh-largest planet in our solar system. It is known as the *Red Planet* because its surface is rich in iron oxide—rust—and so it appears red from Earth.

- Jupiter is the largest planet in the solar system; it has sixteen moons and is more than 1,000 times larger than Earth.

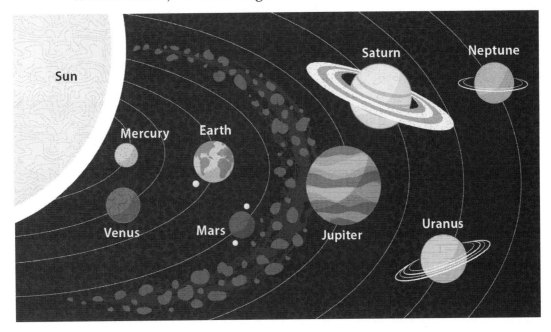

Figure 4.6. The Solar System

▸ Saturn is the second-largest planet in our solar system, known for the icy rings that encircle it.

▸ Uranus is the third-largest planet in our solar system.

▸ Neptune is the fourth-largest planet in the solar system.

The Next Generation Science Standards include explicit strands regarding space in first grade, when students are asked to make observations and describe patterns of the sun, moon, and stars. However, a basic understanding and identification of Earth, the moon, and the sun can be introduced in prekindergarten, as can space exploration. Many art projects, such as having students create a moonscape model out of modeling clay, or drawing/coloring the planets, are both developmentally appropriate and a great way to integrate fine motor skills development with basic science concepts.

SAMPLE QUESTION

10) **Which astronomical bodies generate their own light?**

A. stars

B. planets

C. comets

D. moons

Answers:

A. **Correct.** Stars—including the sun, which is a star—generate their own light. Planets, comets, and moons all reflect light from the sun.

B. Incorrect. Planets are large, natural objects that orbit stars; they do not generate their own light.

C. Incorrect. Comets are chunks of ice or dust that orbit the sun and do not generate their own light.

D. Incorrect. Moons revolve around a planet and do not give off their own light; instead, they reflect light from the sun, which makes them appear to shine.

SEASONS AND WEATHER

Weather and seasons are an important part of any preschool or kindergarten classroom, and rightly so since they help students observe what is somewhat predictable in the natural world—seasons—and what is often hard to predict—weather. Various tools can help scientists make observations about weather. A **thermometer** measures the air temperature and is a great tool to help students as young as kindergarten track and record the temperature. More advanced tools, such as **barometers**, which measure air pressure and are often used to help predict rain, and **anemometers**, which measure wind speed, can be useful for older students to make and record observations. Younger students might observe wind speed and direction from a wind sock, or track the rain over a period of days or weeks with a rain gauge.

Earth makes one complete **orbit** around the sun every 365 days, and this is called a year. A **day** is a twenty-four-hour period—the time elapsed for the earth to rotate once on its axis such that the sun appears at the same place in the sky the next day. Some people living near the equator have close to twelve hours of light and twelve hours of darkness each day.

Seasons happen because of the tilt of Earth's axis toward and away from the sun. Because the earth's axis tilts at 23.5 degrees, most of the planet's inhabitants experience varying amounts of light and darkness dependent upon the time of year. During the summer, the northern half of the earth is tilted toward the sun, making daytime longer. During winter, the northern half of the earth is tilted away from the sun, making nights longer. The opposite happens in the southern half, so when it is summer in the Northern Hemisphere, it is winter in the Southern Hemisphere.

December
winter in Northern hemisphere
summer in Southern hemisphere

June
summer in Northern hemisphere
winter in Southern hemisphere

Figure 4.7. Seasons

Explicit instruction in seasons generally begins in preschool, and students will appreciate the seasons with thematic units on holidays and celebrations within these seasons. Bulletin boards, classroom decorations, and class- or school-wide celebrations (fall/spring carnivals, etc.) are all useful to help students recognize and look forward to certain seasons. Older students can begin to appreciate that seasons are relative and that not all places on Earth experience the same season at the same time.

Weather, particularly sunlight, should be emphasized in kindergarten. Beginning in first grade, students should make observations about different amounts of daylight at various times of the year. In second and third grade, observations and patterns about the weather, seasons, and sunlight can be expanded to include the way that these patterns impact all life on Earth.

A variety of tools and hands-on activities can be used to help students explore the weather and seasons. Simple observation and recording activities are appropriate for all age groups, with teacher scaffolding as necessary. These activities often work well when integrated with math activities, such as recording data in a table and recognizing patterns over time. Even prekindergarten students can participate in these types of activities with the aid of pictures.

Young students should also develop vocabulary to describe weather. This can be reinforced by asking students, for example, whether it is colder today than it was yesterday, or having them tell you whether the day is hot or *very* hot. These are good questions to help get very young students talking about the weather. Older students might benefit from hands-on activities, such as experimenting with a globe and a flashlight to better understand Earth's tilt, and even creating models showing the orbits of the earth, the sun, and the moon.

SAMPLE QUESTIONS

11) Ms. Bess, a third-grade teacher, points to the United States and South Africa on the globe and asks her class the following question: "Our longest day is June twenty-first, and our longest night is December twenty-first. What is the longest day and night in South Africa?" What is the correct response?

A. The longest day and night are the same in South Africa as in the United States.

B. The longest day in South Africa is September twenty-second, and the longest night is March twenty-first.

C. South Africa has twelve hours of light and twelve hours of darkness each day.

D. The longest night in South Africa is June twenty-first, and the longest day is December twenty-first.

Answers:

A. Incorrect. In the Southern Hemisphere, the longest days and nights are reversed.

B. Incorrect. In most locations, these two dates generally have an approximately equal number of light and dark hours.

C. Incorrect. Places near the equator have this, but South Africa is in the Southern Hemisphere, not near the equator.

D. **Correct.** Because it is in the Southern Hemisphere, the longest day and night are reversed in South Africa.

12) **A prekindergarten instructor wants to begin teaching her students about weather. What is the best activity for this age group?**

  A. building a model of the earth, the sun, and the moon and relating it to the seasons

  B. taking the class outside to make observations about the weather, such as hot, cold, windy, etc.

  C. explaining seasonal variations in the Northern and Southern Hemispheres with orbital diagrams

  D. having students fill in a compare-and-contrast chart showing the climate of different regions of the US

Answers:

  A. Incorrect. This activity is not developmentally appropriate for a prekindergarten class and is not about weather.

  B. Correct. This is an appropriate activity to help students begin to use weather-related vocabulary.

  C. Incorrect. This is not developmentally appropriate for a prekindergarten class.

  D. Incorrect. A compare-and-contrast chart is not developmentally appropriate for a prekindergarten class, and this one is more about overall climate than weather.

PROPERTIES OF EARTH'S MATERIALS

Earth is made up of minerals, rocks, soil, and water. **Minerals** are naturally occurring substances formed in the earth that are not animals or plants. Examples of minerals are elements such as gold, silver, and iron, and combinations of elements, such as salt. **Rocks** are solid masses made up of minerals. Rocks form much of the earth's **outer crust**—the thinnest layer of the earth's surface—including cliffs and mountains.

Fossils can also make up some of the earth's surface. Fossils are impressions or remains left by plants or animals that lived a long time ago. They might be imprints of footprints, shells, or nests—known as trace fossils or body fossils—or the preserved remains of organisms themselves. Fossils are formed by replacing original organic material with minerals. This allows them to be preserved from decay.

> **HELPFUL HINT**
>
> Luster describes how light reflects off the surface of a mineral. Terms to describe luster include *dull*, *metallic*, *pearly*, and *waxy*.

Soil is formed slowly as rock breaks down into tiny pieces near the earth's surface and combines with organic matter. Soils have properties of texture and color and the capacity to hold water and grow plants. Soil provides a home for many animals, such as insects, spiders, and worms as well as bacteria and other living things. Soil affects the atmosphere by releasing gases, such as carbon dioxide, into the air. It is important because it cycles nutrients including carbon and nitrogen. Soil also helps filter and clean the water.

Water is a tasteless, odorless, and nearly colorless liquid. Many substances dissolve in water, so water in nature is rarely pure. Earth's water is always changing states from vapor to liquid to ice and back again. This **water cycle** affects Earth's materials. The water cycle describes the existence and movement of water on, in, and above the earth. These are the parts of the water cycle:

▶ precipitation: Water falls to the earth as rain, snow, sleet, or hail.

▶ evaporation: Water changes from liquid to gas as it is heated by the sun.

▶ condensation: Water vapor changes from a gas to a liquid and forms water droplets as it cools.

▶ runoff: Water drains from a high point of land and flows into an existing body of water.

▶ accumulation: Water collects on the earth's surface creating oceans, streams, and lakes.

▶ transportation: Water is absorbed by a plant, carried through to the leaves, and then turned into vapor and released into the atmosphere. Water can cause the earth's surface to break down through weathering and erosion, which create cliffs, canyons, and other rock formations.

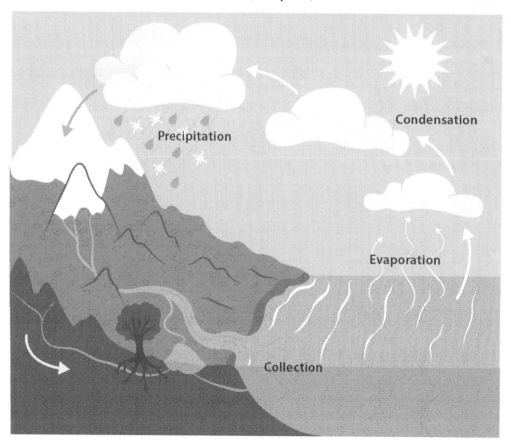

Figure 4.8. The Water Cycle

Changes in the earth's surface can happen quickly or slowly, and students should begin to make this distinction in second grade. Slow processes include:

- ▶ weathering: Wind, water, and ice cause large rocks to break up into smaller rocks.
- ▶ erosion: Rock and soil are carried from one place to another. Human actions, such as deforestation and construction, can accelerate erosion.
- ▶ deposition: Layers of sediment are deposited on one another, building up land mass. Deposition can lead to many different formations depending upon where it occurs. Ocean sandbars and river deltas are both the products of deposition, which happens after erosion.

Other changes in the earth's surfaces happen very suddenly. These include:

- ▶ earthquakes: Earthquakes are the release of energy when two blocks of the earth slide past one another. They are most likely to occur along boundaries of tectonic plates—large pieces of the earth's crust and mantle that fit together like a puzzle over the earth's surface.
- ▶ volcanoes: These are eruptions caused when magma within the earth reaches its surface. Volcanoes also occur along plate boundaries.
- ▶ landslides/mudslides: These are large amounts of earth and rock that move down a slope. These occur most frequently in coastal and mountain areas, but they have been recorded in all fifty states.

At all levels, students should see the earth as a naturally changing environment, though human interactions with the planet can also cause changes. This might happen as the result of human-generated pollution that impacts the water cycle or rapid deforestation that leads to erosion. Students must be encouraged to be responsible stewards of both the earth's resources as well as the materials of the earth itself.

> **HELPFUL HINT**
>
> **Weathering** is the process of breaking large rocks into smaller rocks over time. **Erosion** is the movement of weathered rock and soil from one place to another. Both are caused by wind, ice, water, and gravity.

SAMPLE QUESTIONS

13) Which of the following changes the earth's surface slowly?

- A. volcanoes
- B. earthquakes
- C. wildfires
- D. weathering

Answers:

A.   Incorrect. Volcanoes are eruptions that result in sudden changes to the earth's surface.

B.   Incorrect. Earthquakes can happen suddenly and therefore change the earth's surface within moments, not slowly.

C.   Incorrect. Wildfires result in sudden changes to the earth's surface.

D.   Correct. Weathering changes the earth's surface slowly; the other processes change the earth's surface quickly.

14)   **Mrs. Hart teaches second grade in Houston, Texas. One of her students asks her the following question: "Why don't we have any earthquakes here?" What is her best response?**

A.   "The climate here is too humid, so we do not have earthquakes."

B.   "Unlike some other places, our city is not located near a plate boundary, so we do not usually get earthquakes."

C.   "Because of erosion caused by tropical storms in the Gulf of Mexico, we are unlikely to experience earthquakes."

D.   "We do not have earthquakes because we are at such a low elevation."

Answers:

A.   Incorrect. Earthquakes are not related to humidity.

B.   Correct. Earthquakes occur most frequently along boundaries between tectonic plates.

C.   Incorrect. Earthquakes are not related to erosion.

D.   Incorrect. Earthquakes are not related to elevation.

LIFE SCIENCE

Life science focuses on biology—the study of life and living organisms—and on the changes that all living things undergo. It covers topics including characteristics of organisms, such as what plants and animals need to survive; life cycles, the different stages of the lives of plants and animals; and ecosystems, how living things interact with each other and their environment.

CHARACTERISTICS OF ORGANISMS

An **organism** is an individual living thing, such as a plant, an animal, or a bacterium. Organisms have five characteristics that nonliving things do not have:

▶   Organisms are made up of cells.

▶   Organisms collect and use energy.

▶   Organisms grow and develop.

▶ Organisms can reproduce.

▶ Organisms respond to changes in their environment.

A **cell** is the smallest unit of organization in a living thing. A cell contains a nucleus and is surrounded by a membrane. The cell contains the organism's DNA and can make copies of itself. Some organisms are made up of more than one cell. These organisms' cells have specific roles. For example, hair cells function to grow and repair hair, and that is their only job. A group of similar cells can form a **tissue**. Tissues make up

organs, such as lungs, which perform specific duties. An **organ system** is a group of organs that work together for one or more purposes, such as the respiratory or digestive system.

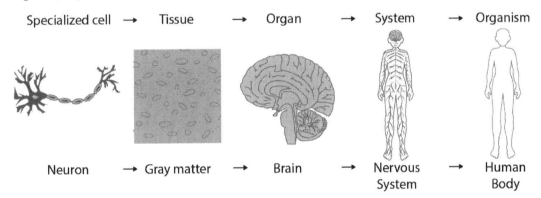

Figure 4.9. The Biological Hierarchy

Organisms collect and use energy. Cells, however, cannot survive by themselves. They need **nutrition** to grow, maintain balance, repair themselves, reproduce, move, and defend themselves. Nutrition is the act or process of taking in nutrients in order to grow and survive. Living organisms can either make their own food or depend on others to make food for them. Plants produce their own food through the process of photosynthesis. Other organisms eat plants to get energy.

The third characteristic of organisms is that they grow and develop. Living organisms begin life as a single cell. **Growth** is the increase in size and mass of an organism. For example, immature plants and animals are very similar to, but not exactly like, their parents.

Another characteristic of organisms is that they reproduce. **Reproduction** is the process by which new organisms are developed. Living things do not need to reproduce in order to survive; they need to reproduce to ensure that their species does not become extinct. Though it is not imperative, most organisms will go to great lengths to ensure they are able to reproduce.

The last characteristic of an organism is that it responds to changes in its environment. For example, if people hear a loud noise and wake up, the scare might make their hearts beat faster, and they might breathe faster. When this happens, the heart pumps more blood to the brain, which makes the people become fully alert. This response helps the people stay safe in a threatening or dangerous situation. Also, organisms can respond to their environment through **movement**. For example, geese temporarily move from the north to the south in winter because of their **sensitivity** to the cold. Sometimes the movement becomes permanent if the organism's habitat has changed such that its survival is no longer possible in its current location.

Even beginning in kindergarten, students should begin thinking about what different plants and animals (including humans) need to survive and how they can change the environment to meet their needs. This can be illustrated by a gopher digging a hole in which to live or a human digging a well from which to obtain water. In first grade, students should begin thinking about how the behaviors and structure of organisms help them survive and thrive. For example, fish have gills to enable them to breathe underwater, and mother bears aggressively protect their young to ensure survival. In second grade, students should start considering broader interactions among organisms, such as animals spreading plant seeds from one location to another. By third grade, students should be considering a broad range of environmental conditions that help organisms survive and how some organisms thrive while others do not, even though they are in the same environment.

SAMPLE QUESTION

15) A third-grade teacher wants to illustrate that the same environment can be perfect for one organism but harmful to another. Which example might she use?

A. fish and coral living in an ocean environment

B. camels and cactuses living in a desert environment

C. humans and pigeons living in a city environment

D. humans and deer living in a city environment

Answers:

A. Incorrect. Fish and coral will both thrive in an ocean environment.

B. Incorrect. A desert environment is suitable for both of these organisms.

C. Incorrect. Living in a city environment can work well for both humans and pigeons.

D. **Correct.** Deer would not be able to find the vegetation they need to eat in order to survive and might be hit by cars in an urban environment. On the other hand, humans do just fine in an urban environment. The other choices describe organisms that are well-suited to their environments.

LIFE CYCLES

A life cycle is a series of **stages**—or steps—in the process of growth and development during the life of all living things. **Development** is the steps along the way of an organism's transformation from a single cell to its mature form. Plants and animals **reproduce**; **parents**—a mother and father—produce young, or **offspring**. Offspring are the children or young of a particular human, animal, or plant. Life cycles are not the same across all living things, but they do all start with **birth** and end in **death**.

The reproduction of many plants—the flowering plants—results in a **seed**, from which the offspring plant grows into a new plant. A seed starts to grow and sprout when the conditions of the soil are just right, including the temperature and the amount of water available. When the seed **germinates**, or starts to grow, a **seedling** begins to appear. A seedling is a young tree or plant grown from a seed. The seedling continues to grow and eventually becomes an adult plant, a process called **maturation**. Once the plant becomes mature, it starts to make flowers. Flowers contain the reproductive organs of the plant, allowing seeds to be created. The flowering plant life cycle then begins again.

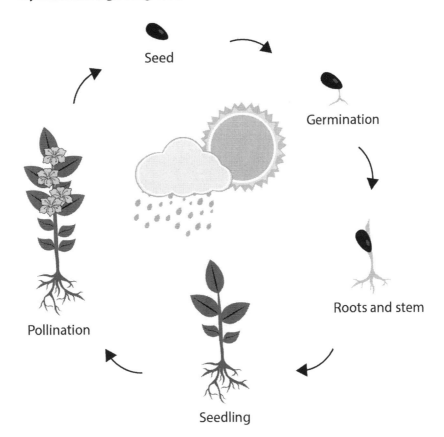

Figure 4.10. The Plant Life Cycle

Investigating how plants use their structures to survive is a first-grade objective per the Next Generation Science Standards. Experiments with plants pertaining to water and sunlight are recommended for second grade. Of course, various activities that allow even younger students to observe plant growth and development, such as school gardens or simple classroom plants, are appropriate at all ages.

HELPFUL HINT

Use the acronym *LAWN* to remember what plants need: **L**ight, **A**ir, **W**ater, **N**utrients.

Some animals develop through a process called **metamorphosis**—a series of physical changes—to become an adult. For example, a butterfly starts off as an **egg** and then **hatches** as a **larva**. Larvae—known as *caterpillars* in the case of butterflies—are very different from their parents. At the end of the larval stage, a butterfly becomes a **pupa**, surrounded by a hard **chrysalis**, or cocoon. This is the middle stage of the butterfly's development. Pupae do not move or eat. Once the butterfly is fully developed into its adult form, the case around the pupa cracks open. The butterfly emerges to search for food and for other butterflies to mate with, and the cycle begins again.

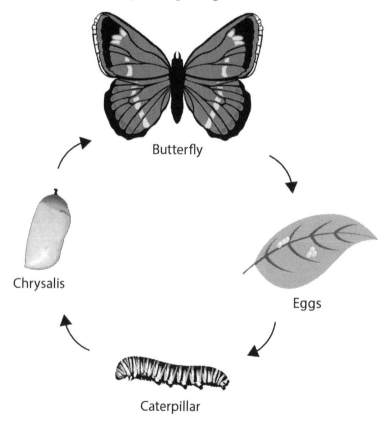

Figure 4.11. The Butterfly Life Cycle

Teaching basics about life cycles is a fabulous way for even preschool students to become interested in nature. Students can be encouraged to look for (but not touch!) eggs, cocoons, or buds in the natural environment. Students of all ages can also become highly engaged in the life cycle of the plant through class or school-wide projects, such as a garden. Gardens provide a unique opportunity to integrate a health and wellness curriculum into a science curriculum as students try different healthy, organically grown foods straight from the school garden. Health and wellness are also a key part of teaching about the human life cycle. Research has proven that healthy habits encouraged by teachers as early as the preschool years are often likely to be carried on throughout much of a student's life.

In addition to the life cycle of specific organisms, older students—namely those in second and third grade—should begin to understand the impacts that environmental changes may have on animal and plant species. Some organisms can withstand these changes while others cannot. Those that cannot will either relocate to a new environment or die out entirely.

> **QUICK REVIEW**
>
> What other ways can health and wellness be integrated into early childhood science instruction?

Extinction of a species can be likened to the end of its life cycle. While there is some debate as to the appropriateness of discussing upsetting themes, such as the decimation of habitats at the hands of humans, most research suggests that if conservation efforts are to be effectively carried out among future generations, they must be taught in the early childhood years. The key is to present information to students in a way that will first encourage their interest and appreciation for the natural world; this interest will then extend to a desire to protect it.

SAMPLE QUESTIONS

16) A third-grade teacher using the Next Generation Science Standards sees this strand: "Develop models to describe that organisms have unique and diverse life cycles, but all have in common birth, growth, reproduction, and death." What would be an appropriate activity to address this standard?

    A.   creating a diagram of the life cycle of a star

    B.   creating an infographic of a mosquito and frog life cycle and comparing the two

    C.   planting a lima bean seed in a plastic bag with a wet paper towel and observing its growth

    D.   watching a video on asexual reproduction in bacteria

Answers:

    A.   Incorrect. A star is not a living organism, though it does have a life cycle of sorts.

    B.   **Correct.** Working with an infographic will help students see that both a mosquito and a frog are born, grow, reproduce, and then die. It is also developmentally appropriate for third-grade students.

C.   Incorrect. Planting and studying a lima bean will help students observe a plant life cycle, but it will not allow them to compare it to another life cycle.

D.   Incorrect. This video might have some relevance, but it is not drawing a direct comparison to another life cycle.

17)   Which of the following occurs during germination?

A.   The plant becomes mature.

B.   The plant makes flowers.

C.   The plant makes and releases seeds.

D.   The seed begins to sprout.

Answers:

A.   Incorrect. Maturation is when the plant becomes mature.

B.   Incorrect. A plant makes flowers after the maturation phase.

C.   Incorrect. After the plant flowers, it makes seeds.

D.   Correct. Germination is the phase of the plant's life cycle when the seed begins to sprout.

ECOSYSTEMS

An **ecosystem** is a large community of living organisms and the physical environment they live in. All living things need energy to grow, move, and reproduce; that energy comes from food. The feeding relationship between organisms in an ecosystem is described in a **food web**, which shows how each organism gets nutrients and energy. Each individual strand in the web is called a **food chain**. The food chain starts with plants. Green plants make their own food through a process called **photosynthesis**, during which they use sunlight to change water and carbon dioxide into food. Plants are generally referred to as **producers**, while those organisms that eat them are called **consumers**.

CONSIDER THIS

Ask students what would happen if all the decomposers disappeared from an ecosystem.

A food chain might start with grass, which rabbits eat. Rabbits are **herbivores**—animals that feed only on plants. The rabbit is **prey**—an animal that is hunted and eaten by another animal, such as a snake. Snakes are **predators**—animals that hunt and eat other animals for food. The snake eats the rabbit, and later, a **carnivore**—an animal that eats mainly meat, such as a hawk—eats the snake. Other animals, like some humans and bears, are **omnivores**, meaning they eat both plants and meat.

After the remains of dead animals are left behind by predators, decomposers—like **fungi** and bacteria— play an important role. Fungi are organisms that appear similar to plants but cannot make their own food using sunlight. Fungi consume plants, animals, and other living matter. Examples of fungi include mushrooms, yeasts, and mold. Fungi help **decompose** dead plants and animals. When fungi eat dead plants and animals, they release nutrients and minerals back into the soil; these will then be used by plants.

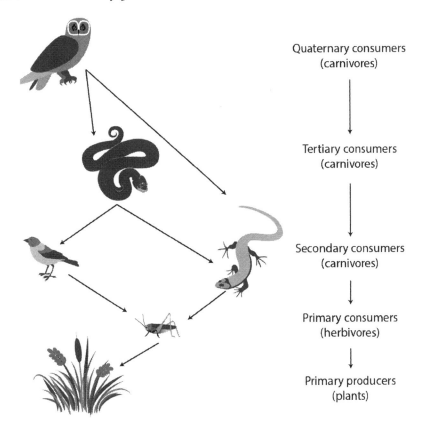

Quaternary consumers
(carnivores)

Tertiary consumers
(carnivores)

Secondary consumers
(carnivores)

Primary consumers
(herbivores)

Primary producers
(plants)

Figure 4.12. The Food Chain

Diverse ecosystems exist throughout the planet and have different varieties of plants and animals. Even in kindergarten, students can begin a simple study of this concept by matching animals with their habitats or natural environments. Deer and bears, for example, might live in a forest habitat whereas killer whales and jellyfish live in an ocean environment. Beginning in first grade, students should be considering how plants and animals use their own bodily structures to respond to their habitat in order to survive and grow.

HELPFUL HINT

Biotic components are alive: they can move, grow, reproduce, eat, and drink. **Abiotic** elements are not alive.

SAMPLE QUESTIONS

18) **Which of the following is an example of an herbivore?**

A. green algae

B. dolphin

C. cow

D. bird

Answers:

A. Incorrect. Algae are plants that make their own food; they do not eat plants.

B. Incorrect. Dolphins are carnivores that eat meat.

C. Correct. Cows eat only plants, so they are herbivores.

D. Incorrect. Birds eat both plants and other animals, so they are omnivores.

19) **A second-grade class is conducting an experiment to test the following hypothesis: fungi will grow more quickly when exposed to sunlight. How might the class best set up the experiment?**

A. observe the height of mushrooms both in open fields and in forest habitats

B. leave one petri dish in the refrigerator and keep one on the counter

C. compare fungi growth on a hamburger bun to that on a piece of wheat bread

D. leave one piece of bread on the windowsill in sunlight and leave another in a dark place

Answers:

A. Incorrect. This is not the best choice since there may be other factors aside from exposure to sunlight that will impact the growth of the mushrooms.

B. Incorrect. This experiment introduces another variable—cold. An experiment should only change the one variable it is designed to test.

C. Incorrect. This experiment would determine which type of bread grows fungi the most quickly, not the effect of sunlight on fungi growth.

D. Correct. This would change only one variable and would allow the hypothesis to be tested by exposing one piece of bread to sunlight and not the other.

ENGINEERING, TECHNOLOGY, AND APPLICATIONS OF SCIENCE

Engineering, technology, and applications of science are closely connected and influence each other. Scientists use technology and engineering to facilitate their research and find solutions to problems. When engineers need to create something, such as a new type of car, they depend on the **design process** to lead them. The design process is the process by which new technologies are created. It is very similar to scientific investigation. Both build on evidence and reason and follow a logical sequence of steps to solve problems and find answers. The steps include:

- ▶ identify the problem
- ▶ brainstorm
- ▶ design
- ▶ build (redesign, test, evaluate, repeat)
- ▶ share a solution

Students should be participating in simple engineering projects starting in pre-kindergarten. This may begin with very simple tasks, such as building a tall tower out of blocks that will not fall. It can then progress, in kindergarten, to testing two different designs to see which one works better. In first and second grade, students should begin to analyze the data from these tests. In third grade, students can begin proposing their own solutions and designs to solve real-world problems.

For example, a teacher might give the class a real-life scenario such as the following: A family owns a cabin that floods each year when heavy summer rains come. This year, they want to protect their cabin from the water. The flood waters are expected to be about one inch.

The teacher can distribute a scaled model house and a variety of supplies to each student. The students will then have to brainstorm ideas for how to engineer the cabin to withstand the flood waters. Next, they may draw a design or write out their plans. Then, they will augment their model cabin with the flood-withstanding features and test it, perhaps by placing it in a tub with one inch of water. At this point, they can evaluate how much their model cabin flooded and what modifications they should make. They then redesign and test again. Once a design is successful, they can share it with others.

> **QUICK REVIEW**
>
> How can students be encouraged to conserve resources and reduce waste in schools?

Students should also be exposed to technology, even as early as prekindergarten. While various schools and programs may have different expectations regarding the use of computers, they will all most likely encourage students to be proficient in simple computer operations during the early childhood years. Many elements of computer science have been adapted to accommodate young learners. Students as young as kindergarten age can learn basic drag-and-drop programming, and older students can learn a variety of computer languages with sufficient instruction and practice.

As much as possible, students should not see science in a vacuum. Instead, they should be given multiple opportunities to apply scientific principles throughout the school day. Ideas for this include having students make hypotheses and conduct simple tests throughout the day, allowing them to make astute observations about their environment. Teachers should also encourage students to learn about different careers that involve the application of scientific principles and how these professionals study and improve the world around us.

QUICK REVIEW

How is technology integrated into your state's science standards?

SAMPLE QUESTION

20) A kindergarten teacher wants to make sure her students are proficient with basic computer technology by the end of the year. What is one objective that is reasonable for them to meet?

A. using Java and Python

B. recording video on a tablet

C. turning on a computer

D. learning to type

Answers:

A. Incorrect. These computer languages are not developmentally appropriate for a kindergarten student.

B. Correct. This is an appropriate objective for kindergarten students. It might also aid students in recording observations.

C. Incorrect. This is too simple for an end-of-year goal for kindergarteners.

D. Incorrect. Most kindergarteners will not have the fine motor skills for this skill yet.

Physical Education and Health

Teaching physical education and health aims to give students the skills and confidence to become physically active and remain so throughout their lives. A high quality physical education and health program incorporates lessons that focus on student development and their changing movement abilities. Teachers must also consider the maturity level of students, their fitness level, and their motor skills.

TEACHING PHYSICAL EDUCATION

Physical education teachers should expose students to a wide variety of health- and skill-related fitness activities. Health-related fitness includes flexibility, body composition, cardiovascular fitness, muscular strength, and endurance. Skill-related components include balance, power, speed, coordination, and agility.

When designing lessons, teachers should keep in mind the **FITT** (frequency, intensity, time, type) **principle**. This acronym describes guidelines for a fitness plan, and it can be applied to the whole class or to individual students if necessary.

Frequency refers to how often students should exercise. For example, lifestyle exercises may be scheduled more often rather than endurance ones. The **intensity** of the activity describes how hard students need to work during each class. **Time** refers to how long students should participate in the activity. Students should participate in at least thirty to sixty minutes of age-appropriate physical activity daily, ten minutes of which should be moderate to vigorous activity. The **type** of activity describes the kinds of activities students practice or play. Teachers should create different lessons incorporating a wide variety of lifestyle

> **HELPFUL HINT**
>
> Each class and grade level's fitness goal will be different, and modifications may be needed to match a lesson plan with the students' current fitness level.

and recreational activities, active aerobics, flexibility, sports activities, and strength and muscular endurance exercises.

In early childhood, learning movement fundamentals requires movement concepts and fundamental motor skills. Teaching **movement concepts** helps children increase their understanding of body awareness and management. There are four movement concepts:

1. body awareness
2. spatial awareness
3. qualities of movement
4. relationships

The objective of **body awareness** is for students to explore the body's capabilities. In early childhood, students learn to identify and understand the locations of different body parts. They also practice the many shapes and positions they can form with their bodies. Teachers should help students gain an awareness of body movements and how the body can be used to communicate.

Spatial awareness is understanding where the body can move. Teachers should provide ample opportunities for students to explore the spatial qualities of movement. Examples include self-space, general space, pathways, range, and the direction of movement. Students should not only recognize these examples, but also respect the space of others, travel through space in a purposeful manner, and adjust their range of movement depending on the task.

The goal in teaching the **qualities of movement** is for students to understand how balance affects movement and the qualities of static and dynamic balance. Teachers should also help students generate and modify force to accomplish assigned tasks as well as differentiate among speeds so they can move more quickly or slowly. As students progress through the elementary grades, teachers should encourage them to accomplish movements within a certain amount of time and space.

HELPFUL HINT

Developing body management skills means integrating agility, coordination, balance, and flexibility to create effective movement.

Managing **relationships** in movements helps students understand how the body and its parts work together and with objects. Ultimately, students should move more effectively around individuals or with a group of people.

Developing student understanding and execution of **fundamental motor skills** should include a wide variety of exercise and games. Skill development should be emphasized, especially the importance of mastering basic skills to build more sophisticated ones. At the elementary level, teachers should emphasize student locomotor, non-locomotor, and manipulative skills to develop their motor skills.

1)   A preschool teacher asks her students to make the shape of each letter in the alphabet with their bodies. Which of the following movement concepts is she working to improve in her students?

A.   body awareness

B.   spatial awareness

C.   qualities of movement

D.   relationships

Answers:

A.   **Correct.** Having students form letters with their bodies helps them understand the way their bodies move and form shapes.

B.   Incorrect. Spatial awareness activities involve students learning about the space their bodies take up and how to move their bodies through the space around them.

C.   Incorrect. Qualities of movement activities emphasize control over balance, force, and time.

D.   Incorrect. Relationship activities emphasize the relationships between the body and objects or other people.

LOCOMOTOR AND NON-LOCOMOTOR SKILLS

Locomotor skills are the numerous ways the body can move through space. They include walking, skipping, running, jumping, sliding, galloping, and leaping. Students should be given ample time to practice skills repeatedly after observing a proper demonstration.

When teaching students walking skills, teachers should demonstrate that each foot alternates and that there is always one foot touching the floor. Instruct students to point toes straight ahead, keep their eyes forward with their heads up, and with their weight transferred from the heel to the ball of the foot. Students can also practice walking at different speeds, on their toes, or with bent legs.

Sliding involves students moving sideways with a leading foot. Students should focus on keeping the weight on the balls of their feet, eyes focused on the direction of travel, with hips and shoulders pointing to the front. This **locomotor pattern** is commonly used in sports such as softball, basketball, and racquet sports. In the younger grades, the focus should be on introducing the basic movements so students develop proficiency in different sports as they get older.

Students must understand that **galloping** is similar to sliding, but it is done forwards and emphasizes an upward motion. Ensure that students make high gallops and that one foot is always in front of the other.

Jumping and hopping are both rhythmic locomotor skills and used in activities such as dance and common games. **Jumping** entails pushing off the ground with both feet, whereas hopping involves pushing off with one foot. Teachers should help students develop these skills by teaching them how to jump by pushing off and landing with bent knees on their toes. **Hopping** is different in that students use one supporting leg that is bent to push off with the balls of the feet. Have students practice their hopping and jumping skills by moving in different directions and with their arms out, high to the side. Leaping is a similar airborne action; students move over an object leading with one foot and landing on another.

Finally, teachers should help students learn **skipping** by introducing the basic components in the younger grades. They should have been taught how to slide and hop before learning to skip. Students should practice marching with the knees high while hopping on the opposite foot at the same time. This is a rhythmical movement, and the focus should not be on speed but rather on mastering the rhythm of stepping and hopping. Once students develop more proficiency in skipping, they should master it by the middle elementary grades.

Non-locomotor skills are movements that do not require moving through space. These include bending, stretching, twisting, turning, pushing and pulling. As students develop their movement skills, teachers should give children ample opportunities to explore them, as well as combine them with locomotor skills so these can be applied to all physical education activities.

> **QUICK REVIEW**
>
> How would a lesson plan that focuses on locomotor skills be different from one that focuses on non-locomotor skills? What materials would you need? How would you set up the space for the class?

SAMPLE QUESTION

2) **Which of the following is a feature of a hop?**

   A. Alternate legs move in front of one another.

   B. Using the ball of one foot, a person pushes off from the ground on one leg.

   C. The individual uses one foot to push off the ground and lands on the other.

   D. Both legs are bent; the toes push off the ground at the same time.

Answers:

   A. Incorrect. This is walking.

   B. Correct. Hopping also requires students to keep their heads forward and arms out. The leg that is not pushing off the ground is usually slightly bent.

   C. Incorrect. This is leaping.

   D. Incorrect. This is jumping.

MANIPULATIVE SKILLS AND GAME SKILLS

Manipulative skills differ from locomotor and non-locomotor skills in that they involve students using objects like jump ropes and balls. These skills include throwing, catching, striking, and kicking. Many of these skills are taught through sports or standalone lessons such as drills.

Manipulative skills tend to be more challenging for children and should only be introduced when children are more proficient with locomotor and non-locomotor skills. Teachers should understand that focusing on how the body can move through space is more important for students in the younger grades than the students' ability to manipulate an object.

Game skills are a natural progression from manipulative skills; many manipulative skills relate to specific games. Teaching students **game skills** allows them to connect motor skill development and games they play. It also gives them an opportunity to practice skills in a team setting. This can include making decisions together and accepting individual differences in a group setting. Teaching game skills also helps students develop large muscle groups. Finally, game skills allow students to experience success and a sense of accomplishment.

> **HELPFUL HINT**
>
> Since hand-eye coordination is more difficult at farther distances, striking is one of the last skills students develop. The length of the object that children use to strike further complicates learning the skill. Teachers need to modify equipment so that lower elementary students can more easily develop this skill.

Teachers help students master game skills by guiding them on the techniques of the game skill and providing consistent feedback on their performance. One of the best ways to develop a game skill is through observation in a controlled setting. As students gain more experience, they can observe skills in games, giving them more context. Students should also experiment with performing the skill in different ways, moving in different ranges and directions. Students will learn that certain techniques or skills do not apply to all games, or even all parts of a game.

Mini games or drills provide the necessary environment for students to further develop game skills. These skills should be used repeatedly, mimicking the teacher's demonstration.

SAMPLE QUESTIONS

3) Which of the following activities would most likely be achieved independently by first-grade students?

A. catching a ball

B. striking a ball with a bat

C. skipping

D. leaping

Answers:

A. Correct. Students in first grade can demonstrate different skills that involve moving and staying still. The other skills are all learned in later elementary grades.

4) **Which of the following statements most appropriately describes the purpose of teaching game skills?**

A. Game skills help students increase their awareness of their own bodies.

B. Game skills help students link motor skill development to the games they play.

C. Game skills teach students about the role of stress in their bodies.

D. Game skills teach students to respect others.

Answers:

A. Incorrect. All physical education activities help students be aware of their own bodies.

B. Correct. Game skills help students master skills beyond physical development, including connecting motor skills to specific games.

C. Incorrect. Students learn about physical stress through the study of health, not by learning game skills.

D. Incorrect. Respect for others can be taught through many subjects in school.

SAFETY

During physical education lessons, **safety** for teachers and students must be taken into consideration. Teachers should check the area before any activity or game begins to ensure there are no dangerous objects or hazards. Ensure that participants understand a signal from the teacher indicates the beginning and end of play. Teach students that it is important to respect others and the equipment; students must follow commands and avoid grabbing or pushing. A warm-up period before starting any activity will prevent injuries. For the sake of safety, teachers should also consider omitting skills that might put students in harm's way.

Teachers must consult with a school nurse or a health professional regarding the needs of students with health conditions like asthma or diabetes; teachers should also be aware of the effects of medication students take and symptoms of health emergencies. Lessons and physical activities may be modified to accommodate physical and social needs.

SAMPLE QUESTION

5) **Which of the following will most likely reduce the number of accidents in a physical education class?**

    A.   posting signs on proper etiquette

    B.   instructing students to arrive on time for class

    C.   asking students to monitor one another during class

    D.   incorporating a warm-up period to prevent injuries during activities

Answers:

    A.   Incorrect. Posting signs will not necessarily prevent accidents.

    B.   Incorrect. Punctuality does not necessarily prevent accidents.

    C.   Incorrect. A teacher should monitor students to prevent any accidents. Students are not responsible for class safety.

    D.   **Correct.** A teacher should incorporate activities into the lesson to ensure the safety of all students. Warming up will help prevent injuries.

EQUIPMENT

Choosing the right equipment for an early childhood physical education class is essential for students to develop their skills at an appropriate pace. Equipment should be matched to the confidence, size, and skill level of the student so that he or she is motivated to actively participate in class. For example, younger students who are not proficient in coordination might need short and lightweight equipment that can be more easily manipulated or handled.

Pedometers are useful tools; these devices reliably measure a student's physical activity levels. They enhance instruction by providing accountability, revealing students' activity levels and consequently providing feedback on the effectiveness of instruction. This feedback can then be used to create or modify lessons to ensure that students receive quality instruction.

Teachers should also ensure that there is enough equipment so that students are engaged at all times. Having enough equipment ensures that students have equal opportunities to practice and reinforce skills taught in class; sufficient equipment also prevents potential classroom management problems. In the case of equipment shortage, teachers should select a variety of activities that use different equipment so students are not left idle. Teachers can also create activities to engage some students in observing and giving feedback to others who are demonstrating skills they have learned.

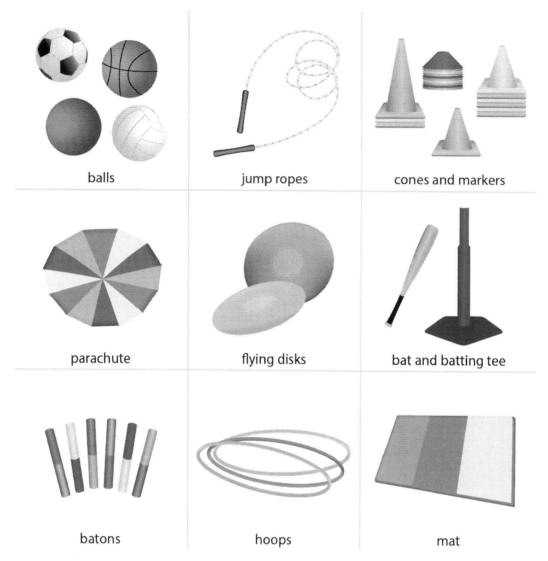

Figure 5.1. Physical Education Equipment

balls   jump ropes   cones and markers

parachute   flying disks   bat and batting tee

batons   hoops   mat

SAMPLE QUESTION

6)   Which of the following pieces of physical education equipment would be most appropriate for a class of three-year-old children?

   A.   basketball

   B.   scooter

   C.   parachute

   D.   jump rope

Answers:

   A.   Incorrect. A basketball is too large for a three-year-old child to effectively manipulate.

   B.   Incorrect. Three-year-old children will have trouble following the rules necessary for the safe use of scooters.

C.   **Correct.** Three-year-old children are capable of playing many different games with a parachute (e.g., Popcorn, Around the World).

D.   Incorrect. A three-year-old child does not have the motor skills necessary to use a jump rope.

TEACHING HEALTH

Lessons on healthy living are integral to a well-rounded physical education and health curriculum. While it is important for students to practice motor development skills, a good physical education and health curriculum also shows students the benefits of a healthy lifestyle. Improved physical fitness and knowledge of proper nutrition helps students in other areas of life, including self-discipline, cooperation, stress reduction, goal setting, and better relationships with peers.

At the elementary level, lessons on health help students learn about wellness and unhealthy behaviors. They gain the ability to explain the importance of physical activity, what contributes to disease in the body, and how nutrition, stress and substance abuse affect their growth and well-being.

> **HELPFUL HINT**
>
> Planting a garden is a great hands-on activity for teaching early elementary students about food and nutrition.

Teaching students about the physical systems in the body is a great introduction to the theories of health and gives them the fundamental knowledge to better understand **nutrition** and fitness. In the early elementary grades, the focus should be on the elements of a **balanced diet**. Looking at the healthy eating plate and identifying nutrients helps students learn how their choices affect their bodies.

Teachers can also address disease prevention and control. Students learn about practical ways to prevent disease, such as practicing **personal hygiene**, identifying symptoms of diseases and how they affect the body, and how to prevent diseases. Students may also learn about injury prevention and safety. Topics would include basic safety rules, reacting to emergencies, and understanding strategies for self-protection.

Figure 5.2. MyPlate Food Guide

Beyond the physical body, students also need to understand that their **mental health** contributes to social and emotional well-being. Students should learn different strategies and skills to improve their relationships with others and themselves. Topics can include:

- friends and family
- effective communication
- appropriate emotional responses
- assuming responsibility for their own decisions

Older students will learn about stress, its effects on the body, and identifying resources and constructive ways of dealing with it.

Learning about **substance abuse** helps older students understand the impact drugs can have on their lives. Lessons should help students understand how alcohol and other types of drugs (including some types of medications) affect the body when abused; students should learn about decision-making. More specifically, lessons can examine media, peer pressure, and other external factors (such as laws) that impact decision-making. Equally important are lessons on internal factors like addiction.

SAMPLE QUESTION

7) **Which of the following methods is NOT an appropriate activity for teaching students about the benefits of nutrition?**

   A. showing students a picture of the USDA food plate and creating a balanced meal using the guidelines

   B. showing students a picture of the food pyramid and creating a balanced meal using the guidelines

   C. showing students possible side effects when they eat too much sugar

   D. showing students the types of food that can help to fight disease

   Answers:

   A. Incorrect. The USDA food plate is a useful tool to illustrate healthy food choices.

   B. **Correct.** The food pyramid was replaced by the MyPlate guidelines to demonstrate healthy food choices.

   C. Incorrect. Teaching about the side effects of sugar would be an appropriate lesson in nutrition; it shows the impact of food choices on the body.

   D. Incorrect. Discussing the benefits of various foods is an appropriate lesson; students are learning the value of good nutrition.

The Arts

PURPOSE AND FUNCTION OF THE ARTS

The arts, including visual arts, music, and performance, is a tool for children to learn about themselves and the world around them. Early childhood arts teachers present art as a lens through which to understand the world. To create well-rounded arts classes, teachers provide students ample opportunities to create and reflect on their own creations, to respond critically to other people's works and their contributions to the human experience, and to critique art in relation to its cultural and historical context.

Teachers can also use the arts to make connections between other subjects. A successful early childhood lesson plan will incorporate concepts from history, math, science, and language lessons. For example, children who are learning about ancient Egypt can learn about the many types of art produced in that culture. Children can then create their own Egyptian art by sculpting and painting masks, building pyramids out of paper blocks, or crafting jewelry.

SAMPLE QUESTION

1) An arts teacher is working with a second-grade teacher to coordinate a lesson on punctuation. Which of the following activities would NOT be appropriate for the arts teacher to include?

    A. Have students use different colors and brushes to paint punctuation marks.

    B. Have students work in groups to create posters that describe the purpose of each punctuation mark.

    C. Help students create a dance with different movements for each punctuation mark.

    D. Use a rhythmic tune or beat that emphasizes punctuation while reading a book.

Answer:

A. **Correct.** The arts lesson should focus on the use of punctuation, not just its shape. The other choices are all appropriate activities that would help students learn about punctuation.

ART CRITICISM

Children can learn to use the language of art to make judgments about their own artwork and that of others—to engage in **art criticism**. In preschool and early elementary school, critiques can be conducted through discussion. To help students appreciate and think critically about art, teachers should engage students with questions like "What do you think of when you see this picture?" or "What makes you feel that way about this song?" These questions can help teachers lead children through the process of art criticism.

The four major areas of art criticism are description, analysis, interpretation, and judgment. In **describing** a work of art, make sure students avoid using expressive words like *beautiful* or *ugly*. Instead, help them describe the piece as objectively as possible. Examples include using the title of the piece, observing technical qualities (e.g., what tools or instruments were used), noting recognizable symbols or images, and addressing the elements of art present.

HELPFUL HINT

Trying to protect children from making mistakes can diminish creativity, so allow children to experiment with the tools and techniques of art creation. Children should also be encouraged to think critically about their own work but shouldn't be scared away from expressing themselves through their art.

An **analysis** of the artwork entails discerning and describing how the piece is organized. Students should investigate the principles of art, such as emphasis, repetition, and contrast. In visual arts, students can also consider the relationships between or among subjects, if applicable; they may also consider the relationship between the piece and the viewer, including how the piece affects the viewer when it is perceived from different angles. In addition, analysis may involve comparing the piece with other works of art.

When students are ready to **interpret** the artwork in question, they should discuss how the work impacts them and describe its unique qualities. For example, students may use expressive language (e.g., descriptors like *funny, sad,* and *beautiful*). They could also discuss how the work reminds them of personal experiences, world events, or issues they have encountered in their studies.

Finally, students should **judge** the artwork and justify their opinion of it. Whenever possible, students may compare the artwork with other pieces they have studied. They may even explain whether they think the work is original and justify their explanation.

SAMPLE QUESTION

2) A kindergarten student is critiquing an art piece. She talks about the artwork and how it reminds her of a sad time in her life. Which of the following areas of art criticism is she using?

A. description

B. judgment

C. interpretation

D. analysis

Answers:

A. Incorrect. In describing an artwork, the critic addresses art as objectively as possible.

B. Incorrect. In using judgment, the critic justifies his or her opinion on the artwork.

C. **Correct.** Interpreting an artwork entails discussing the unique qualities of a piece and how the piece reminds a person of events in his or her own life.

D. Incorrect. In analysis, a critic describes how a work of art is organized.

ART HISTORY

Art history should also be taught in early childhood so students can gain an understanding of how artists and art made contributions to culture and society. In studying art history, students learn how artists interact with their contemporaneous cultures, respond to historical events and social change, and address other artistic movements. Art history lessons should encourage students to ask why an artist created a certain piece of art, how it was used, and what its purpose was.

Art history for young children means exposing students to significant artists, not expecting them to write essays or conduct independent research. For example, teachers can decorate the classroom with printouts or posters of important artworks. If possible, take students on field trips to galleries, museums, and performances so they can gain an appreciation of art.

> **HELPFUL HINT**
>
> Art history for young children shouldn't be confined to the visual arts. Play songs and pieces of music from different time periods and cultures for the class.

As students study individual artists and their bodies of work, encourage them to consider the mind of the artist as he or she created the work, and how the artwork relates to its time period. Teachers should provide as much relevant background as possible so students can use that knowledge to view and discuss the artwork. Even young children can benefit from exposure to the art and music of different civilizations important throughout human history.

Teachers can also use art history to help students explore world history and other cultures. Students can be taught about art from ancient civilizations such as ancient Egypt, the ancient Mayans, ancient Ethiopia, classical Greece and Rome, and more. They can also be introduced to modern art from various cultures around the world.

Teachers can also engage students with art history by having them create art from different cultures and time periods. Students can use supplies like pipe cleaners, wood craft sticks, cardboard, and construction paper to build their own versions of ancient pyramids and temples. To help build motor skills, have children use clay or play-dough to make their own sculptures during a lesson on classical civilization. Watercolors, tempera paints, and pastels are also great tools for young students inspired by Claude Monet or Jackson Pollock to make their own impressionist- and modern-style artworks.

SAMPLE QUESTION

3) **Which of the following best describes why students should study art history?**

A. A strong grasp of art history helps students improve their skill in art techniques.

B. A knowledge of art history helps students understand art criticism.

C. Studying art history gives students a break from creating art.

D. Art history helps students understand how an artwork addressed its contemporaneous society.

Answers:

A. Incorrect. Studying art history can help students recognize and evaluate how other artists apply different techniques; it does not necessarily help students improve their own skills.

B. Incorrect. There are numerous other ways to help students understand art criticism, including understanding how to describe an artwork.

C. Incorrect. This is not the most appropriate reason to study art history.

D. **Correct.** Studying art history helps students to understand why an artist created the artwork he or she did.

VISUAL ARTS

The **visual arts** includes drawing, painting, sculpting, and photography. While the tools and techniques used in these art forms can be very different, they all rely on the same foundational elements and principles.

A good understanding of the elements and principles of art is necessary for the creation and analysis of art. Teachers should show children that artists use these elements and principles to make decisions when creating their own art, and that students should apply this knowledge to their own works.

ELEMENTS AND PRINCIPLES OF ART

Art is created through the use of line, shape, form, value, texture, space, and color. Together, these are known as the **elements of art**.

Line in art is called a moving dot: it can control the viewer's eye, indicate form and movement, describe edges, and point out a light source in a drawing. Artists use different line qualities and contours to suggest form. To indicate value or a light source, artists use cross-hatching lines in varying degrees.

A closed contour is what creates **shape**, which is two-dimensional. A shape can create balance and affect the composition, establishing positive and negative spaces. Different types of shapes include regular, or geometric, and organic, or freeform, shapes. When students understand the basics of shapes, they can create complex forms by combining simple organic and regular shapes.

Form is like shape except it is three-dimensional. Creating form requires an understanding of how light reflects upon an object, or its **value**. Teachers should help students understand where the highlight, the reflected light, the mid-tone, the core shadow, and the cast shadows are in order to create an illusion of form. Having students create a value scale and understand how it applies to objects they see is also helpful. Value also helps to create **texture**, which refers to how an object would feel if someone were to touch it. Students can develop their sense of texture through exposure to a wide variety of objects and by understanding how light reflects off rough, smooth, matte, and shiny surfaces.

> **HELPFUL HINT**
>
> To engage children, have them create and critique art that relates to topics that are familiar to them, such as family, friends, sports, holidays, and animals.

Creating an illusion of **space** can help students in creating an artwork on a two-dimensional surface. Students should experiment with different techniques such as overlapping shapes, shape placement, sizes of shapes, and perspective to see how objects can appear closer or farther away.

The color wheel is primarily used to teach students the theories of **color**. Early childhood teachers will focus on the types of colors:

- **Primary colors** (red, yellow, and blue) cannot be made using other colors.
- **Secondary colors** are made by mixing primary colors (yellow + blue = green).
- **Tertiary colors** are made by mixing one primary color with half the saturation of a second primary color (blue + 1/2 red = violet).

The color wheel also shows **complementary colors**, which appear opposite each other on the wheel. When paired together, complementary colors offer a stark contrast that is pleasing to the eye.

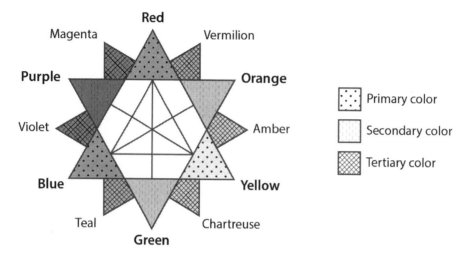

Figure 6.1. The RGB Color Wheel

The **principles of art** refer to the composition of the elements of art within a piece of work. These principles include:

- balance
- unity
- contrast
- movement
- emphasis
- pattern
- proportion

In order to create **balance** in an artwork, colors, forms, shapes, or textures need to be combined in harmony. Harmony also helps to create **unity** in a piece of work by creating a sense of wholeness.

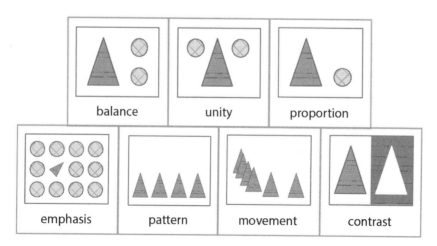

Figure 6.2. Principles of Art

Artists generate **contrast** by using various elements of art, like shapes, form, colors, or lines, to capture the viewer's attention and draw it toward a certain part of the work. **Movement** guides the viewer's eye through a composition, usually to highlight areas of contrast or emphasis. Repeating occurrences of a design element, such as shapes, forms, or textures in an art piece, are called **patterns**. Finally, **proportion** describes the way the sizes of objects appear. For example, objects that are farther away appear smaller and have less detail than objects that are closer.

SAMPLE QUESTIONS

4) A first-grade teacher wants to show students how complementary colors can be used when painting. Which of the following colors should she NOT use as an example?

    A. blue and orange

    B. red and blue

    C. purple and yellow

    D. red and green

    Answer:

    B. Correct. Red and blue are not directly opposite on the color wheel. The other choices are all complementary colors.

5) A kindergarten teacher has his students paint a picture that includes animals of different sizes. What principle of art is the teacher introducing to his students?

    A. pattern

    B. movement

    C. proportion

    D. unity

    Answer:

    C. Correct. Having students draw animals of different sizes introduces them to proportion, or the way the size of elements in an artwork relate to each other.

TEACHING ART

In early childhood education, art teachers should consider student capabilities, classroom management, and curriculum.

Children in prekindergarten may not yet be able to use certain tools, and a kindergartener is probably not ready for an in-depth discussion of the elements of art. However, even the youngest children can mix different colors of paint or play-dough to create new colors, learning about the color wheel. Students can learn about proportion, balance, and unity by creating their own scenes—pictures of their homes, families, pets, and possessions.

Children in prekindergarten and kindergarten have a wide range of motor skills, and teachers should consider this in classroom management. Not every student will be able to use every art tool. Some students may need the teacher's assistance in learning how to manipulate paintbrushes or scissors; the teacher may even need to dedicate a lesson to using certain tools depending on how many students need guidance.

While younger students are generally less self-critical than older students, any student might be dissatisfied with his or her creation. If students express concern over having made a "mistake," the teacher can help them find ways to improve their artwork to their liking. Just telling a student that the artwork is fine the way it is can be frustrating for some children who are seeking guidance. Offer solutions and be encouraging, not judgmental. Still, mistakes are part of art, and teachers should emphasize that the process is as important as the product. Accidents will also happen, especially with the youngest children: be prepared for paint to spill and equipment to fall.

Visual arts education for young children can be cross-curricular. For instance, creating animals is a great way to integrate student learning about science and math. Children learning about different shapes like triangles, quadrilaterals, and circles can apply their skills as those shapes transform into the ears of a cat, the eyes of an owl, or the body of a dog. Older students can draw shapes; younger students with less-developed motor skills can experiment with making collages from cut-out pieces of construction paper, or they can even cut the paper themselves, depending on ability. Students learning about specific animals or plants can create them in the art room or develop informational posters displaying facts they have learned.

SAMPLE QUESTION

6) Kimba, a kindergartener, does not know how to use the safety scissors the students will employ to cut construction paper. She states that she is not allowed to handle scissors at home because they are dangerous. How should Mrs. Rodriguez, the art teacher, respond?

A. find a different activity for Kimba while the rest of the class uses scissors

B. spend a class discussing and demonstrating the proper use of scissors and scissors safety

C. explain to Kimba that her mother is incorrect and that scissors are safe to use

D. guide Kimba individually on safety scissors usage and explain they are safer than other scissors

Answer:

D. Correct. Mrs. Rodriguez should explain that the scissors in the art room are safe for children and are not the same as other scissors. She should not devote an entire class to scissors safety unless most of the other students are in the same situation as Kimba. If the other students need to focus on scissors too, the teacher should find a more age-appropriate way to explore the topic because a lecture will bore kindergarteners. Kimba should not be isolated from the rest of the class, nor should her mother's parenting choices be invalidated.

MUSIC

The early childhood music curriculum focuses on listening and responding to music others have created. Students learn the basic elements of music and have an opportunity to engage in musical history studies and participate in music ensembles.

Teaching music in the early childhood is important to help students enhance skills that they can transfer to other subject areas. Students who are exposed to music education tend to do better in language development (such as reading tests) than students who are not. Music education helps to develop the left side of the brain, which is critical to processing language. Furthermore, research has shown links between spatial intelligence and music studies, which means that students learn to visualize different elements working together and to recognize patterns, corresponding with the problem-solving skills needed in mathematics.

It is also important for music teachers to help students make connections between music and other disciplines and the real world. To do so, teachers must vary lessons. For example, listening to music can teach students about different musical genres and expose students to musical history. Music can also be connected with literature: students may learn to conduct research for a music-related project and in the process draw upon knowledge learned in different classes. Lessons on music culture may also tie into social studies.

To make real-world connections, teachers help students recognize the impact of music in their everyday lives. Teachers expose students to music from popular culture, such as commercials, movies, and television shows. Teachers can also help students understand the emotional aspects of music—by using songs to remember significant events, for instance. Studying informational texts is another way for students to understand music in real-world contexts.

ASPECTS OF MUSIC

Pitch can be high or low, and **scales** are created by organizing patterns of pitches with intervals in between. Having students listen to many pitches and practice the different types of scales offers them a more practical approach to learning. Usually teachers start by using a number system to help younger students learn the notes, then move onto *solfeggio* (*do, re, me, fa, so, la, ti, do*) as they progress.

Rhythm governs time in music. It is a specific pattern in time—a tempo—much like a steady pulse. This pattern is organized into meter, which arranges these pulses into groups. These groups then can be further divided into two, three, or four smaller units. To help students develop an understanding of rhythm, teachers begin by using familiar songs or nursery rhymes and have the students clap along. The students feel and count the beats in a song, learning to distinguish when notes should start and end. Then students can understand the rhythmic patterns of the song. Students can progress to recognizing rhythm just by listening to a song, or creating one by playing a musical instrument.

Melody describes the size of the intervals of the contour (rising or falling)—the tune of a song. As such, it is the main focus of a song and a way for a composer to communicate with his or her audience. **Harmony** relies on the melody and is the use of pitches or chords simultaneously: the notes that support melodies. To develop the concept of melody, teachers should have students listen to and consider how a melody rises and falls, or have them compare melodic contours. These actions create melodic personality. Teachers can also introduce the names and sounds of notes first to help children develop a sense of melody.

> **DID YOU KNOW?**
>
> Music instruction can be incorporated into many areas of childhood education. For example, preschool children learn with music when they first begin to memorize the English alphabet. Eventually, they will figure out that the song they use for the ABCs is the same as "Twinkle, Twinkle, Little Star."

The **timbre**, or **tone**, is the musical characteristic that distinguishes between different instruments. When discussing timbre, expose students to as many sounds as possible. Students can describe the sound by naming the instrument (once they have learned it) or by using different terms. Words can include *brassy, bright, raspy, shrill, dark,* or *buzzy.* As students become more advanced, they can group different timbres according to instrument type, whether it be woodwind, brass, string, or percussion. Help students understand that the timbre does not change even if the same instrument is played at different pitches and volumes.

Dynamics refers to the loud or soft parts of a piece of music. They can change gradually or suddenly (crescendo or decrescendo) or have a large dynamic range if there are very soft and incredibly loud passages in the composition.

Combining melody, rhythm, and harmony creates the **texture** in a composition, as these all determine the overall quality of the sound. Texture includes the number of layers and how these relate to one another. There are different types of musical textures. **Monophonic** is made of one voice or line with no accompaniment. **Polyphonic** includes many musical voices that imitate or counter one another, including the rhythm or melody. An example of this would be songs popular during the European Renaissance or the baroque period. **Homophonic** consists of a main melody that is accompanied by harmonic chords. An example of this would be a singer with a piano accompaniment. The texture would be considered homo-rhythmic if all parts have a similar rhythm. Teachers should introduce one texture at a time so students have a chance to listen to and develop their understanding of how to accurately identify textures. Students can also perform different songs to get a feel for how different textures work.

SAMPLE QUESTION

7) A second-grade teacher asks her students to listen to several musical instruments and identify which instruments produce similar sounds. Which aspect of music are the students learning?

A. timbre

B. loudness

C. pitch

D. rhythm

Answers:

A. **Correct.** Also called tone, timbre is used to distinguish between instrumental sounds.

B. Incorrect. The loudness of an instrument refers to the dynamics of a piece of music.

C. Incorrect. An instrument's pitch refers to the location of notes on a music staff.

D. Incorrect. Rhythm is the pattern of the timing in a piece of music.

TEACHING MUSIC

When teaching music, it is important for teachers not only to select and use manipulatives but also to choose developmentally appropriate materials in the classroom. Children in preschool and early elementary school will not have developed the fine muscle control that would allow them to play more complicated instruments. Teachers should select items such as Orff instruments and other simple percussion instruments; these are easier to play and help students visualize pitch and rhythm while they develop their motor skills.

Later, recorders are introduced when students are able to physically play them. This simple instrument helps students develop necessary skills for more advanced instruments, such as breathing techniques. Teachers can also use the recorder to teach a wide variety of songs and ensembles using one instrument.

> **HELPFUL HINT**
>
> Instruction and practice with techniques like playing the recorder and painting with brushes help build children's fine motor skills.

When choosing appropriate music for students to sing, teachers should select simple pieces, such as nursery rhymes. As students progress through the elementary grades, more complex pieces should be selected. These musical works should include the elements of music students need to master at that grade level, as well as a wide variety of musical styles. Choosing different contemporary and historical pieces of music helps students to compare music based on the historical context and the intent of the composer.

Teachers also must consider the different aspects of a musical piece when selecting one that is developmentally appropriate. Vocal demands should be considered to ensure that a song is not too difficult for students to master. Rather than singing scale patterns, students find it easier to sing skips, particularly descending skips. Teachers should also consider the level of rhythm patterns and the tempo. It is more difficult for younger students to sing fast songs and to move the voice quickly with difficult rhythm patterns; complex rhythm patterns are appropriate only for older classes. Furthermore, most elementary school students struggle with singing multiple notes on one syllable and repeating the same note, so this should be avoided. A song's length should also be considered. The younger the student, the shorter the song. Generally speaking, songs with four beats of four phrases are usually appropriate.

> **HELPFUL HINT**
>
> Call-and-response songs are popular and appropriate for early childhood choruses.

Selecting songs with lots of repetition is beneficial for younger students. Teachers should look for songs that have repeating melodies, rhythms, and words. However, younger children frequently struggle with songs that have repeating words but changing melodies. When reviewing lyrics, teachers must choose texts that are relevant to student experiences and that use appropriate vocabulary.

SAMPLE QUESTION

8) Which of the following instruments is most appropriate to use in a preschool classroom?

   A. recorder

   B. xylophone

   C. flute

   D. double bass

Answers:

A. Incorrect. Preschool students will not have developed the fine motor skills needed to play the recorder.

B. Correct. Orff instruments are appropriate for younger students as they develop the fine muscle control that will enable them to play more complex instruments later.

C.   Incorrect. Students may not have practiced the proper breathing techniques necessary to play a woodwind instrument.

D.   Incorrect. Preschool students do not have the appropriate motor skills to play a double bass.

the Diverse Needs
nts

LANGUAGE LEARNERS

ood classrooms are diverse places that include children from many
kgrounds. Students may speak English fluently, speak English only at
another language at home, or have little experience with English at all.
es early-childhood classrooms very linguistically and culturally diverse
ecause of this, early-childhood teachers must strive not only to create environments that are accepting and embracing of diversity but also to build cultural competency among students and the school community at large. **Cultural competence** is the awareness of one's own cultural identity and the ability to understand, appreciate, and respect different cultural norms.

Promoting cultural competency requires opening the classroom to different cultures. Students of different cultures and their families have much to share with the class and the school community. An Indian American family might show a kindergarten class traditional Indian clothing, music, and dance as part of a unit on different places around the world. A Chinese American family might share a special holiday and its traditions, such as the Lunar New Year, with the class. The more that students are exposed to different cultural elements in contexts where they can ask questions and feel safe to explore, the more likely they will be to embrace their differences as a fundamental part of well-rounded citizenship.

Teachers should also be respectful when they interact with families from different backgrounds who might have differing expectations of their children's educational experiences. When teachers model tolerance, understanding, and interest in broad cultural perspectives, students are likely to follow. Even in more homogeneous school environments where one dominant culture prevails, teachers must still make an effort to introduce students to cultural diversity any way that they can. As the United States continues to become more diverse, all students need to practice developing cultural competency from a young age, even if they are born into somewhat non-diverse communities.

In addition to coming from different cultural backgrounds, some students may have **limited English proficiency,** which is a limited ability to read, speak, write, or understand English based on English not being one's primary language. Students who enter an early-childhood classroom with limited English proficiency will need extra support. They will need **differentiation,** or different techniques and adaptations to instruct students with varying needs. Teachers may have to provide visual cues and directions alongside explicit instruction in vocabulary and oral-language skills.

These students, like all young students, will need multiple opportunities to practice listening and speaking. They will also need multiple opportunities to show what they know independently of their language skills. The **Universal Design for Learning,** a learning framework popular in many schools today, emphasizes giving students:

- **multiple means of representation**, or multiple ways of gaining new knowledge

- **multiple means of expression**, or multiple ways to show what they know

- **multiple means of engagement**, or multiple ways to motivate and engage students in their learning

Students who have limited English proficiency, for example, might learn certain science concepts better visually, such as through graphics and videos, if they find the vocabulary in the science textbook challenging. They might also need accommodations or modifications during assessments to ensure that they can fully demonstrate their knowledge.

For example, an elementary school student who has just arrived in the United States speaking very little English might receive a math assessment containing extra math problems with only numerals. Meanwhile, the rest of the class would receive an assignment divided between numerals-only problems and word problems. This lets the student demonstrate knowledge of mathematical concepts independently of their English language skills. This type of differentiation can go a long way to build student confidence and student interest in the classroom environment. It also prevents students from becoming disengaged in school while they build the skills to communicate in English.

Since early childhood is when students best learn new languages, many schools have programs designed to develop **dual language learners**, which is defined as those who are learning two languages simultaneously. This may take the form of a language-immersion program where young English-speaking children are placed in an environment where another language is spoken for part or most of the day. These programs are generally made up of students with a monolingual English background and students with some proficiency in a second language, with the goal for students to develop both languages through classroom instruction and social interaction with their peers.

Dual language programs can also take another form where students who speak only English at home are placed in a completely immersive environment to quickly become proficient in a second language. These programs have become very popular in many large cities as the need for a workforce that is fluent in more than one language continues to grow.

Young children whose home languages are not English will be dual language learners in most typical, majority English education programs. These young children, who are still developing skills in their home languages as part of the natural arc of child development, will also be developing skills in a second language. Teachers working with dual language learners must promote English language skills while supporting the ongoing development of the children's home languages. This **bilingualism**, or the ability to speak two languages fluently, is a huge benefit to the child that should be nurtured. Children who develop two or more languages simultaneously have been found to have advantages in socio-emotional development, early language and literacy, and overall cognitive development.

These students should also be encouraged to pursue **biliteracy**, or the ability to proficiently read and write in two languages. While language-immersion programs will likely offer this component explicitly, all early-childhood teachers can encourage students and families to read and write in both English and their home languages as appropriate so as to develop these proficiencies. Some districts and schools offer classroom curriculum resources in languages other than English to encourage this, and many educational publishers and technology companies offer resources in commonly spoken second languages, such as Spanish. Above all, when there are students who are learning English, teachers should not push them to discard their heritage languages or to stop developing them.

Children who are learning two languages may engage in **code switching**, or alternating between two languages or dialects. It occurs most often in children when they begin a sentence in one language but complete it in another. This is a somewhat remarkable thing, and it shows that these children are maintaining grammatical rules in both languages. Code switching is natural, normal, and expected, and it is no cause for concern. Rather than chiding students for code switching, teachers should use these opportunities to expand students' vocabulary and knowledge in both languages, dependent, of course, on the teacher's proficiency in the children's native languages. Constantly correcting students for code switching undermines their overall development and does not validate their need to communicate.

Students in the primary grades who have already developed fluency in their home languages but who have limited English proficiency are not considered dual language learners but rather **English language learners (ELLs)**, which is defined as students who need specialized instruction in English and other academic subject areas due to a lack of English proficiency. Instruction for these students will also vary considerably based on the program. However, most research suggests that best practices include helping students obtain English proficiency quickly while providing appropriate support and differentiation so that students can continue learning across content areas. It is important for teachers, especially of young students who may feel nervous in a new environment at first, to make English language learners feel comfortable in the classroom. Teachers can do that by using strategies such as using visuals and predictable routines and by not forcing students to speak until they are ready.

Some students will go through a **silent period** where they may not speak much, and this is normal in learning a new language. Some students may also be reluctant to practice newly acquired English language skills for fear of making mistakes, so teachers should make sure the classroom is a safe space where all attempts to use the new language are validated and praised.

Partnering with families, a key part of any successful early-childhood classroom, can be more challenging with English language learners if their parents also have limited English proficiency. However, teachers should never discount the value of creating trusting relationships with all families, irrespective of their home languages. Having classroom newsletters, websites, and other communications translated into other languages and having a translator available for parent conferences can increase communication with families and help overcome language barriers to parent involvement. Since research indicates a strong positive correlation between a solid home–school connection and student engagement in school, every effort should be made to reach out to families through all available means. Some schools in large urban areas have school administrative staff (such as social workers, parent engagement representatives, and school culture officials) for this express purpose, and some even offer English as a second language classes for parents as part of a community school model.

SAMPLE QUESTIONS

1) A first-grade teacher is monitoring the lunchroom when she sees a student, Juan, with a package of food labeled in the student's home language. What might be an appropriate response?

    A.   asking Juan to write an English translation of the packaging

    B.   saying to Juan, "That looks yummy! What are you eating?"

    C.   asking Juan to show his food to the native English speakers at the table

    D.   asking the other students at the lunch table to describe the interesting packaging in English

Answers:

    A.   Incorrect. This is not developmentally appropriate for a first grader, particularly one who might have limited English proficiency.

    B.   **Correct.** This shows interest in Juan's culture and encourages him to engage in conversation, further developing his oral language skills.

C. Incorrect. While this might help Juan develop some oral language skills, choice B is a better option as it is an open-ended question that sparks conversation.

D. Incorrect. This might spark some conversation, but choice B is still the best option as it encourages Juan to practice speaking, and it shows interest in his food.

2) A third-grade teacher is working on a social studies unit about comparing different communities and ways of life. He wants to help his class develop cultural competency as part of this unit, and he also wants to make a connection between home and school. Which activity would be most useful to meet these goals?

A. organizing a cultural festival where families showcase different parts of their cultural heritages

B. asking students to do research on their cultural heritages and present their information to the class

C. encouraging students to check out nonfiction books on different parts of the world

D. having students create labels for different parts of the school in languages other than English

Answers:

A. **Correct.** Organizing a cultural festival develops cultural competency as students learn about and develop an appreciation for cultural differences, and bringing families into the classroom helps make the home–school connection.

B. Incorrect. A cultural research activity might help develop cultural competence when students present to the class, but it does not necessarily make a connection between home and school.

C. Incorrect. A reading assignment will not help create a home–school connection, and it also does not directly promote cultural competence.

D. Incorrect. Multilingual labelling might help develop cultural competence as students appreciate other languages. However, it does not help create a home–school connection.

STUDENTS WITH SPECIAL NEEDS

The **Individuals with Disabilities Education Act (IDEA)** is the main piece of federal legislation that governs special-education services. Part B of IDEA covers students from the age of three to twenty-two, and it provides guidelines to schools to help address the needs of special-education students. IDEA establishes the framework for identification, parental rights, placement decisions, modifications and accommodations, and behavior supports. It also covers transitioning to adulthood and the process for handling disputes between parents and schools. Part C provides state-run early-intervention services for children from birth to age three.

IDEA mandates that all students be educated in the **least restrictive environment (LRE)**, meaning that students with special needs should be educated with their peers to the fullest extent they are able. This provision creates a more inclusive environment where all students fully participate, and it also means that the early-childhood classroom will likely contain students with a variety of special needs who will need differentiated instruction.

IDEA defines thirteen types of disabilities for which students are eligible to receive special services.

- **Specific learning disabilities (SLD)** is a broad category that includes processing disorders that affect a student's ability to read, write, speak, or do math (such as dyslexia, dysgraphia, and dyscalculia).

- **Speech or language impairments** include communication disorders that cause children to having trouble forming or comprehending words.

- **Other health impairments** include any condition that limits children's strength or alertness (such as ADHD, Tourette's syndrome, and illnesses such as diabetes).

- **Autism spectrum disorder (ASD)** is a development disorder whose key traits include poor communication skills, repetitive behaviors, resistance to change in environment or routine, and sensitivity to sensory stimuli.

- **Intellectual disabilities** cause students to have below-average intellectual functions and adaptive functioning, meaning that their capacity to function independently is diminished (such as Down syndrome and fetal alcohol syndrome).

- **Emotional disturbances** include several mental health conditions such as bipolar disorder, obsessive-compulsive disorder, and oppositional-defiance disorder.

- Children with **multiple disabilities** have more than one condition that cannot be accommodated in a program designed for only one of those conditions.

- **Deafness** is "a hearing impairment that is so severe that the child is impaired in processing linguistic information through hearing, with or without amplification."

- **Hearing impairments** affect children's hearing but do not fall under the definition of deafness.

- **Visual impairments** include blindness and partial sight.

- **Deaf-blindness** is defined as having visual and hearing impairments.

- **Orthopedic impairments** (physical disabilities) limits children's physical functioning (such as epilepsy, muscular dystrophy, and cerebral palsy).

- A **traumatic brain injury** is caused by an accident or outside force. This category does not include congenital or degenerative brain injuries.

Because IDEA provides for special services for any student with a health impairment that limits his or her functioning, it is important to recognize that students with special needs may have many complex conditions that affect their learning, so teachers must focus on inclusion and accommodation rather than limitations.

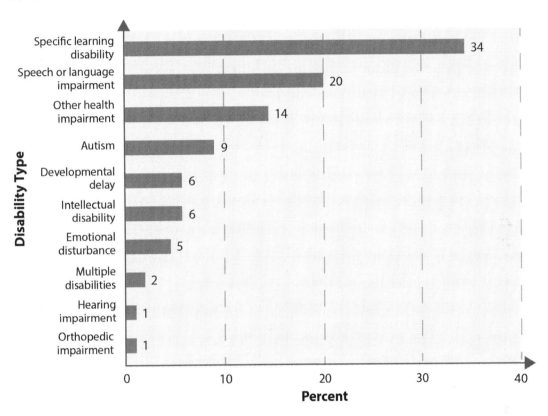

Figure 7.1. Percentage of Students with Disabilities

IDEA provides for early identification and intervention concerning children with special needs through federal grants to states. Students under age three who have been identified as needing special services because of a developmental delay or health condition that might lead to an educational delay will be provided with an **individualized family services plan (IFSP)**. This plan will outline the services that the child will receive from doctors, social workers, and other early interventionists. These services must take place in a natural setting where the child will feel comfortable, and this setting is often the child's home.

The plan is typically highly collaborative, and it involves a team of practitioners and parents. Teachers of very young children in an early-childhood setting may be called on to participate in progress monitoring and development of students being served by an IFSP. The goals of the plan are reviewed every six months and updated annually. Typically, IFSPs differ in eligibility in that they tend not to cover specific learning disabilities. But all states have their own criteria for eligibility, and states have varying definitions for what constitutes a developmental delay. Young children who receive services through an IFSP may or may not continue to need and receive special services once they turn three. The IFSP team will normally meet then to decide whether a child needs services under an individualized education program (IEP).

An **individualized education program (IEP)** is similar to an IFSP, but it is for students between the ages of three and twenty-one. The IEP determines what the child's particular learning needs and goals are and how the school will accommodate and provide for the growth of the student. It also lays out how progress will be tracked and measured.

Teachers at the early-childhood grade levels should also be highly aware of the collaborative nature of the IFSP and IEP. They will be collaborating with any number of specialists: speech therapists, physicians, diagnosticians, social workers, and district and school personnel, just to name a few. Of course, they will also be collaborating, first and foremost, with the parents of each student with an IFSP or IEP. Parents of students with special needs often experience a range of emotions, particularly if they feel that their children's unique needs are not being addressed adequately. It is paramount to act proactively, communicate, and document each child's progress toward their goals.

Students with special needs with an IEP may need a combination of **modifications**, or changes in what they learn, alongside **accommodations**, or changes in how they are taught. Modifications change the learning goal or objective itself, while accommodations simply change how an individual student goes about meeting a goal or objective.

Modifications and accommodations can happen as part of both instruction and assessment. For example, a third-grade student with the diagnosed specific learning disability of dyslexia might be allowed to use a spell-checker for a writing assignment. That is an accommodation. However, if he or she is given the task of writing only three sentences while other students are asked to write five sentences, that is a modification. Similarly, a kindergarten student with a speech or language impairment might be tested on their letter sounds in a different way from their peers. That is an example of an assessment modification. If the same student is not assessed on letter sounds entirely, that is an example of an accommodation.

STUDY TIPS

Accommodation = help

Modification = change

Accommodations help a learner meet the learning goal. Modifications change the learning goal.

One very helpful type of accommodation for many students is assistive technology. **Assistive technology** can include a calculator that helps a student with dyscalculia solve math problems and seat cushions that help students with physical disabilities sit more comfortably at their desks. This technology, both low- and high-tech, can help students with a variety of special needs participate more fully in classroom activities and meet IEP objectives.

Students with certain disabilities may benefit greatly from systems and devices that can be used for **augmentative and alternative communication**, which are techniques to aid those with communication-related disorders. Students might use various low-tech aids, such as a picture board to communicate through pointing or gesturing. They may also use more high-tech devices, such as speech-generating devices or applications. These devices or programs can help students communicate in the classroom, which can be critical to helping students meet IEP goals for social learning.

When instructing students with special needs, teachers should be mindful of evidence-based best practices. Students with intellectual and learning disabilities are often served best with systematic and explicit instruction. Instruction that is **systematic** follows a sequence of mastering each component before moving to the next. For example, systematic math instruction would involve learning to count before learning to add. **Explicit instruction** is very clear and direct. An explicit math lesson might involve the teacher modeling and explaining as she works through each step of a problem. Explicit instruction also frequently employs the "I do, We do, You do" model where the teacher first models, then the student and teacher do the task together, and then the student does the task independently.

Another popular and research-validated strategy for addressing the needs of the inclusive classroom with students of varying learning needs is **peer tutoring**. This strategy pairs students to reinforce key concepts. There are several peer tutoring models with **ClassWide Peer Tutoring (CWPT)**, where students are divided into tutoring groups with differing skill levels, being the most popular. Variations include **Peer-Assisted Learning Strategies (PALS)**, where ability grouping is less emphasized. Peer tutoring has been found to be quite effective in getting more students one-on-one assistance and giving struggling readers more opportunities for practice and immediate feedback. It has also been found to promote self-confidence and to help students develop positive social relationships with their peers.

SAMPLE QUESTIONS

3) Which of these is an accommodation that might be used for a first-grade student who is blind?

    A.   having the student focus more on oral reading and less on writing

    B.   excusing the student from participating in visual art projects

    C.   providing the student with more time at the sensory table

    D.   giving the student reading material in braille

Answers:

A. Incorrect. Shifting focus to a different skill would be a modification, not an accommodation. It represents a change in what the student is learning.

B. Incorrect. Excusing the student from participation in an activity altogether is a modification and not an accommodation.

C. Incorrect. If the student is learning the same things at the sensory table that other students are learning, but in a different way, this might be an accommodation. However, sensory tables are more developmentally appropriate in preschool classrooms than first-grade classrooms.

D. Correct. The student is still learning the same material, only in a different way.

4) **Randy, a third grader, has been diagnosed with the specific learning disability of dyscalculia. This disability makes it very hard for Randy to recall math facts. What accommodation might his math teacher use for certain assignments?**

A. She might give Randy more time to complete these assignments.

B. She might put Randy with a peer tutor for more help.

C. She might allow Randy to use pre-printed math fact tables.

D. She might give Randy shorter assignments with fewer problems.

Answers:

A. Incorrect. This does not address Randy's disability directly.

B. Incorrect. Peer tutoring likely will not help Randy with recalling math facts, though it might help with other math skills.

C. Correct. This will allow Randy to complete the assignment with the aid of the fact table when he gets stuck on recalling a certain fact.

D. Incorrect. This is an assignment modification, not an accommodation.

GIFTED AND TALENTED STUDENTS

The early-childhood classroom will likely also have students who are **gifted and talented**, or those who have abilities significantly above the norm for their age. These students, estimated at around 6 percent of the public-school population in the United States, need special instruction to fully develop their talents. These talents may lie in a variety of domains: the arts, sciences, social skills and leadership, or overall cognitive abilities. Unlike students with other special needs for whom services are federally mandated, most decisions surrounding identification and services for gifted and talented students happen on the state level or sometimes even on a district or school level. Programs for these students vary considerably from place to place, but the most common are:

▶ specialized schools designated for gifted and talented students

- specialized magnet schools for the arts, sciences, or other pursuits that attract children with talents in these areas
- district- or school-wide gifted-and-talented programs that generally involve special instruction in pull-out programs
- grade advancement beyond the students' ages
- class grouping strategies

Gifted and talented students also receive modifications and accommodations within the regular classroom such as:

- purposeful and meaningful assignment extensions and enrichment activities
- differentiated curriculum
- curriculum compacting

Research shows that whatever structure a gifted program takes, even if it is the classroom teacher consistently differentiating instruction, it is vital that there be some program in place for these students. Ensuring that all members of the class are being adequately challenged and given multiple opportunities to learn new things each day can certainly be tough when balancing the needs of many learners. Studies have shown that teachers tend to focus more on students performing below grade-level expectations because of pressures related to benchmark or statewide-standardized testing. However, encouraging gifted students' pursuits in youth has been very strongly correlated to their achievement over the lifetime.

Curriculum compacting is one of the simplest and most effective ways to provide meaningful educational experiences for gifted students. Using this method, students who have already mastered certain skills can move on to new material without wasting time reviewing material that they find rudimentary. In a kindergarten class, for example, a gifted student who is already a fluent reader may become bored with the memorization of high-frequency sight words. This student can then be given an extension or enrichment activity more appropriate to their current skill level, such as writing and illustrating a short "book" using ten high-frequency sight words. A third-grade student who has shown

> **DID YOU KNOW?**
>
> Some research suggests that gifted students develop asynchronously. One domain, such as their cognitive or language development, may be quite advanced, while other domains, such as socio-emotional or physical development, may lag behind. This means that gifted and talented students need just as much differentiation across all domains of early learning as any other students.

mathematical giftedness might, instead of continuing to work on third-grade objectives that she has already mastered, begin working with the fourth-grade math textbook. The key is eliminating parts of the curriculum that the student has mastered and replacing those elements with engaging, challenging activities and assignments that are more appropriate for the student's current developmental level.

Another component of successful gifted and talented instruction, which can be used in conjunction with curriculum compacting, is **grouping**. This simply means that students with similar giftedness are placed in a group and complete certain classroom activities together. This can also help with practical concerns as teachers differentiate instruction. Grouping could be used as part of learning-center rotations in a kindergarten classroom, for example, and this lets the teacher provide more calibrated instruction at the appropriate level for each group. In the elementary grades, grouping can give teachers a chance to modify cooperative learning assignments for the needs of gifted and talented learners.

Early-childhood educators also need to avoid common pitfalls in instructing gifted and talented students. These students, like all students with diverse needs, should be included in whole group activities and instruction as much as possible without excessively isolating them. They should also not be expected to work on the exact same material as other students, only faster or more accurately. The curriculum must be thoughtfully differentiated so that they are still challenged and they are not participating in assignments that they find boring or rudimentary.

Gifted and talented instruction needs to be thoughtful and purposeful. While it can be challenging to devise a new set of objectives for gifted students beyond the existing multiple sets of objectives for the class and the grade at large, enrichment activities for gifted and talented students should have a purpose and goal in mind. Having a student simply read independently (assuming that the student's interests lie elsewhere) while the remainder of the class practices the weekly spelling words will likely not drive engagement or promote a feeling of belonging. And while gifted students can and should use their talents to help their peers who might be struggling with a particular skill, they should not become full-time peer tutors at the expense of their own learning.

QUICK REVIEW

What is your school's, district's, or state's policy on identifying gifted and talented students?

Early-childhood educators need to be proactive and supportive in the identification of gifted and talented students. While the process for identifying gifted students will vary widely by state, district, and program, most involve teacher input in the form of checklists, recommendations, or portfolio collection. Teachers should be prepared to help other personnel to identify these students through honest and candid feedback when requested.

SAMPLE QUESTIONS

5) Mark, a second grader, is an academically gifted student in Ms. Hayes's math class. Mark knows his addition and subtraction, but during practice time, he becomes extremely disruptive to those around him. What is Ms. Hayes's best course of action?

A.   moving Mark forward a grade

B.   applying ability grouping

C.   using curriculum compacting

D.   creating a behavioral-modification plan

Answers:

A.   Incorrect. This is likely not Ms. Hayes's choice to make, and we do not know whether Mark's academic giftedness warrants skipping the entirety of second grade.

B.   Incorrect. Grouping would only help if the group worked on something other than addition and subtraction since Mark already knows those well.

C.   Correct. Curriculum compacting would allow Mark to move on to new material while the rest of the class continues to learn about addition and subtraction.

D.   Incorrect. Mark is likely acting out because he is bored, so using curriculum compacting is a more helpful solution than a behavioral-modification plan.

6)   **Myra is a third grader who is very artistically gifted. Her art teacher, Mr. Wong, wants to nourish this gift and encourage Myra to grow in her artistic ability. Which instructional strategy would best meet his goal?**

A.   Mr. Wong should instruct Myra to research famous artists.

B.   Mr. Wong should ask Myra to draw several pictures for each picture that the other students draw.

C.   Mr. Wong should give Myra instruction and practice in new media and techniques.

D.   Mr. Wong should encourage Myra to teach other students her drawing techniques.

Answers:

A.   Incorrect. A research project is an enrichment activity that does not align with the teacher's goal to encourage Myra to grow in her artistic ability.

B.   Incorrect. If Myra has already mastered the material, asking Myra to do more work at the same degree of difficulty as the other students is not productive, and it does not aid in her development.

C.   Correct. Teaching Myra new skills will help her develop her artistic ability in new ways.

D.   Incorrect. Having Myra teach other students will not directly help her to develop her own artistic ability.

Practice Test

TEST I

Read the question, and then choose the most correct answer.

1

Which skill is being developed during an activity for first graders in which they identify the sounds that consonant digraphs *ch*, *sh*, and *th* make?

- A. print awareness
- B. phonics
- C. phonological awareness
- D. word recognition

2

Which of the following is NOT an example of environmental print?

- A. a brand name on a tube of toothpaste
- B. the school name printed on the marquis outside
- C. the words *Writing Center* affixed to the classroom writing center
- D. a page in a new storybook that is read aloud to students for this first time

3

Which of the following words has the onset italicized?

- A. pl-*ate*
- B. *br*-oom
- C. in-*ter*-est
- D. fair-*y*

4

When asked what he thinks about a classmate's artwork, a toddler responds, "Mary's good art!" Which of the following phases of oral language development is the toddler likely in?

A.   babbling phase

B.   holophrastic phase

C.   two-word phase

D.   telegraphic phase

5

Which of the following words would be appropriate for a preschool child to use as a practice word to begin copying letters from an environmental source?

A.   the word *blimp* as dictated to her

B.   the child's name written on a piece of paper for her to copy underneath

C.   the word *McDonald's*, which she retains the spelling of from memory

D.   the word *elephant*, which she writes after she is shown a picture of an elephant

6

Which of the following is a characteristic of a print-rich classroom?

A.   a daily read-aloud time

B.   many labeled objects

C.   lots of pencils, pens, and markers

D.   a library stocked with picture books

7

Mrs. Cortez is quietly reading a book to Henry, a three-year-old student who did not fall asleep during nap time. As she reads, Mrs. Cortez points to each word on the page. Which of the following is the teacher trying to accomplish?

A.   reinforce Henry's print awareness

B.   keep a steady pace and rhythm as she reads

C.   lull Henry to sleep

D.   focus Henry's attention toward reading the words along with her

8

Which of the following statements is true about phonemic awareness?

A.   It generally has to be explicitly taught.

B.   It is natural and intuitive.

C.   Most students will master it at the same rate.

D.   Students do not need it to begin reading.

9

Mr. Scott writes the following words on the board:

blimp
roar
grin

He asks his class to make a new word out of each word by removing a part of the existing word. Which of the following concepts is the teacher trying to develop in his students?

A. the alphabetic principle

B. phoneme deletion

C. phoneme substitution

D. phoneme segmentation

10

Which of the following is true of beginning phonics instruction that might occur in a kindergarten classroom?

A. It usually involves lots of oral exercises.

B. It relies heavily on sight word knowledge.

C. It presumes students have a knowledge of Latin and Greek roots.

D. It does not require knowledge of letter-sound correspondence.

11

Which of the following is a non-decodable word?

A. bread

B. fly

C. what

D. plan

12

Mr. Smith's second-grade class is going to read a story aloud. He wants to emphasize that the narrator has a different point of view from the other characters. Which of the following should he do to emphasize this point?

A. read the entire story himself and point out when the narrator is speaking

B. have students read in a different voice when reading/speaking as the narrator versus when reading/speaking as the characters

C. have students label the text for each line that is spoken by the narrator

D. have students read very slowly when reading the narrator's lines so they can really appreciate the narrator's points

13

Which of the following concepts should be taught alongside phonics to ensure that students will be able to read quickly and fluently?

A.   print awareness

B.   sight word recognition

C.   stroke order

D.   spelling

14

Max is a high-achieving second grader who has scored 100 percent on almost every spelling and phonics assignment. He used to really enjoy reading seatwork time because he completed his work more quickly than all of the other students. However, lately he seems very bored with the assigned work. Once he finishes his work, he usually disrupts others. Which of the following is the best way the teacher can help Max?

A.   ask the administration to move Max to third grade since he has clearly mastered second-grade material

B.   enlist his parents' help to improve Max's behavior after he is finished with his work

C.   have him write the reading work over again to improve comprehension and motor skills

D.   give Max a modified version of the reading work where his assignment is slightly more challenging

15

Jenine is a second-grade student targeted for extra reading practice. One day, the teacher listens to her read a paragraph out loud and notices that Jenine is reading very slowly. Which of the following parts of fluency does Jenine need help with?

A.   rate

B.   prosody

C.   accuracy

D.   phonemes

16

When should students be introduced to simple poetry with rhyme that is read aloud?

A.   in second or third grade

B.   in third grade only

C.   in preschool

D.   as soon as students are decoding words on their own

17

Mrs. Perez is teaching her first-grade class about meter in poetry. Which of the following activities would be most appropriate to help her students understand this concept?

- A. independently label each line of the poem with an *A, B, C,* or so on to indicate the rhyming pattern
- B. read in a different voice for each character in the poem
- C. copy each line of the poem multiple times until they pick up its meter
- (D.) clap to the beat of a poem that she reads aloud

18

Which of the following describes quantitative text measurements?

- A. the frequency with which certain words are used
- B. the overall structure of the text and how it is organized
- C. the layout of the text, including graphics, font, spacing, and so on
- (D.) any quantifiable criteria for which a number can be calculated

19

Mark, a third grader, is having difficulty identifying the main idea of texts he reads. Mrs. Martinez wants to give him extra practice with this skill when he completes his weekly oral reading assessment. Which of the following is the best way for Mrs. Martinez to incorporate the identification of the main idea into Mark's weekly oral fluency assessment?

- (A.) stopping him after he reads each paragraph and asking, "What was that paragraph about?"
- B. assigning him longer passages to read so that he can practice with more advanced texts
- C. having Mark read only nonfiction texts since the main idea is easier to identify
- D. giving Mark passages with varying themes so that he has more exposure to different genres

20

Mr. Clark is giving his third-grade students lots of practice making inferences, and he wants to make sure they back up their inferences with textual evidence. Which of the following activities should he use to help his students practice this skill?

- A. teaching his students about bias
- B. having students highlight or underline the part of the text that led them to a certain inference
- C. having his students write a summary of each story they read
- D. having students rewrite the ending of a story per what they though should have happened

21

Mr. Harrison wants his third-grade class to practice writing a problem-solution piece in the second person. Which of the following assignments would best meet his goal?

A. a drama that groups of students write collaboratively

B. a letter that each student writes to the principal proposing a solution to a school-wide problem

C. a letter that each student writes to his or her parents thanking them for being good parents

D. an essay that explains and solves an environmental problem

22

Mrs. Estrada is helping her students brainstorm for a collaborative class-wide writing assignment. She has helped the class come up with the following chart, which she has written on the board:

People and Dogs

Both can live in "houses"	Dogs spend most time outside; people spend most time inside
Both sometimes eat meat	People use silverware; dogs do not use silverware
Both like to run around	People run for exercise; dogs run to chase things

Which of the following text organizational structures is the class likely using?

A. cause and effect

B. problem-solution

C. compare and contrast

D. description

23

Mr. Blake wants to give his kindergarten class an introduction to the idea of first-person point of view, so he reads a story about a dinosaur who wants to be a ballerina. The story is told in the voice of the dinosaur. After he has read the story to the class, Mr. Blake asks a series of questions. Which of the following questions introduces students to the first-person point of view?

A. Why did the dinosaur want to become a ballerina?

B. What character told the story we just read?

C. Where did the story take place?

D. What did you like most about the story?

24

Which of the following is an example of pretend reading?

- A. a student decoding a simple sentence with simple CVC words
- B. a student reading a picture book by telling the story based on the picture cues
- C. a student reading a passage orally with limited expression
- D. a student checking out a book from the library but never looking at it

25

Which of the following is the first oral presentation many students give during their school career?

- A. the first oral report a teacher assigns
- B. the first time a teacher asks a new student to get up and introduce herself
- C. their first experience with show and tell
- D. a monologue they read

26

A second-grade class has just finished reading a short story. The teacher wants his students to compare the short story to a different interpretation of the same story. Which of the following activities would best meet his goal?

- A. reading the story again but in a different accent
- B. taking students to see a stage play based on the story
- C. having students read critical interpretations of the story
- D. having students compare the story to a passage in their science textbook

27

Mrs. Smith is reading a story set on Valentine's Day to her kindergarten class, which includes both students born in the United States and students who are not as familiar with American holidays. Which of the following can she conclude about the knowledge demands of this story, and what might she do to prepare her students for these demands?

- A. The story will be easy for all students to understand because most American holidays such as Valentine's Day are universal.
- B. She should give her students some background on the holiday first because not all of her students will have had experience with this holiday.
- C. The book has very low knowledge demands and will only require the focus and attention of her students.
- D. The story easily fits in with what all of her students already know, so it is a perfect choice per its knowledge demands.

28

Which of the following is an activity that will help students develop their procedural knowledge of writing?

A.   handwriting practice

B.   drawing or scribbling to communicate an idea

C.   writing a letter to a friend to tell about a vacation experience

D.   reading a story aloud

29

Which of the following word pairs shows both a CV and VC pattern?

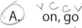

A.   on, go

B.   off, pin

C.   clap, up

D.   big, bad

30

Which of the following is an example of expository writing?

A.   a poem about a family of birds

B.   a short story set in the nineteenth century

C.   a brochure on a language and literacy conference

D.   a teen fantasy novel

meant to tch abt

by coming evnr.

31

Mrs. Jett notices that her third-grade student Jo often leaves out the articles *a, an,* and *the* from her writing. A conference with Jo's parents recently revealed that this could be because her native language does not use articles. Which of the following revision strategies might be helpful for Jo?

A.   reading her work aloud

B.   pairing her with another English language learner for peer review

C.   having her memorize a list of prepositions

D.   pairing her with a native English speaking partner for peer review

32

Which of the following situations requires passive listening?

A.   sitting in the audience at an assembly

B.   having a conversation with a friend

C.   a server taking an order at a restaurant

D.   an employee discussing job performance with a supervisor

33

A teacher has decided to create a class-wide digital literary sampler to show parents the hard work his class has done over the course of a unit on narrative writing. Which of the following phases in the authorship cycle is the teacher addressing?

A. brainstorming

B. editing

C. drafting

D. publishing

34

How might a teacher publish the pictures and emergent writing created by her preschool students in such a way that shows growth over the course of the year?

A. posting it on the classroom bulletin board

B. keeping it in a portfolio that is shared with parents

C. having students go back and revise their letter strings

D. videotaping student performances at the dramatic play center

35

A second-grade teacher asks her class the following question: "Do you think this story was written mainly for children or adults?" Which of the following is the teacher asking her students to consider?

A. the intended audience

B. the organizational structure

C. the theme

D. the point of view

36

Mrs. Spellman has asked that her third-grade class begin to focus their research topics into three questions to explore. Aisha, who has selected dance as her topic, is having a hard time coming up with three questions. Which of the following is the best way for Mrs. Spellman to help Aisha develop three questions to research?

A. ask Aisha when she started dancing and why she likes it so much

B. direct Aisha to change her topic if she cannot find three questions

C. have Aisha list what types of dance she might want to know more about

D. instruct Aisha to create a word web of the terms she associates with dance

37

A teacher is working on a unit on forming the past tense of verbs with his second-grade class. Which of the following would be the most appropriate writing assignment to ensure sufficient practice with this skill?

A. writing a paragraph that compares and contrasts cars and trucks

B. writing a paragraph about what they did over the winter break

C. writing a description of their living room

D. writing a persuasive paragraph about their favorite color

38

A teacher has a first-grade class full of students of varying literacy skills and levels of English proficiency. She wants to make use of a new digital storytelling software program purchased by the school, but she has concerns that not all of her students will find it easy to type words and use illustrations in their stories. How can she differentiate instruction so that all of her students can participate in this activity?

A. encourage students to add words to their stories as they see fit but do not make this a requirement

B. give students the first two words of each sentence she expects them to write

C. let some students create a fiction story and have others create a nonfiction story

D. have some students use the software and have others write and draw their stories on paper

39

Which of the following is NOT a technique associated with active listening?

A. nodding in agreement

B. restating what the speaker said

C. showing empathy and understanding

D. interrupting the speaker

40

The teachers at a particular school do not enjoy the program coordinator's professional development presentations because she mumbles when she speaks. Which of the following parts of formal speaking does she need to practice?

A. dialect

B. articulation

C. active listening

D. types of questioning

41

One of a teacher's third-grade students writes the following sentences:

I gave my sister a gift. My sister asks if you know what it is.

Which of the following concepts does the teacher need to review with the student?

  A.   sentence fragments

  B.   shifts in pronoun person

  C.   lack of pronoun agreement

  D.   use of a pronoun without an antecedent

42

Mr. Ramirez's co-teacher has asked that he help introduce the following new vocabulary to his third-grade class to help prepare students for an upcoming math lesson:

parallel, congruent, rhombus, trapezoid

Which of the following concepts is being developed in the students?

  A.   content-specific words

  B.   multiple-meaning words

  C.   different registers

  D.   figurative language

43

Which of the following words has a prefix?

  A.   antihero

  B.   goldsmith

  C.   graciousness

  D.   understandable

44

Which of the following is a simile?

  A.   He was taller than a building.

  B.   The engine panted and gasped.

  C.   The sun was like a glistening gem.

  D.   The house was a decaying corpse.

45

Which of the following sentences has a dark and dreary tone?

A. The silly little boy ran as fast as he could, chasing the rabbit the entire way down the hill.

B. The simple man sat every day at the same table doing the same job for the same clients.

C. The dark moon shone dimly on the horizon outlining the storm's path as it moved toward the town.

D. No one knows why she was such a strange girl. Maybe it was her upbringing. Maybe it was her nature.

46

Mrs. Gonzalez teaches toddlers in the classroom next to Mrs. Fox. Mrs. Fox can frequently hear Mrs. Gonzalez narrating her own actions: for example, "Now I am washing my hands before I prepare snack" and "I must put on my coat before I go outside." Which of the following explains why Mrs. Gonzalez is likely doing this?

A. She is exposing her students to oral language and new vocabulary.

B. She wants to serve as a good role model for her students.

C. She is helping her students see the moral in all that they do.

D. Her students only listen when she speaks at a very high volume.

47

Hannah is four and in Mr. Lawrence's prekindergarten class. Mr. Lawrence is having a conference with Hannah's mother, who has expressed concern that Hannah frequently misspells words that she uses to label pictures she draws. Which of the following is the advice Mr. Lawrence should give Hannah's mother?

A. have Hannah focus on a few target spelling words each week until she begins to label her pictures correctly

B. not to worry since Hannah is in the invented spelling phase, which is a natural part of literacy development

C. not to worry since Hannah is receiving lots of targeted phonics practice in school but to have Hannah go back and correct these pictures

D. have Hannah focus on learning new vocabulary each day as this will help with her overall spelling development

48

Which of the following should be included in effective phonics instruction in a kindergarten classroom?

A. a solid foundation of letter-sound correspondence

B. an emphasis on silent reading

C. identification of main ideas

D. early practice with chapter books

49

Which of the following words cannot be spelled through simple phoneme segmentation?

A. up

B. bigger

C. not

D. help

50

The first week of school, a kindergarten student named Mary has very few basic skills. She cannot hold a pencil, does not understand directions, and seems to have had no previous schooling. She does not seem able to use many of the learning materials in the classroom, including the books in the literacy center. Mary's instruction should start with which of the following concepts?

A. phonological awareness

B. the alphabetic principle

C. decoding

D. print awareness

51

Matt, a second grader, is working with the school counselor on appropriate behavior. One of the strategies Matt has been given is to count to ten before acting when he is angry. What skill is the counselor helping Matt develop?

A. self-concept

B. interpersonal relationships

C. self-regulation

D. conflict resolution

52

Mr. Howard wants his first graders to work on the development of self-identity. Which activity would be most appropriate?

A. having each student write down a nice thing about each member of the class and then sharing these affirmations

B. assigning students an essay to write on the roles of each of their family members

C. asking students what they want to be when they grow up and why

D. having students role-play resolving conflict through compromise

53

Ms. Watts wants to prepare a unit on community helpers for her prekindergarten class. She wants to include a hands-on exploratory activity as part of this unit. Which activity would best meet her goal?

A. inviting an attorney to speak to the class

B. reading a story about the role of the police in keeping the community safe

C. getting students to brainstorm different community helpers

D. allowing students to try on the protective equipment firefighters use

54

Ms. Pi, the school's Mandarin teacher, wants to partner with the kindergarten classroom teacher to help students develop appreciation for Chinese culture outside of language. Which activity would be most appropriate?

A. organizing a Chinese New Year celebration

B. having students create a poster about different dress and hairstyles in China

C. displaying an infographic comparing Taiwan, Hong Kong, and mainland China

D. showing a video on Mao Zedong

55

Which of the following describes a relationship of economic interdependence?

A. a subsistence farmer growing all of the food his family needs

B. a desert country importing food from the US while exporting oil there

C. a local shopkeeper selling basic goods to his community

D. a family in which the members make all of their own clothing

56

What physical location has been determined to be the location of the prime meridian?

A. Greenwich, United Kingdom

B. Moscow, Russia

C. New York City, United States

D. Juneau, United States

57

Miss Greene is searching in her curriculum resources for a map to introduce her second-grade class to the idea of a legend. Which map would be the best resource for her to use?

A. a political map of the United States showing each state in the same color

B. a topographical map showing different elevations

C. a map that uses corncob icons to denote the major corn-producing states in the United States

D. a map that includes latitude and longitude

58

The idea that the law, rather than government officials themselves, is what governs a nation is known as what?

A. justice

B. the rule of law

C. natural law

D. equality

59

A teacher in Los Angeles asks her first-grade class the following question: "Do you have more shorts and short-sleeved shirts at home or more coats and sweaters? Why?" These questions would most likely precede a discussion on

A. the way climate impacts people.

B. different clothing choices among different cultures.

C. standards of modesty in dress that vary by culture.

D. the way in which one's social conditions impact him or her.

60

Ms. Wilson knows that George, unlike the rest of her kindergarten students, did not attend any sort of preschool or prekindergarten program. Because of this, George has trouble adjusting to certain classroom routines during the first few weeks of school. Ms. Wilson assists George by giving him more verbal cues and help with transitions than she does with other students. What concept is Ms. Wilson promoting?

A.   equality

B.   tolerance

C.   natural consequences

D.   equity

61

Which of the following is a part of a child's microsystem?

A.   government

B.   ethnicity

C.   mosque

D.   parent-teacher relationship

62

How are Supreme Court justices selected?

A.   through an election

B.   nomination by the House with approval by the Senate

C.   appointment by the president

D.   nomination by the president with confirmation by the Senate

63

Mr. Grant happens upon Jada, a third-grade student, struggling to get started on an assignment. What can he do to promote her self-awareness and metacognition?

A.   help her to get started by creating a graphic organizer for her

B.   pair another student with her to help

C.   ask her to read the directions aloud

D.   ask her which part she does not understand

64

A first-grade teacher notices that one of her students is able to read a difficult book aloud when her friend, the best reader in the class, sits next to her and helps her with some of the more challenging words. What concept is this teacher observing?

A. the formal operational stage

B. abstract thought

C. the zone of proximal development

D. the chronosystem

65

Which classroom setup is most conducive and appropriate to promoting social interaction among second-grade students?

A. individual desks

B. assigned spots on a carpet

C. group or paired seating

D. students seated in front of computer terminals

66

A second-grade class has just read a story about a young girl whose family moved from Oklahoma City to Lagos, Nigeria. Which question might help spark appropriate discussion about recognition of and appreciation for cultural differences?

A. Why did the family move to Lagos?

B. What is the population of Lagos?

C. Have you ever been to a big city?

D. How is Lagos different from Oklahoma?

67

A third-grade teacher walks her students through each step of a new concept and offers assistance throughout until students can handle this concept on their own. What technique is she using?

A. metacognition

B. secondary socialization

C. emotional regulation

D. scaffolding

68

A second-grade teacher is trying to help her students learn how to use a compass rose. She gives each student a map of the United States with a compass rose. She asks students to follow a series of instructions. Which instruction might she include?

A. Point to the state that is directly above Texas.

B. Point to the capital of Florida.

C. Point to the only state that is an island.

D. Point to the state that is directly to the west of Utah.

69

Ms. Perez, a first-grade teacher, is working on map and globe skills with her class. To assess student knowledge of key concepts, she is calling students up one by one during independent work time to determine their level of proficiency with place identification. Which places would be most appropriate for Ms. Perez to ask students to identify on the large classroom maps?

A. Canada, Mexico, and the Antarctic Ocean

B. the United States and their home state

C. the capital of their home state and major cities like Los Angeles, New York, and Chicago

D. the Great Lakes and the Mississippi River

70

A second-grade teacher asks her class the following question: "What kind of houses would people living in forests most likely build?" What is she trying to help students understand?

A. the relationship between conservation and resource depletion

B. economic interdependence

C. how people relate to their environment

D. the way the global economy and the environment impact each other

71

Mrs. Markel's third-grade class reads an article about a community of people in a rain forest environment who are experiencing dramatic changes in their way of life because loggers are cutting down the trees in their home. What concept is Mrs. Markel imparting on her class?

A. that economic development is never as important as maintaining biodiversity

B. that part of global citizenship is taking action

C. that humans are dependent on their environments

D. that there can always be compromise when different cultures interact

72

Ms. Robbins is teaching her prekindergarten class about the phrases "next week," "next month," and "next year." Which example would best help students understand these phrases in context?

A. I have a big meeting next week.

B. Halloween is next month.

C. Next year we will all be one year older.

D. Next month we will be starting a unit on animals.

73

Ms. Graham wants to present balanced information about the "settlement of North America" to her first-grade class. Which strategy best meets this goal?

A. teaching students about concepts of colonial oppression of native peoples in the Hispanic Southwest

B. teaching students both about the Pilgrims and the Native Americans

C. reading a book about Christopher Columbus's heroism

D. having students make Pilgrim hats out of various art supplies

74

A kindergarten teacher in the rural Midwest has a class that is not diverse. She wants to introduce the concept of diversity to her students. Which activity would be most appropriate?

A. having students compile statistics on the ethnic makeup of the state's population

B. organizing a discussion about the history and achievements of the civil rights movement

C. reading a book titled *All Kinds of People* that features people of various ethnicities

D. encouraging students to share their own experiences with people of various religions

75

A third-grade class is writing a persuasive letter to a local company that is polluting a nearby river, asking it to be more environmentally responsible. They are including the economic impacts of the pollution as part of their overall argument. Which of the following might they include as an economic impact the pollution might have?

A. destroying local bird species

B. decreasing tourism

C. limiting biodiversity

D. not preserving the river for future generations

Read each constructed-response question carefully. Then, write a response that addresses all components of the question.

Scenario #1:

A third-grade teacher gives students the following assignment:

1. Write an autobiographical paragraph in the first person with at least eight sentences that has both an introductory sentence and a concluding sentence.

2. Ensure that your paragraph uses time expressions ("first," "next," "then," "last," and so on) to help the reader follow the order of events.

> Max was born in 2011 in Boston. First, he has three brother. Named Mark, Pat, and Ethan. He like ride bikes and eating pizza! His' favorite show is watching baseball on TV. Next, he will be an astronaut when he grows up. He also like swimming. Hopefully, he will get good grade this year. This is all about Max.

Tasks:

I. Evaluate the student's work, listing strengths and errors.

II. Explain how you would help the student correct one of the errors.

Scenario #2:

A first-grade teacher is assessing social studies learning through an individual map skills/oral assessment as a benchmark assessment. Below are her notes from working with Jilian.

Skill	Met Standard?	Notes
Can point to the United States on the map/globe	Yes	Originally pointed to Russia but when realized the globe could spin, corrected herself.
Can point to Georgia on the map/globe	Yes	Pointed to Alabama and when asked to try again, pointed correctly to Georgia
Can put finger on Georgia and then point to a state that is north of Georgia	Yes	
Can put finger on Georgia and then point to a state that is west of Georgia	Yes	
Can locate the Atlantic and Pacific Oceans	No	Inverted Atlantic and Pacific Oceans
Identifies a picture of Benjamin Franklin and can name an accomplishment	Yes—identify No—accomplishment	Said he invented the light bulb
Identifies a picture of Thomas Jefferson and can name an accomplishment	No—identify No—accomplishment	Shrugged and would not guess even when prompted

Tasks:

I.   Evaluate the student's current proficiency level, listing strengths and opportunities.

II. Explain how you would reteach ONE core concept to the student and assess mastery of this core concept.

Test II

Read the question, and then choose the most correct answer.

1

A kindergarten teacher puts five blocks on the table and asks the students how many blocks there are. She then gives one block each to five students and asks the class how many blocks there are now. Which mathematical concept is the teacher demonstrating?

- A. cardinality
- B. subitizing
- C. decomposing
- D. number conservation

2

A third-grader teacher is teaching her class strategies to confirm their answers when performing simple operations of division with remainders such as $10 \div 3$. Which strategy would be most helpful to her students?

- A. using a number line
- B. using a dot plot or scatter plot
- C. drawing the number of objects and then partitioning
- D. drawing the problem as fractions and then multiplying

3

A prekindergarten student is given a pile of small objects and asked to complete the following task: "Make two piles of objects that are the same." The student is then asked: "Why did you put these objects together in one pile and those objects together in another pile?" What concept is the student being asked to demonstrate?

- A. one-to-one correspondence
- B. cardinality
- C. patterning
- D. classifying and sorting

4

Decomposing helps reinforce which of the following mathematical concepts?

- A. place value
- B. cardinality
- C. addition
- D. skip counting

5

A first-grade teacher gives each student a handful of dimes and asks them to count out seventy cents. What underlying mathematical concept must students have first mastered to enable them to complete this activity?

A.   working with nonstandard units of measurement

B.   decomposing whole numbers

C.   commutative property of addition

D.   skip counting by tens

6

Which of the following activities with measurement would be appropriate for a first-grade class working with US customary units?

A.   measuring the length of each student's shoe in inches with a ruler

B.   calculating the area of the classroom using a yardstick

C.   finding the mass of several library books using kilograms

D.   converting the amount of soda in a bottle from ounces to liters

7

A third-grade teacher draws the figure below on the board and asks her students to shade in a fraction that is equivalent to $\frac{2}{8}$.

Which student response is correct?

A.   C.

B.   D.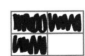

8

Mr. Reyes asks his third-grade class to calculate how much money would be left if a person bought a pack of gum for $1.68 and paid with a $10 bill. Aside from measurement, what math skills is this problem assessing?

A. skip counting and percentage

B. ratios and borrowing

C. place value and decimals ✓

D. order of operations and place value

9

A second-grade teacher gives students unit cubes and a large empty cube. She asks them to count out how many unit cubes fit in the empty shape. What concept is the teacher introducing to her students?

A. area

B. perimeter

C. volume

D. surface area

10

A third-grade teacher writes the following problem on the board:

4,000 + 200 + 80 + 3

She then asks students to write this as a single number. What concept is she asking students to demonstrate?

A. decomposing a number

B. composing a number

C. the lattice method

D. doubling

11

Mrs. Hawkins's second-grade class is working on a project to determine how many students have pets at home versus those who do not. What would be the best way for her class to represent the data?

A. percentage

B. ratio

C. fraction

D. stem-and-leaf plot

12

Harriet solves a math problem in meters, but the teacher asks that the answer be converted into centimeters. What must Harriet do with her answer to make the conversion?

A.   multiply by 100

B.   divide by 100

C.   multiply by 10

D.   divide by 10

13

Mrs. Adams asks her third-grade class to write an equation to match the following problem:

Alex went to the store to buy hamburger buns for a cookout. He needed thirty-six hot dog buns. Each package contained twelve buns. How many packages does he need to buy?

Which equation is correct?

A. $12 \times 3 =$

B. $12/36 =$

C. $36 \div 12 =$

D. $12 \div 36 =$

14

Ms. Greene is scaffolding her prekindergarten students during block play. She helps one student form a pattern of one yellow block, one green block, one yellow block. What can be said about Ms. Greene's instructional strategy?

A.   She is encouraging number conservation through manipulatives.

B.   She is encouraging sequencing through manipulatives.

C.   She is encouraging subitizing through cardinality.

D.   She is encouraging the development of one-to-one correspondence.

15

A kindergarten student is working at a math center where he must write the number 6 and then glue six objects onto the page. What skill is he demonstrating?

A.   subitizing

B.   use of manipulatives

C.   cardinality

D.   patterning

16

A first-grade teacher wants to help her students develop strategies to solve subtraction word problems using visual representations. Which strategy would be most appropriate?

  A. decomposing numbers

  B. using a number line

  C. drawing an array — multiplication.

  D. using fact families

17

A third-grade teacher wants her class to practice measuring the classroom using the metric system. Which measurement tool should she give them to use?

  A. ruler

  B. yardstick

  C. meter stick

  D. tape measure in inches

18

Which of the following geometric concepts would be most appropriate to introduce to a kindergarten class?

  A. surface area

  B. perimeter with unit cubes

  C. attributes of shapes

  D. circumference and radius

19

Which of the following is an example of a physical change?

  A. baking a cake — chemical.

  B. boiling water

  C. burning wood

  D. rust on a bike

20

A second-grade class is learning about the properties of two-dimensional shapes. Which of the following activities would best reinforce the concept of perimeter?

  A. using playdough to make solid figures 3D

  B. working on a jigsaw puzzle

  C. using toilet paper tubes to create a windsock 3D

  D. throwing a basketball through a hoop 3D.

↓ look into!

21

Mrs. Lovett is teaching her students how to use reciprocals to divide fractions. She asks four students to divide $\frac{5}{6}$ by $\frac{2}{3}$. Which of the following students correctly completes this operation?

A. Juan: $\frac{5}{6} \div \frac{2}{3} = \frac{7}{9}$

B. Reggie: $\frac{5}{6} \div \frac{2}{3} = \frac{6}{5} \div \frac{2}{3} = \frac{12}{15}$

C. Madison: $\frac{5}{6} \div \frac{2}{3} = \frac{5}{6} \times \frac{3}{2} = \frac{15}{12} = \frac{5}{4}$

D. Amir: $\frac{5}{6} \div \frac{2}{3} = \frac{15}{18} + \frac{12}{18} = \frac{27}{18}$

$\frac{5}{6} \div \frac{2}{3}$ 5

$\frac{5}{6} \cdot \frac{3}{2}$ $\frac{15}{12} = \frac{5}{4}$

22

A preschool teacher is introducing his students to one-to-one correspondence. Which of the following activities should he use in his classroom?

A. counting each toy as it is put away in a toy box

B. matching socks from a laundry basket

C. playing Go Fish to match cards with similar numbers

D. asking students to identify the color of a ball

23

Miguel usually receives a $5 allowance each week and currently has $10 saved. If he does not receive his allowance the next week, he will have $10 when that week is over.

Which of the following properties is demonstrated by this scenario?

A. identity property

B. commutative property

C. distributive property

D. associative property

24

A second-grade teacher is teaching her student to count money. Which of the following skills should students have before starting the lesson?

A. decomposing numbers

B. subitizing

C. division

D. skip counting

25

Mrs. Collins asks her students to skip count by fives to 100. Which of the following basic skills is necessary for the students to complete the task?

A.   rote memorization of numeric words

B.   writing numbers

C.   matching patterns

D.   sorting objects

26

Which of the following concepts do students need to understand in order to answer the following question?

What is the largest three-digit number you can make using the digits 3, 6, and 8?

A.   rounding

B.   place value

C.   decomposing

D.   subitizing

27

A first-grade class is beginning a unit on basic addition. Which of the following should the teacher use to introduce the topic?

A.   a calculator

B.   a number line

C.   manipulatives

D.   written equations

28

Mrs. Johns is teaching fact families and writes $23 - 10 = 13$ on the board. All of the following are part of the fact family she has introduced EXCEPT

A. $23 - 13 = 10.$

B. $10 + 13 = 23.$

C. $13 + 10 = 23.$

D. $23 \times 10 = 230.$

X

A

29

Mr. Jones is teaching equivalent fractions. Which of the following skills could he use to show an application of this skill?

A. reducing a very large fraction

B. finding the reciprocal of a fraction

C. drawing a visual fraction model

D. working with unit fractions

30

When learning about improper fractions, students are asked to decompose the fraction $\frac{14}{3}$. Which of the following students has decomposed the fraction properly?

$4\frac{2}{3}$

A. Angel: $1\frac{4}{3}$

B. Dina: $\frac{3}{3} + \frac{3}{3} + \frac{3}{3} + \frac{3}{3} + \frac{2}{3} = 4\frac{2}{3}$

C. Roberto: $4\frac{1}{3}$

D. Danny: $\frac{3}{14}$

31

Which of the following equations could a teacher use as an example of the commutative property of addition or multiplication?

A. $5 + 3 = 4 + 4$

B. $5 + 3 = 3 + 5$

C. $5 \times 3 = 15 \times 1$

D. $5 + 3 = 3 \times 5$

32

In order to demonstrate an application of the distributive property, Mr. Lopez presents the following problem and asks students to write an equation that solves the problem.

At a party, six girls and nine boys order hotdogs for $2 each. How much money was spent for hot dogs?

Which of the following students has written the correct equation?

A. Julie: $2 \times 6 + 9 = \$21$

B. Samuel: $2 + 6 + 9 = \$17$

C. LaShawn: $2 \times (6 + 9) = 2 \times 6 + 2 \times 9 = \$30$

D. Omar: $2 \times 6 \times 9 = \$108$

33

A teacher writes 65 + 35 = 35 + 65 on the board. Which of the following properties of addition is she demonstrating?

A.   distributive property of addition

B.   commutative property of addition

C.   identity property of addition

D.   associative property of addition

34

Emerson Elementary School has an on-campus store where students can purchase snacks. Which of the following activities involving the store would NOT be a good way to teach a second-grade class about money or the value of money?

A.   having students calculate the tax on certain items

B.   explaining how price tags are used to show the cost of an item

C.   encouraging them to find an item within a given budget

D.   using play money to shop in the store

35

Mrs. Lee is preparing to teach her students concepts related to time. Which of the following is NOT a reason she should begin her lesson with an analog clock rather than a digital clock?

A.   Analog clocks can be easily manipulated by students.

B.   Analog clocks only show twelve hours.

C.   Analog clocks have hands that constantly move.

D.   Analog clocks can be used to demonstrate skip counting by fives.

36

A third-grade class is divided into groups and asked to collect quantitative data for a class project. Each group submits its plan to the teacher. Which group will need to be redirected?

A.   group A: test scores of students in a class

B.   group B: costs of different airline fares

C.   group C: income of people in a company

D.   group D: the favorite color of members in a family

37

A second-grade teacher wants to have her students collect data and create a bar graph. Which of the following would be the best question for her to give her students?

A. How does the temperature outside change during the day?

B. What percentage of students like different types of ice cream?

C. What is the relationship between a plant's age and height?

D. Which classroom has the largest number of students?

38

Mrs. Hayes has targeted one of her kindergarten students for more practice with counting bears because he struggles with jumping ahead as he counts objects. Which of the following learning objectives is Mrs. Hayes most likely working to help this student achieve?

A. one-to-one correspondence

B. ability to skip count by two

C. sorting objects by shape

D. patterning and sequencing

39

A first-grade teacher wants to set up a math center to help his students meet the objective of subitizing quantities up to ten. Which learning material would be the best for him to include in this center?

A. an abacus

B. multiplication tiles

C. dot pattern flash cards

D. addition fact flash cards

40

Miss Wyatt's second-grade class is completing word problems that ask for students to "round the answer to the nearest tens place." She notices that most students have the correct answer until they get to the final step of rounding and sees that they are rounding the number to the nearest ones or hundreds place. Which underlying concept does Miss Wyatt need to reteach?

A. place value

B. addition and subtraction

C. whole numbers

D. composing numbers

41

Maria is a kindergarten student going through math learning center rotations. At the teacher-led table, her teacher asks her to show the equation 2 + 2 with blocks and to count aloud as she adds. Other than addition, what concept is Maria practicing and demonstrating for her teacher?

A.   composing numbers

B.   one-to-one correspondence

C.   number conservation

D.   subitizing

42

Which of the following is an example of a structural adaptation in animals?

A.   A lizard has camouflaged skin.

B.   A skunk sprays a toxin to scare away the prey.

C.   A spider spins a web to trap food.

D.   A bird migrates south in the winter.

43

Which of the following Earth science topics is developmentally appropriate for kindergartners?

A.   the four seasons

B.   shifting continents and landforms

C.   geological formation of different types of rocks

D.   ozone depletion

44

Which animal would live in a temperate forest?

A.   kangaroo

B.   sloth

C.   dolphin

D.   deer

45

Which of the following is the most appropriate activity for teaching prekindergarten students about states of matter?

A.   drawing a model of each state of matter

B.   sorting objects or pictures into the different categories

C.   writing what they learned about the states of matter

D.   having students independently make a root beer float to see the states of matter

46

A first-grade teacher sets up a science center with an activity related to floating objects. The students have a bowl of salt water and a bowl of fresh water to put small objects in. Which of the following concepts is the teacher trying to help students better understand through the science center?

A.   the states of matter

B.   the differences between freshwater and saltwater habitats

C.   density

D.   the scientific process

47

A first-grade teacher sets up a science center with an activity that has four candy canes and four glasses, each filled with a different liquid. The liquids are warm water, cold water, oil, and vinegar. The students are instructed to hypothesize which liquid they think will dissolve a candy cane the quickest and then test their predictions.

The teacher is trying to encourage student predictions on which of the following?

A.   physical properties

B.   physical change

C.   density

D.   reactions

48

A preschool teacher with a class of three-year-old students is teaching them about clouds. Which of the following is the most appropriate activity?

A.   The teacher gives the students paint to depict the different types of clouds.

B.   The teacher has the students draw and label the different types of clouds.

C.   The teacher has students independently make the four types of clouds using cotton balls.

D.   The teacher gives students shaving cream to make clouds on their tables.

49

As a quick assessment of lesson vocabulary, a third-grade teacher writes the following definition on the board:

the amount of water vapor in the atmosphere

The teacher then asks students to write on their whiteboard the vocabulary word related to the definition. Which of the following students is most correct?

A.   Luke, who wrote *humidity*

B.   Phillip, who wrote *atmosphere*

C.   Justine, who wrote *temperature*

D.   Kelli, who wrote *precipitation*

50

Mrs. Bevels is teaching her lower elementary students about weather. What measuring tool should she have available to teach her students how to measure air pressure?

A.   barometer

B.   wind vane

C.   anemometer

D.   thermometer

51

A first-grade teacher sets up a science center with an activity that asks students to dissect owl pellets. Which of the following is the teacher trying to develop in students through the center?

A.   vocabulary

B.   classification

C.   hypothesis

D.   observation

52

Which of the following is an example of a producer?

A.   zooplankton

B.   grass

C.   fish

D.   grasshopper

53

Which of the following hands-on activities will be most effective in introducing kindergartners to the concept of the five senses?

A.   placing an object in a paper bag and having students use all their senses to decide what the object might be

B.   reading a story about the five senses and having a discussion

C.   placing objects in a free-choice center for students to explore on their own with their senses

D.   reading a story, having students observe an object, and then discussing the object

54

Which of the following project-based learning activities would be most effective in teaching second graders the life cycle of a plant?

A. The students use an interactive computer program to see the life cycle of a plant.

B. The students plant a seed and record what happens as the plant grows.

C. The students draw a diagram and label the parts of the plant.

D. The students listen to a story and learn about the life cycle of a plant.

55

A second-grade teacher is teaching her students about simple machines. Which of the following is the most hands-on, developmentally appropriate activity?

A. The teacher puts students in groups and the students write a report on a simple machine.

B. The teacher reads a book and then hands out a sorting worksheet. The students must sort the machines into the correct category.

C. The teacher puts students in groups and they create a simple machine using materials provided; then they present their machine to the class.

D. The teacher puts students in groups and asks them to research the history of the automobile.

56

A second-grade teacher is instructing her students about landforms. Which of the following agents causes the change in appearance of the earth's surface in a gradual manner by causing rocks to be broken down into smaller pieces?

A. erosion

B. weathering

C. earthquakes

D. deposition

57

Which of the following is a characteristic of the sun?

A. The sun has water in its atmosphere.

B. The sun holds all the planets in place.

C. The sun has no atmosphere.

D. The sun takes twenty-four hours to rotate.

58

Which of the following is an example of a translucent object?

A.   a book

B.   a glass of water

C.   a t-shirt

D.   a car window

59

Which of the following is an example of a mixture?

A.   sand and water

B.   salt and water

C.   sugar and water

D.   amalgam dental fillings

60

As a quick assessment of third-grade lesson vocabulary, Mrs. Burns writes the following definition on the board:

energy that is stored and is waiting to work

Mrs. Burns then asks students to write on their whiteboard the vocabulary word related to the definition. Which of the following students is most correct?

A.   Joy, who wrote *kinetic energy*

B.   William, who wrote *thermal energy*

C.   Tamara, who wrote *mechanical energy*

D.   Justin, who wrote *potential energy*

61

As a quick assessment, a third-grade teacher writes the following question on the board:

What landform is created from the erosion of sediment by moving water?

The teacher then asks students to write on their whiteboard the vocabulary word related to the definition. Which of the following students is most correct?

A.   Tiesha, who wrote *an island*

B.   Hillary, who wrote *a sand dune*

C.   Johnny, who wrote *a delta*

D.   Reba, who wrote *a canyon*

62

Which of the following is a characteristic of stratus clouds?

A.   often gray

B.   big and tall

C.   high in the sky

D.   puffy

63

A first-grade teacher is teaching her students about constellations. Which of the following is the most appropriate activity?

A.   The teacher reviews constellations. Then, the students write five facts about what they have learned from the lecture.

B.   The teacher reviews constellations and the students use marshmallows and tooth picks to create various constellations, such as the Big Dipper.

C.   The teacher puts students into groups; each group has pictures of constellations and facts. The students must match the constellation to the fact.

D.   The teacher shows the students a video about constellations, then the students write two facts about what they learned.

64

Which of the following is a physical education activity aimed at increasing student cardiovascular fitness and endurance?

A.   stretching before sprinting as fast as possible

B.   walking on a balance beam while holding something in one's hands

C.   doing jumping jacks for several minutes without stopping

D.   learning how to shoot a basketball

65

A kindergarten teacher hoping to integrate physical education into everyday instruction tosses a beanbag to students each morning during circle time. Which skill is she helping her students develop?

A.   spatial awareness

B.   fundamental motor skills

C.   body awareness

D.   self-care skills

66

It is raining, and Mrs. Jansen's prekindergarten class cannot go outside for recess. She decides to work on their non-locomotor skills in the classroom instead. Which activity would be best?

A.   hopping in place

B.   jumping from one taped-off place on the floor to another

C.   focusing on inhalation and exhalation

D.   stretching

67

A first-grade student on the playground is observed to be sliding in a forward and upward motion with one foot in front of the other. Which locomotor pattern is she using?

A.   galloping

B.   skipping

C.   hopping

D.   pivoting

68

A third-grade physical education teacher notices that one of his students has lower levels of overall endurance and a harder time completing activities designed to build cardiovascular fitness. What modifications might he make for this student?

A.   excusing the student from all activities outside of stretching

B.   decreasing the time and intensity of the student's exercises

C.   encouraging the student to develop greater body awareness

D.   helping the student to develop more fundamental motor skills

69

Which lesson on personal hygiene would be most appropriate for a kindergarten class?

A.   a discussion on brushing teeth

B.   talking about the importance of deodorant use

C.   how to apply hair conditioner

D.   a lesson on toenail trimming

70

A second-grade teacher asks her students to mix one drop of red paint with two drops of blue paint to create the color blue-violet. What concept is she teaching her students?

A. secondary colors

B. tertiary colors

C. complementary colors

D. primary colors

71

A kindergarten teacher gives students small paintbrushes for an activity because she wants them to work on more detailed painting. One student named Mila, however, is behind the rest of the class in fine motor skills. What modification might the teacher make?

A. give Mila a different activity such as making a play-dough figure

B. give Mila a larger paintbrush or a paintbrush with a sponge on the end

C. have Mila finger paint instead of using a brush

D. encourage Mila to make her painting abstract instead of realistic

72

A preschool teacher gives her students egg-shaker maracas to shake while she plays the morning welcome song. Which musical concept is she encouraging students to develop?

A. timbre

B. pitch

C. rhythm

D. tone

73

Which method of assessment is most useful to track student progress in visual arts?

A. observational notes

B. portfolios

C. summative assessment

D. oral assessment

74

Mrs. Walker has various swatches of colored fabric. She holds different color combinations up in pairs and asks the class to raise their hands if they think the color combinations look pleasing together. Which concept is Mrs. Walker likely trying to teach her class?

A.   secondary colors

B.   art criticism

C.   contrast

D.   complementary colors

75

What would be the most appropriate activity for a prekindergarten class to participate in as they listen to a new piece of music?

A.   identifying the different instruments they hear

B.   stating whether the piece is polyphonic or homophonic

C.   clapping along with the rhythm of the piece

D.   describing the pitch of the piece

Answer Key

TEST I

1)

A. Incorrect. Print awareness is when children begin to recognize that oral language and written language are related.

B. Correct. Phonics is when children begin to correlate sounds with letters or groups of letters.

C. Incorrect. Phonological awareness is identifying and manipulating the sounds of spoken language.

D. Incorrect. Word recognition is the ability to recognize and read words effortlessly.

2)

A. Incorrect. Environmental print is any print in a student's natural environment.

B. Incorrect. The school marquis is in a student's everyday environment.

C. Incorrect. This is in the everyday environment of the classroom.

D. Correct. This is a new exposure to print, not one found in the student's everyday environment.

3)

A. Incorrect. The onset is the initial consonant sound of the word.

B. Correct. The onset is the initial consonant sound, in this case the blend *br*.

C. Incorrect. The onset is the initial sound.

D. Incorrect. The onset is the initial sound.

4)

A. Incorrect. The toddler is beyond babbling.

B. Incorrect. Holophrastic speech is single word.

C. Incorrect. The sentence has three words.

D. Correct. This sentence lacks the preposition *at* and is indicative of the telegraphic phase.

5)

A. Incorrect. *Blimp* is a very challenging word for a preschooler (*b*'s and *p*'s). Also, it is not developmentally appropriate to ask most preschoolers to spell from oral dictation.

B.   Correct. Copying is a key stage in learning to write, and a child's name is a word with which she is generally already familiar.

C.   Incorrect. *McDonald's* is a challenging word, and although it is a common environmental print word, a preschooler most likely has not memorized its spelling.

D.   Incorrect. *Elephant* is a challenging word, and a preschooler will not know the spelling of this word based on a picture.

6)

A.   Incorrect. Reading aloud is important but not necessarily characteristic of a print-rich classroom.

B.   Correct. Labeling objects in the classroom such as a *door, whiteboard, cubby*, and so on will make a classroom rich in environmental print.

C.   Incorrect. An abundance of writing utensils is important but not necessarily in direct relation to providing a print-rich classroom environment.

D.   Incorrect. Picture books do not contain enough print to characterize a print-rich classroom.

7)

A.   Correct. Understanding that words are what is read on a page is an important part of print awareness.

B.   Incorrect. This would help Mrs. Cortez, not necessarily Henry, and this is likely not the primary reason for her pointing.

C.   Incorrect. This would not lull him to sleep necessarily.

D.   Incorrect. It is most unlikely that Henry is able to read the words.

8)

A.   Correct. Phonemic awareness does not come naturally. This is why people who cannot read can still use oral language.

B.   Incorrect. It must be taught. Most research suggests that intentional activities such as exposing students to rhymes are necessary to help children fully develop this skill.

C.   Incorrect. Students will develop phonemic awareness at a different speed based on many factors.

D.   Incorrect. Students need to be able to understand and use sounds to sound out words and read.

9)

A.   Incorrect. The alphabetic principle relates to letter and sound knowledge.

B.   Correct. His students will delete a sound from each word to make a new word.

C.   Incorrect. Phoneme substitution would involve substituting one sound for another.

D.   Incorrect. Phoneme segmentation involves sounding out words.

10)

A.   Correct. Phonics involves connecting written language to spoken sounds.

B.   Incorrect. Sight words are not sounded out phonetically.

C.   Incorrect. Knowledge of root words is part of advanced instruction, not beginning phonics.

D.   Incorrect. Letter-sound correspondence is crucial for phonics study.

11)

A.   Incorrect. Once students master the consonant blend *br* and the short vowel pattern *ea*, they can decode the word *bread*.

B. Incorrect. Once students master the consonant blend *fl* and the long *i* sound, the word *fly* is decodable.

C. Correct. Using standard decoding strategies, the word *what* would incorrectly rhyme with *cat*, so it is not decodable.

D. Incorrect. *Plan* is composed of a simple onset consonant blend *pl* and the rime *–an*.

12)

A. Incorrect. This is not the best strategy and might bore the students.

B. Correct. This will help students understand that the narrator is telling the story from a different point of view.

C. Incorrect. This is not a read-aloud activity.

D. Incorrect. Read-alouds should always be designed to increase fluency through rate, accuracy, and prosody.

13)

A. Incorrect. Print awareness is important but should be mastered before phonics instruction.

B. Correct. Memorizing sight words through multiple exposures will help students read more quickly and fluently.

C. Incorrect. Stroke order is not related to reading but to writing.

D. Incorrect. Spelling will not help with reading rate and fluency.

14)

A. Incorrect. Changing grades may not even be possible; furthermore, it is the teacher's responsibility to accommodate gifted students in his or her classroom.

B. Incorrect. This might help but should not be the teacher's only course of action since Max is bored with the work being assigned to him.

C. Incorrect. Having Max write the work over again will seem like a punishment for finishing quickly because he has mastered the material.

D. Correct. Max is clearly asking for and ready for more challenging work.

15)

A. Correct. Rate is the speed at which one reads.

B. Incorrect. Prosody is the expression with which one reads.

C. Incorrect. Accuracy is how correctly one reads.

D. Incorrect. Phonemes are sounds and do not apply directly to measuring a student's reading fluency.

16)

A. Incorrect. Students should be introduced to rhyme well before second grade.

B. Incorrect. Students should be introduced to rhyme well before third grade.

C. Correct. Many developmentally appropriate books for preschoolers are written in simple poetry; this helps develop phonological awareness.

D. Incorrect. Students do not need to be decoding on their own to enjoy listening to poetry.

17)

A. Incorrect. This activity would likely be too challenging for first graders to do independently.

B. Incorrect. Differentiating characters in this way would not help students recognize meter.

C. Incorrect. Copying lines of the poem would not necessarily help students recognize meter.

D. Correct. Clapping to the beat of the poem is a developmentally appropriate way to introduce this concept to first graders.

18)

A. Incorrect. Although word frequency is a part of a quantitative text measurement, it is not the only measure.

B. Incorrect. Text structure is a qualitative measurement.

C. Incorrect. Text layout is a qualitative measurement.

D. Correct. This definition describes a quantitative text measurement.

19)

A. Correct. This will give Mark extra practice identifying the main idea during oral reading assessments.

B. Incorrect. This will likely only frustrate Mark if he is having trouble identifying the main idea in simpler texts.

C. Incorrect. Mark needs exposure to and practice with many different types of texts.

D. Incorrect. This approach does not address identifying the main idea directly.

20)

A. Incorrect. Although teaching about bias might help avoid faulty inferences, it does not necessarily help with identifying textual evidence for an inference.

B. Correct. This activity gives students direct practice with supporting an inference with evidence from the text.

C. Incorrect. This activity does not pertain to identifying textual support

for an inference; an inference involves reading something and then drawing a conclusion based on what one has read. Writing a summary merely helps students recall what they have read.

D. Incorrect. This activity does not necessarily pertain to inferences. This would be an appropriate activity to help students think creatively or determine whether they were satisfied with the conclusion of a story. However, it does not help them draw conclusions based on things not explicitly stated in the text.

21)

A. Incorrect. This assignment would not necessarily have a problem-solution structure and would not be written in the second person.

B. Correct. This assignment would meet both goals of being written in the second person and defining a problem and its solution.

C. Incorrect. This assignment would be written in second person but would not be a problem-solution structure.

D. Incorrect. This assignment would have a problem-solution structure but would not be written in the second person.

22)

C. Correct. This chart shows the class is writing about the similarities and differences between people and dogs.

23)

A. Incorrect. This is a question about character motivation, not point of view.

B. Correct. If the students answer correctly, they will have identified the dinosaur as the first-person narrator protagonist.

C. Incorrect. This is a question about setting.

D. Incorrect. This question might help establish the students' point of view toward the story, but it does not address the first-person point of view within the story.

24)

A. Incorrect. This is actual reading.

B. Correct. Pretend reading is "reading" based on memory or pictures cues.

C. Incorrect. This is simply oral reading without prosody.

D. Incorrect. This is not reading at all.

25)

A. Incorrect. Students usually have practice with this far sooner.

B. Incorrect. Show and tell typically predates this.

C. Correct. Show and tell is a great early introduction to giving and listening to an oral presentation.

D. Incorrect. Show and tell usually comes first.

26)

A. Incorrect. This might give a different interpretation but would be hard to implement, and second-grade students would likely not make the connection.

B. Correct. This would allow students to see if their interpretation of the story as read is similar or dissimilar to the theatrical production.

C. Incorrect. This would not be developmentally appropriate for second graders.

D. Incorrect. This would not be a different interpretation of the same story.

27)

A. Incorrect. This story demands a basic understanding of the holiday, which some of her students may not have.

B. Correct. She needs to help her students meet the knowledge demands of the story to enable them to fully understand it.

C. Incorrect. The book has high knowledge demands per her student population, and she must ensure her students have the background information they need.

D. Incorrect. She cannot assume all of her students have a background with this holiday.

28)

A. Correct. Procedural knowledge involves how to write letters, words, and so on.

B. Incorrect. This is part of conceptual knowledge, or understanding the purpose of writing.

C. Incorrect. This is about generative knowledge, or being able to generate writing to accomplish a purpose.

D. Incorrect. This is a way to share or publish writing with others.

29)

A. Correct. *On* is a VC and *go* is a CV pattern.

B. Incorrect. *Off* is a VC but *pin* is a CVC pattern.

C. Incorrect. *Clap* is CCVC and *up* is a VC pattern.

D. Incorrect. Both words are CVC.

30)

A. Incorrect. A poem is not usually designed to inform.

B. Incorrect. A short story is narrative writing.

C. **Correct.** This expository writing is designed to inform the reader about an upcoming event.

D. Incorrect. A teen fantasy novel is narrative writing.

31)

A. Incorrect. This might not help Jo recognize her errors with missing articles since she is not a native English speaker.

B. Incorrect. This might not help her depending on the other student's proficiency with the use of articles.

C. Incorrect. This will not help her use articles appropriately.

D. **Correct.** This might aid Jo in finding the places she needs to insert articles.

32)

A. **Correct.** Passive listening calls for the listener to listen without conversing.

B. Incorrect. This situation calls for active listening; to hold a conversation, one must respond.

C. Incorrect. This calls for active listening as the waiter or waitress will need to confirm understanding with the customer.

D. Incorrect. This calls for active listening; the employee will need to respond to feedback.

33)

A. Incorrect. Brainstorming is the first phase in the authoring cycle when students generate ideas.

B. Incorrect. Editing involves revising work to make it more readable.

C. Incorrect. The students have already drafted the pieces.

D. **Correct.** Publishing student work involves sharing it with others.

34)

A. Incorrect. Posting student work on the classroom bulletin board will not show student growth over the course of the year.

B. **Correct.** Keeping student work in a portfolio that is shared with parents shows student growth over time.

C. Incorrect. Having students revise their letter strings is not appropriate for emergent writers and is not a way to publish student work.

D. Incorrect. Videotaping student performances does not pertain to writing.

35)

A. **Correct.** The teacher is asking the class to consider the intended audience for the text.

B. Incorrect. This question is about audience, not organizational structure.

C. Incorrect. This question is about audience, not theme.

D. Incorrect. This question is about audience, not the point of view.

36)

A. Incorrect. This might help Aisha think more deeply about the topic, but it will not necessarily help her determine three research questions.

B. Incorrect. Dance is a good topic because Aisha is interested in it. She just needs further prompting from Mrs. Spellman.

C. **Correct.** This is the start of the second phase of the research process in which students find background information and conduct a preliminary search on their topic.

D. Incorrect. This is not part of the research process and is more of a word-association activity that might lead to a descriptive, but not research, piece on this topic.

37)

A.   Incorrect. This paragraph would most logically be in the present tense.

B.   Correct. This paragraph would most logically be written in the past tense and would provide practice with forming the past tense.

C.   Incorrect. This paragraph would most logically be written in the present tense.

D.   Incorrect. This paragraph would most logically be written in the present tense.

38)

A.   Correct. This approach will help make this activity inclusive for all students. She can encourage more highly skilled students to add more words to their stories as she sees fit.

B.   Incorrect. This approach will not help low-level students who might not be able to complete these sentences.

C.   Incorrect. This approach will not necessarily accommodate lower-level students.

D.   Incorrect. This approach might create a sense of difference that the teacher does not wish to impart. Additionally, all students can generally benefit from educational technology.

39)

A.   Incorrect. Physical gestures like nodding are part of engaging with the speaker and showing agreement and understanding.

B.   Incorrect. Restating what the speaker said shows understanding, a crucial part of active listening.

C.   Incorrect. Showing empathy is a very important part of active listening.

D.   Correct. Listeners should always wait for the speaker to finish before speaking when actively listening.

40)

A.   Incorrect. A dialect is a way of speaking uniquely to a group of people. Mumbling is a problem that can affect any group of people.

B.   Correct. Articulation refers to clarity of speech.

C.   Incorrect. She is speaking, not listening.

D.   Incorrect. Mumbling and lack of articulation make the presentations arduous, not necessarily the wrong types of questioning.

41)

A.   Incorrect. Both of these are full sentences.

B.   Correct. The student has unnecessarily shifted to the second person, *you*, when there is no need for such a shift.

C.   Incorrect. All of the pronouns agree with their antecedents.

D.   Incorrect. It is clear that *it* refers back to *gift*.

42)

A.   Correct. The students need a basic knowledge of the meaning of these words before they can apply them in math class.

B.   Incorrect. Multiple-meaning words are homonyms. These math words are not homonyms like *interest* (engagement in something) and *interest* (money earned from savings).

C.   Incorrect. Registers are patterns of speech associated with a certain social situation.

D.   Incorrect. These are literal words with a concrete and not abstract meaning.

43)

A.   Correct. *Anti–* is a common prefix that means *opposite of* or *against*.

B.   Incorrect. Goldsmith is a compound word: *gold + smith*.

C.   Incorrect. *–ness* is a suffix.

D.   Incorrect. *–able* is a suffix.

44)

A.   Incorrect. This is a hyperbole, where something is greatly exaggerated.

B.   Incorrect. This is personification, where a nonhuman object is given human qualities such as the ability to pant and gasp.

C.   Correct. Similes make comparisons using the words *like* or *as*.

D.   Incorrect. This is a metaphor, where two unlike things are compared without using *like* or *as*.

45)

A.   Incorrect. The word choice here does not contribute to a dark or dreary tone. It is rather descriptive and matter-of-fact.

B.   Incorrect. The tone here is one of monotony through the repetition of the word *same*.

C.   Correct. The words *dark*, *dimly*, and *storm* contribute to a dark and dreary tone.

D.   Incorrect. The short sentences create some anticipation and uncertainty as to why she was a strange girl, but the word choice does not create a dark and dreary tone.

46)

A.   Correct. She is narrating her own actions as a way of talking to her students and exposing them to lots of oral language and new words.

B.   Incorrect. She probably does want to be a good role model, but this is not necessarily why she is narrating her actions.

C.   Incorrect. These are simple classroom routines. They do not show a moral or lesson.

D.   Incorrect. This is not why she is narrating her actions, and there is no reason to believe that toddlers only listen or hear when speech is at a very high volume.

47)

A.   Incorrect. This is not developmentally appropriate for a prekindergarten student.

B.   Correct. Her mother likely just needs the teacher's reassurance that this is a natural part of Hannah's development.

C.   Incorrect. Having Hannah go back and correct her pictures may make her less apt to practice drawing and writing.

D.   Incorrect. This is not directly related to Hannah's mother's concern, and she really needs the teacher's assurance that the invented spelling phase is natural.

48)

A.   Correct. Students need to draw on their knowledge bank of letter sounds to decode new words.

B.   Incorrect. Most phonics instruction involves oral language since phonics connects written words to the sounds they make.

C.   Incorrect. This is emphasized in reading comprehension, not phonics.

D.   Incorrect. Phonics study is usually incremental and gradually advances to more complex words and texts.

49)

A.   Incorrect. *Up* is a simple two-sound, VC-pattern word that is easily spelled through sounding out.

B.   Correct. Students would have to know to double the consonant *g*, and simply sounding out the word *bigger* would not generate the correct spelling.

C. Incorrect. *Not* is a simple CVC word that can easily be spelled through sounding out.

D. Incorrect. *Help* is a CVCC word that can be spelled through sounding out.

50)

D. Correct. Mary needs to first understand the basics of reading: that we read books from left to right, top to bottom, and so on. She is not ready for instruction on the other topics.

51)

A. Incorrect. Counting to ten to calm down might indirectly help Matt feel better about himself, but self-concept is not the most direct goal.

B. Incorrect. This activity might help Matt develop interpersonal relationships, but the counselor has a different goal in mind.

C. Correct. Matt is learning to self-regulate his emotions by using this strategy to calm down on his own.

D. Incorrect. This strategy is just helping Matt calm down to avoid outbursts; it is not related directly to resolving conflict with others.

52)

A. Incorrect. This assignment would address self-concept.

B. Incorrect. Writing an essay on family members and their roles would not be developmentally appropriate for a first-grade class and would not address self-identity.

C. Correct. In discussing what they want to be when they grow up, students begin to think about how they fit into society and how they can contribute.

D. Incorrect. Role-playing conflict resolution would help students with developing social competence and developing interpersonal relationships.

53)

A. Incorrect. Listening to a guest speaker is not a hands-on or exploratory activity.

B. Incorrect. Reading a book about a community helper would be an appropriate activity for the unit, but it is not hands-on or exploratory.

C. Incorrect. Brainstorming and discussing community helpers is not hands-on or exploratory.

D. Correct. Handling protective equipment (under supervision) is an effective way for students to explore what it might be like to be a firefighter.

54)

A. Correct. Celebrating Chinese New Year is the most developmentally appropriate activity for a kindergarten class and will help them learn about holidays celebrated as part of Chinese culture.

B. Incorrect. Creating a poster is not developmentally appropriate for kindergarten students.

C. Incorrect. Displaying a geopolitical infographic is not developmentally appropriate for kindergarten students.

D. Incorrect. A video about Mao addresses history and politics more than culture, and it is most likely not appropriate for a kindergarten audience.

55)

A. Incorrect. A farmer growing his own food is independent.

B. **Correct.** Some desert countries cannot grow their own food because of the climate, so they must import food from elsewhere. Likewise, the United States does not have all the oil it needs, so it must import oil.

C. Incorrect. This is intradependence.

D. Incorrect. This family is independent (at least, in terms of clothing).

56)

A. **Correct.** The Royal Observatory in Greenwich has been designated as the location of the prime meridian, or 0°.

B. Incorrect. Moscow is at 38°E.

C. Incorrect. New York is at 74°W.

D. Incorrect. Juneau is at 134°W.

57)

A. Incorrect. A political map will not necessarily help students learn about a map's legend, particularly if the map does not use different colors.

B. Incorrect. A topographical map generally uses concentric rings versus symbols denoted by a legend. Additionally, this map will likely be too complicated for a second-grade class.

C. **Correct.** This map will include a legend explaining that the corncobs are symbols representing areas of corn production.

D. Incorrect. Most maps use latitude and longitude. This map is too general and is not directly related to a legend.

58)

A. Incorrect. Justice is fairness.

B. **Correct.** Rule of law is a key part of our system of government.

C. Incorrect. Natural law refers to morality.

D. Incorrect. Equality is about treating people the same.

59)

A. **Correct.** This discussion is an appropriate way to help students understand that their warm climate impacts the type of clothing they need.

B. Incorrect. This question is not about clothing variance by culture, but by climate.

C. Incorrect. This question does not address how students relate climate to clothing.

D. Incorrect. While one's social condition might impact the ability to purchase clothing, this question is not designed to derive this response insomuch as it is about the type of clothing one needs in a warmer climate.

60)

A. Incorrect. Ms. Wilson is treating George differently, not identically, to the other students.

B. Incorrect. Ms. Wilson is not directly encouraging anyone to accept certain ideas or beliefs they do not agree with.

C. Incorrect. The example does not directly address consequences for George's actions.

D. **Correct.** Ms. Wilson is giving George what he needs to be successful, even if it is different from what she is giving other students.

61)

A. Incorrect. Government is a macrosystem construct.

B. Incorrect. Ethnicity is an element of the macrosystem.

C. **Correct.** A mosque or any other place of worship is a part of a child's microsystem: it is an institution with which the child has direct contact.

D. Incorrect. The parent-teacher relationship is a part of the mesosystem.

62)

A. Incorrect. Supreme Court justices are not elected.

B. Incorrect. Supreme Court justices are confirmed by the Senate but not nominated by the House.

C. Incorrect. Supreme Court justices must be confirmed by the Senate.

D. **Correct.** They are nominated by the president and confirmed by the Senate.

63)

A. Incorrect. Creating the graphic organizer for Jada does not help her recognize what she does and does not understand.

B. Incorrect. Pairing Jada with another student would help Jada develop other skills but not necessarily self-awareness and metacognition.

C. Incorrect. Asking Jada to read the directions aloud might promote in greater understanding but is not related to self-awareness and metacognition.

D. **Correct.** Asking Jada what she does not understand will prompt her to reflect on her own thinking and level of understanding.

64)

A. Incorrect. The formal operational stage is one of Piaget's stages in which children develop abstract thinking.

B. Incorrect. Abstract thought is developed in Piaget's formal operational stage and is not related to this observation.

C. **Correct.** In Vygotsky's zone of proximal development, children are able to do things with the help of a more skilled peer or adult.

D. Incorrect. The chronosystem is part of Bronfenbrenner's model and represents the changes over the life course of a child.

65)

A. Incorrect. Individual desks discourage social interaction.

B. Incorrect. Assigning spots on a carpet is not appropriate for second-grade students, who need a surface to write on.

C. **Correct.** Group or paired seating will encourage cooperative learning and social interaction.

D. Incorrect. Seating students at computer terminals discourages social interaction.

66)

A. Incorrect. This is a question about understanding plot, not necessarily recognizing cultural differences.

B. Incorrect. Lagos is indeed a very large city, but this is not something second graders would necessarily know. This is also related more to population density than to culture.

C. Incorrect. This question is not necessarily related to understanding cultural differences.

D. **Correct.** Asking students to consider the differences between the two locations in the story will encourage students to understand cultural differences among different places in general.

67)

A. Incorrect. Metacognition is thinking about thinking.

B. Incorrect. Secondary socialization is imparting to children how to behave as a member of a group.

C.   Incorrect. The students are not necessarily emotional; they are simply learning a new concept.

D.   Correct. The teacher is meeting students in their zone of proximal development and aiding them until they can complete a task on their own.

68)

A.   Incorrect. By using words like "above," this instruction only addresses relative location, not the cardinal directions per the compass rose.

B.   Incorrect. Locating a state capital is not necessarily related to the use of the compass rose.

C.   Incorrect. Identifying an island is not necessarily related to the use of the compass rose.

D.   Correct. Using a term like "west," one of the cardinal directions, helps students use the compass rose to identify locations on a map.

69)

A.   Incorrect. This is more appropriate for second-grade students.

B.   Correct. This would be a developmentally appropriate expectation for a first-grade student.

C.   Incorrect. This is likely too advanced for a first-grade student.

D.   Incorrect. This is also likely too advanced for first graders who are just learning map skills.

70)

A.   Incorrect. The forest's resources are being used, not conserved. At the same time, it is not clear if resources are necessarily being depleted in any given forest.

B.   Incorrect. The forest community is not necessarily obtaining goods from another community or country.

C.   Correct. The students should understand that people use what is available in their environment. In this scenario, the people would use wood from trees to build houses.

D.   Incorrect. This scenario does not address the global economy.

71)

A.   Incorrect. This article is concerned not with biodiversity but with the changes one group of humans are experiencing.

B.   Incorrect. Global citizenship requires taking action, but there is no reason to believe that Mrs. Markel is advocating for this just by reading the article.

C.   Correct. The people in the rain forest environment are dependent on its resources for survival, so cutting down trees changes their lives dramatically.

D.   Incorrect. It is not clear from this description that the article claims that compromise between cultures is possible.

72)

A.   Incorrect. This example does not help students make a personal connection to this concept of chronology.

B.   Correct. Students are generally excited about holidays, and stating that a holiday is next month—in the future—will help students make this time connection.

C.   Incorrect. Turning a year older is a very abstract concept that a prekindergartner will likely not understand.

D.   Incorrect. Starting a new unit is not as concrete an example as that of Halloween, which young children generally look forward to with great anticipation.

73)

A.   Incorrect. Colonial oppression is far too advanced a subject for a first-grade class.

B.   Correct. The teacher can present a balanced view of both the European settlers and indigenous North Americans by introducing them both as topics.

C.   Incorrect. A book about Columbus is not about North America in particular. One that references his "heroism" does not present a balanced perspective.

D.   Incorrect. This activity is only related to the Pilgrims, not the native peoples who inhabited the area when the Pilgrims arrived.

74)

A.   Incorrect. Compiling a statistical analysis is not developmentally appropriate for a kindergarten class.

B.   Incorrect. A historical discussion about the civil rights movement is not developmentally appropriate for a kindergarten class.

C.   Correct. Reading a developmentally appropriate book on the topic is a simple way to get students to start thinking about diversity.

D.   Incorrect. Kindergarten students in a homogenous rural community will likely have very little experience with people of different religious backgrounds.

75)

A.   Incorrect. Conservation is related to the environment and biodiversity, not economics.

B.   Correct. Pollution might decrease tourism, and this will have economic impacts on the community.

C.   Incorrect. Biodiversity is not directly related to the economy.

D.   Incorrect. Preserving natural resources for the future is not directly related to the economy.

Sample Response #1

I)   The student has followed some of the assignment directions. He has written a paragraph of nine sentences (though one is actually a sentence fragment), and he includes a concluding sentence. He uses a variety of details about himself that aid in providing basic biographical information. He includes time expressions such as "first" and "next." However, "next" is not really an appropriate time expression to introduce a sentence about future hopes. His sentence structure is developing, and his paragraph contains only one sentence fragment along with eight solidly constructed sentences. The paragraph includes a few errors with singular and plural nouns ("three brother" vs. "three brothers" and "good grade" vs. "good grades"). He also has an apostrophe error with the possessive determiner "his," which does not need an apostrophe. Max has also written in the third person instead of the first person. Overall, however, Max has made a good effort at a first draft of a paragraph that can be easily revised to meet specifications.

II)   I would focus on having Max rewrite his paragraph from the first-person point of view. I would have him first circle each time he uses third-person pronouns such as "he" and "his." I would then remind him that he needs to use the first-person pronoun "I" for the paragraph and change each of these instances. I would also direct him to change other words (for verb agreement). I will encourage him to read aloud to a partner or myself to check for subject-verb agreement and other errors after he revises these pronouns.

Sample Response #2

I)   Jilian is developing knowledge of first-grade social studies standards. She was able to self-correct once she realized she had made a mistake identifying Russia instead of the United States, a somewhat similarly shaped country. She has a solid grasp of using the cardinal directions to move north and west. While she initially pointed to Alabama, she clearly had a solid idea of the region in which Georgia is located. The inversion of the Atlantic and Pacific Oceans is somewhat common, and Jilian will hopefully meet this standard with more practice. Jilian does not seem to have retained as much historical knowledge as geographical knowledge, however. While she was able to identify a picture of Benjamin Franklin and knew he was an inventor, she was not able to say correctly what he had invented or any of his other accomplishments. She may be less confident in certain historical knowledge and facts, as evidenced by her unwillingness to take a guess when asked about Thomas Jefferson.

II) I would work to help Jilian grow more interested in historical topics and figures by providing lots of visual literacy and project-based activities. I would, perhaps, have Jilian make a collage featuring pictures she prints out about the lives of Thomas Jefferson and Benjamin Franklin. I might then display her work and other pictures relating to these two figures on a bulletin board in the classroom for reinforcement. I would then use informal assessment to reassess Jilian's understanding by asking her casually if she remembers the name of the person shown and what his accomplishments were.

TEST II

1)

A. Incorrect. Cardinality is figuring out how many objects are in a set. It is not necessarily related to the set changing in composition.

B. Incorrect. Subitizing is the ability to immediately recognize how many objects are in a set without counting them, such as in dot patterns.

C. Incorrect. Decomposing is breaking a number down into its unit parts using place value.

D. **Correct.** The teacher is helping to demonstrate that five objects remain five objects, regardless of how they are arranged.

2)

A. Incorrect. Number lines would be helpful to check answers for addition and subtraction, not for division with remainders.

B. Incorrect. Dot plots represent data; they are not helpful for division with remainders.

C. **Correct.** Students can draw the total number of objects and then partition them into the number of portions per the problem and then see how many are left over. This will help students confirm their answers.

D. Incorrect. This is a very complex way to set up a simple division problem and will result in a decimal remainder. This is not appropriate for a third-grade class performing simple division with remainders.

3)

A. Incorrect. One-to-one correspondence involves counting each object individually.

B. Incorrect. Cardinality involves counting how many objects are in a set.

C. Incorrect. The student is not being asked to put the objects in a pattern.

D. **Correct.** The student is classifying the objects by attribute (shape, size, color, and so on) and then sorting them into respective groups.

4)

A. **Correct.** Decomposing a number refers to breaking it down into its individual place values.

B. Incorrect. Cardinality refers to the number of items in a set.

C. Incorrect. Decomposing a number does not refer to addition.

D. Incorrect. Decomposing a number does involve skip counting.

5)

A. Incorrect. Cents are a standard unit of measurement within American currency.

B. Incorrect. Students are composing and not decomposing seventy cents.

C. Incorrect. Students are not making two addition or multiplication problems equal to one another.

D. **Correct.** In order for students to count out seventy cents with dimes, they must first know how to skip count by tens.

6)

A. **Correct.** This is a developmentally appropriate activity for first graders that uses US customary units (inches).

B. Incorrect. Calculating area is not developmentally appropriate for a first-grade class.

C. Incorrect. This is a suitable activity, but kilograms are metric units, not US customary units.

D. Incorrect. This type of conversion is not developmentally appropriate for a first-grade class.

7)

A. Correct. $\frac{1}{4} = \frac{2}{8}$.

B. Incorrect. $\frac{4}{8}$ is not equivalent to $\frac{2}{8}$.

C. Incorrect. $\frac{2}{4}$ is not equivalent to $\frac{2}{8}$.

D. Incorrect. $\frac{3}{4}$ is not equivalent to $\frac{2}{8}$.

8)

A. Incorrect. This problem does not involve either skip counting or percentage.

B. Incorrect. This problem does involve borrowing because students are subtracting. However, it does not involve ratios.

C. Correct. Students must understand place value and decimals to correctly line up the problem in order to subtract.

D. Incorrect. There is only one operation—subtraction. However, place value understanding is needed.

9)

A. Incorrect. Area refers to a 2-D shape, not a cube, which is a 3-D shape.

B. Incorrect. Perimeter is the outside measurement of a 2-D shape.

C. Correct. The volume is the amount of space a 3-D shape occupies, and the unit cubes are an introduction to this measurement.

D. Incorrect. Surface area is the area of only the surface of a 3-D shape. The unit cubes were put inside the cube, so they are representative of the volume of the cube.

10)

A. Incorrect. This activity is composing a number, not decomposing it.

B. Correct. Students are composing a number based on the units in each place value.

C. Incorrect. The lattice method is a strategy for multiplication.

D. Incorrect. Doubling is a strategy for addition.

11)

A. Incorrect. Second graders who are not yet multiplying and dividing will not be using percentages.

B. Correct. Since there are only two categories (those with pets vs. those without pets), this is best expressed in a ratio.

C. Incorrect. Students would need two fractions to express this value: those with pets as one numerator and those without pets as another numerator. The denominator would be the total number of students in the class.

D. Incorrect. A stem-and-leaf plot shows various values. There are only two values: those with pets and those without pets.

12)

A. Correct. 1 m = 100 cm, so Harriet should multiply her answer by 100.

13)

A. Incorrect. 12 × ? = 36 would be correct, but the 3 is the unknown variable, so this construction is incorrect.

B. Incorrect. This is a fraction and would work only if the numerator and denominator were inverted to show $36 \div 12 \left(\frac{36}{12}\right)$.

C. Correct. This is the equation that matches this word problem, as Alex needs to divide 36 by 12 to find out how many packages of buns he needs.

D. Incorrect. Alex needs to divide the thirty-six buns he needs by the number of buns in each package.

14)

A. Incorrect. Though she is using manipulatives, there is no conservation, as the number of objects would seem to grow as each new block in the pattern is added.

B. Correct. Ms. Greene is encouraging sequencing by color through the use of blocks, which are manipulatives.

C. Incorrect. Subitizing is recognizing how many objects are in a group without counting, and cardinality is finding out how many are in a group.

D. Incorrect. There is no counting of objects, so one-to-one correspondence is not being addressed.

15)

A. Incorrect. Subitizing is looking at a group of objects and knowing instantly how many are there.

B. Incorrect. While the student is using manipulatives to some degree, this is not the best answer because the skill he is demonstrating is not the use of these manipulatives. They are merely the learning materials he is using.

C. Correct. Cardinality is the number of items in a group, so the student is demonstrating this understanding.

D. Incorrect. The student is not necessarily gluing the objects in a pattern.

16)

A. Incorrect. Decomposing numbers is not a visual representation. Further, first-grade students are primarily working with simple

one-digit subtraction problems, so decomposing numbers would not be helpful.

B. Correct. Students can use a number line to illustrate jumps backward to subtract.

C. Incorrect. Arrays are most helpful for multiplication problems.

D. Incorrect. Fact families are not necessarily a visual representation.

17)

A. Incorrect. A ruler is too small to measure the classroom.

B. Incorrect. A yardstick is in US customary units, not metric units.

C. Correct. A meter stick uses metric units and is an appropriately sized tool to use to measure the classroom.

D. Incorrect. A tape measure would be an appropriately sized tool. However, inches are a US customary unit, not part of the metric system.

18)

C. Correct. This is appropriate in that students should know defining and non-defining attributes of shapes. The other choices are too advanced.

19)

A. Incorrect. Baking a cake involves numerous chemical changes as the ingredients interact.

B. Correct. Boiling water is an example of a physical change; the other choices are examples of chemical changes.

C. Incorrect. Burning wood is a chemical change as the wood cannot be changed back to its previous state.

D. Rust on a bike is also a chemical change as the bike cannot be returned to its previous rust-free state.

20)

B.   **Correct.** The shape of the jigsaw puzzle pieces can be used to teach students about perimeter. The other choices focus on three-dimensional shapes.

21)

A.   Incorrect. Juan added the numerators and added the denominators.

B.   Incorrect. Reggie inverted the wrong fraction.

C.   **Correct.** Madison multiplied $\frac{5}{6}$ by the reciprocal of $\frac{2}{3}$ and simplified the result.

D.   Incorrect. Amir turned the problem into an addition problem.

22)

A.   **Correct.** This activity teaches students to associate one object (a toy) to one number.

B.   Incorrect. This activity relates to pattern matching.

C.   Incorrect. This activity reinforces number matching.

D.   Incorrect. This activity relates to learning colors, not mathematical concepts.

23)

A.   **Correct.** Miguel started with $10 and did not receive his allowance: 10 + 0 = 10. This scenario describes the additive property of identity.

24)

A.   Incorrect. Students do not need to know how to decompose numbers when counting money.

B.   Incorrect. Subitizing—identifying the number of objects by sight—is not a skill needed to count money.

C.   Incorrect. Student may need division to complete more complex

calculations involving money, but they will not use it to count money.

D.   **Correct.** Knowledge of skip counting will help children count the different denominations of money by their value (e.g., nickels are skip counted in fives).

25)

A.   **Correct.** Skip counting involves rote memorization of numeric words in the proper order.

B.   Incorrect. Writing of numbers is a follow-up activity.

C.   Incorrect. Pattern matching involves categorizing objects in an environment.

D.   Incorrect. Sorting objects is not a component of skip counting.

26)

A.   Incorrect. Rounding does not involve finding the largest number.

B.   **Correct.** An understanding of place value will lead students to write the number 863.

C.   Incorrect. The problem does not present a number that can be decomposed.

D.   Incorrect. Subitizing does not involve comparing numbers.

27)

A.   Incorrect. Calculators are used at a later stage with older children.

B.   Incorrect. The number line can be used as an extension following basic introduction to addition.

C.   **Correct.** Manipulatives are the best tools to teach children about basic addition.

D.   Incorrect. Written equations are introduced after children have an understanding of addition.

28)

D. **Correct.** This is not a fact family for 23 − 10 = 13. It involves multiplication.

29)

A. **Correct.** A large fraction can be simplified by finding an equivalent fraction.

30)

A. Incorrect. This is an incorrect way to interpret this fraction.

B. **Correct.** $\frac{14}{3}$ can be decomposed to four wholes and a fractional part of $\frac{2}{3}$.

C. Incorrect. This is an incorrect way to interpret this fraction.

D. Incorrect. This is the reciprocal of the original fraction.

31)

A. Incorrect. Although the expressions are equal, the addends are different.

B. **Correct.** The commutative property states that the order of the numbers in an addition or multiplication equation does not matter.

C. Incorrect. Although the expressions are equal, the factors are different.

D. Incorrect. The two expressions are not equal.

32)

A. Incorrect. Julie left out the needed parentheses.

B. Incorrect. Samuel added $2 rather than multiplying.

C. **Correct.** LaShawn's equation correctly applies the distributive property. The total number of children is contained within the parentheses. Since each hotdog costs $2, that total is multiplied by 2.

D. Incorrect. Omar multiplied 6 and 9, but he should have added them.

33)

B. **Correct.** The commutative property states that the order of the numbers in an equation does not matter.

34)

A. **Correct.** Calculating tax is an activity that is too advanced for second-grade students.

B. Incorrect. Explaining the way price tags list cost is a good way to teach children about money.

C. Incorrect. Encouraging children to find an item based on its cost shows them how prices are listed in real life.

D. Incorrect. Using play money is a fun activity to learn about money.

35)

A. Incorrect. This is true: the hands on analog clocks are much easier for students to manipulate than the buttons on a digital clock.

B. **Correct.** Unlike a digital clock, an analog clock can only be used to show twelve hours. This is not an advantage to using an analog clock.

C. Incorrect. This is true: the movement of the hands helps students understand the passage of time.

D. Incorrect. This is true: each number on an analog clock represents five minutes.

36)

D. **Correct.** Since color is a physical characteristic, it is a qualitative observation. The other choices are all numeric, or quantitative, qualities.

37)

A. Incorrect. Showing change over time is best done on a line plot.

B. Incorrect. Comparing percentages is done on a pie chart.

C.   Incorrect. Showing the relationship between two continuous data sets is done on a line plot.

D.   Correct. Comparing the number of items in different categories is done on a bar graph.

38)

A.   Correct. This student is struggling with one-to-one correspondence, or the ability to count and say each object as the object is pointed to or touched.

B.   Incorrect. The student might use counting bears to skip count, but his issue is jumping ahead as he counts, so he needs to work to meet the objective for one-to-one correspondence.

C.   Incorrect. The student could also use counting bears alongside other objects to sort, but since he is jumping ahead as he counts, he is struggling with one-to-one correspondence.

D.   Incorrect. The student could use counting bears (perhaps of different sizes and colors) to practice patterning and sequencing. However, since he is described as counting ahead, he is struggling to meet the objective of one-to-one correspondence.

39)

A.   Incorrect. An abacus would help students develop number sense and an understanding of addition and subtraction, but it would not be the best tool to help with subitizing.

B.   Incorrect. Multiplication tiles help students develop number sense and other math skills but not subitizing.

C.   Correct. Dot pattern flash cards help students subitize, or instantly recognize quantities of objects. This is the best tool to help students practice this skill.

D.   Incorrect. This would help students practice addition facts, not subitizing.

40)

A.   Correct. Students appear to not know which unit is in the tens place, so Miss Wyatt should reteach place value.

B.   Incorrect. Students are doing well with addition and subtraction since they are getting the correct answer prior to rounding. It seems they need a review of which unit is in the tens place to enable them to round up or down as needed.

C.   Incorrect. Presumably students already have some understanding of whole numbers, as they are solving word problems.

D.   Incorrect. Students are not being asked to compose numbers. They are being asked to round to the nearest tens place.

41)

A.   Incorrect. If Maria had been asked to compose a number, the teacher would have asked her to make four, not count out two and two.

B.   Correct. As Maria counts out 2 + 2 with objects, she is using one-to-one correspondence.

C.   Incorrect. Maria is adding quantities together; she is not necessarily demonstrating that quantities go unchanged when rearranged.

D.   Incorrect. Subitizing is recognizing a quantity without counting each individual item.

42)

A.   Correct. A structural adaptation is the way an animal looks, or the body parts or physical features it has in order to survive.

B.   Incorrect. When an animal sprays or shoots a toxin, it is a behavioral adaptation. A behavioral adaptation is the way an animal behaves or acts or what an animal does to survive.

C.   Incorrect. When an animal does something to gather food, it is a behavioral adaptation.

D.   Incorrect. A bird must migrate in the winter in order to survive; this is a behavioral adaptation.

43)

A.   Correct. The students would be able to understand the different seasons. The different seasons are basic and developmentally appropriate for kindergarteners.

B.   Incorrect. Some study of the general ideas of globes and maps would be appropriate, but not the shifting of continents and landforms.

C.   Incorrect. Studying rocks would be appropriate, but not how they are formed geologically.

D.   Incorrect. Ozone depletion is far too advanced for a kindergarten class.

44)

A.   Incorrect. Kangaroos live in an arid desert.

B.   Incorrect. Sloths live in a tropical forest.

C.   Incorrect. Dolphins live in the ocean.

D.   Correct. Deer live in a temperate forest.

45)

A.   Incorrect. Drawing such models would be too advanced for three-year-old students.

B.   Correct. Sorting objects or pictures into different categories is a great activity during which three-year-old students can apply their learning of the states of matter.

C.   Incorrect. Writing about the states of matter would be too advanced for three-year-old students.

D.   Incorrect. Making a root beer float is a fun activity; however, it is not the best activity for prekindergarten students to do independently.

46)

A.   Incorrect. Students might see the different states of matter, but that is not the purpose of the activity.

B.   Incorrect. The students are not learning about habitats in this activity.

C.   Correct. Students are seeing the ability of objects to float in fresh and salt water, which can be used to explain density. Objects will float more readily in the salt water because salt water is denser than tap water.

D.   Incorrect. While the students are learning about experiments, this is not the main purpose of the activity.

47)

A.   Incorrect. The students are incorporating what they know about physical properties, but that is not the main purpose of the activity. Physical properties are how something looks, feels, smells, tastes, or sounds.

B.   Incorrect. The students are incorporating what they know about physical change, but that is not the main purpose of the activity. Physical change is when an object goes from one state to another, such as solid to liquid.

C.   Incorrect. The experiment is not teaching the students about density, which describes how much an object weighs relating to its size.

D.   Correct. The experiment is showing students how a liquid can dissolve an object. Some liquids create a reaction that makes the candy cane dissolve more quickly than others.

48)

A.   Incorrect. The students will be learning basic features about clouds; they will not learn the names of the different types of clouds.

B.   Incorrect. The students will be learning basic features about clouds. They will not learn the names of the different types of clouds, and they will be unable to write the names of the clouds at this stage of development.

C.   Incorrect. The students will be learning basic features about clouds. They will not learn the names of the different types of clouds and might have trouble completing this activity independently.

D.   **Correct.** Allowing these very young students to learn about clouds with shaving cream is a great activity because it allows the students to explore clouds through sensory play.

49)

A.   **Correct.** Humidity is the amount of water vapor in the atmosphere.

B.   Incorrect. The air that surrounds the earth is called the atmosphere.

C.   Incorrect. Temperature is a way to measure heat or cold.

D.   Incorrect. Precipitation is sleet, rain, snow, or hail that falls from the sky and reaches the ground.

50)

A.   **Correct.** A barometer measures air pressure.

B.   Incorrect. A wind vane measures wind direction.

C.   Incorrect. An anemometer measures wind speed.

D.   Incorrect. A thermometer measures the air's temperature.

51)

A.   Incorrect. The main focus of this activity is not to develop vocabulary since the students should have already learned the relevant vocabulary.

B.   Incorrect. The students are not classifying objects.

C.   Incorrect. The teacher never asked students to make a hypothesis prior to their dissection.

D.   **Correct.** The students are making observations as they are dissecting the owl pellets and discovering what they contain.

52)

A.   Incorrect. Zooplankton are tiny animals that are consumers.

B.   **Correct.** Grass is an example of a producer, which is an organism that is able to produce its own food from inorganic substances. The other choices are consumers.

C.   Incorrect. Fish are consumers

D.   Incorrect. Grasshoppers are consumers.

53)

A.   **Correct.** This is a great way to introduce the concept of the five senses. Students can explore first and then learn what the five senses are.

B.   Incorrect. Reading a story is a helpful way to introduce the five senses, but a hands-on experience would be better.

C.   Incorrect. Having students explore in a center is an excellent activity to extend their learning. However, it is not the best way to introduce a new concept, and students might not make the connection between their discoveries and the five senses.

D.   Incorrect. Having the students explore the five senses first and then read a story is a better way for students to learn the concept.

54)

A.   Incorrect. This might be a great alternative if the students cannot physically plant something, but it is not the best way for the students to learn through a hands-on project.

B.   Correct. This is a hands-on lesson that allows the students to see how a plant grows and record their observations.

C.   Incorrect. The students should be able to draw and label the parts of a plant, but this is not the best hands-on activity.

D.   Incorrect. If the students listen to a story, then plant something, it would be a great activity. However, the students are not able to do a hands-on activity, so it is not the best approach for students to learn the life cycle of a plant.

55)

A.   Incorrect. Writing a report would be a better activity for older students.

B.   Incorrect. Reading a book is a good way for students to learn; however, a sorting worksheet is not the best option for second-grade students in this context.

C.   Correct. Having the students create a simple machine is a great way to extend a student's understanding and is developmentally appropriate.

D.   Incorrect. An automobile is a complex, not a simple, machine.

56)

A.   Incorrect. Erosion occurs when small rocks or soil are moved to a new location by wind or water.

B.   Correct. Weathering takes place when rocks are broken down into smaller pieces by the effects of weather.

C.   Incorrect. Earthquakes are the shaking, rolling, or sudden shock of the earth's surface. Earthquakes change the appearance of the earth's surface dramatically, not gradually, so weathering is the better answer choice.

D.   Incorrect. Deposition drops rock and sediment into new places to create landforms.

57)

B.   Correct. The sun's gravity holds all the planets in place. The other choices are not true of the sun.

58)

A.   Incorrect. A book is opaque; it lets no light pass through.

B.   Incorrect. A glass of water is transparent; it lets all light pass through.

C.   Correct. A t-shirt is translucent; it lets some light pass through.

D.   Incorrect. A car window is transparent; it lets all light pass through.

59)

A.   Correct. Sand and water is an example of a mixture. A mixture is any time two or more different objects or materials are mixed but not combined chemically.

B.   Incorrect. The combination of salt and water is an example of a solution—a mixture where one substance is dissolved in another.

C.   Incorrect. Combining sugar and water is also an example of a solution, which is a mixture where one substance is dissolved in another.

D.   Incorrect. Amalgam is an example of a solid solution in which mercury and gold are combined.

60)

A. Incorrect. Kinetic energy is energy that is working.

B. Incorrect. Thermal energy is heat energy. A heater is an example of thermal energy.

C. Incorrect. Mechanical energy is energy of moving parts, like a fan.

D. Correct. Potential energy is energy that is stored and waiting to work.

61)

A. Incorrect. An island is land that is surrounded by water on all sides.

B. Incorrect. A sand dune is created from the deposition of sand.

C. Incorrect. A delta is created from the deposition of sediment at the mouth of a river.

D. Correct. A canyon is created from the erosion of sediment by moving water.

62)

A. Correct. Stratus clouds are often gray.

B. Incorrect. Cumulonimbus clouds are big and tall.

C. Incorrect. Cirrus clouds are high in the sky.

D. Incorrect. Cumulus clouds are puffy.

63)

A. Incorrect. Lecture and recall are not developmentally appropriate for a first-grade class studying constellations.

B. Correct. Having the students build constellations is an appropriate activity for first graders.

C. Incorrect. This activity is too advanced for first-grade students. Most of the students are still learning to read and could have trouble matching pictures of constellations to facts.

D. Incorrect. Watching a video is a great way for students to see constellations, but it is not the best activity for first-grade students. This age group needs a lot of hands-on activities.

64)

A. Incorrect. Stretching is aimed at increasing flexibility and speed.

B. Incorrect. This activity is primarily aimed at developing balance.

C. Correct. Jumping jacks are nonstop aerobic activity aimed at improving cardiovascular fitness and endurance.

D. Incorrect. Shooting a basketball might involve coordination but not necessarily cardiovascular fitness and endurance.

65)

A. Incorrect. Spatial awareness pertains to a body's place in physical space and where it can move.

B. Correct. Being able to catch something thrown is part of fundamental motor skills.

C. Incorrect. Body awareness refers to exploring the body's full capabilities.

D. Incorrect. Self-care skills refer to feeding oneself, dressing, and so on.

66)

A. Incorrect. Hopping in place is a locomotor skill since students are moving through space.

B. Incorrect. This jumping activity is also a locomotor skill.

C. Incorrect. Focusing on breathing in this way is a non-locomotor skill, but it would be very challenging for prekindergarten students.

D. Correct. Stretching is a non-locomotor skill because students are not moving through space and because it can be done easily even in the limited space of the classroom.

67)

A. **Correct.** Galloping is sliding in a forward and upward motion with one foot in front of the other.

B. Incorrect. Skipping is similar to hopping but with forward momentum.

C. Incorrect. Hopping happens one foot at a time.

D. Incorrect. Pivoting is using one foot as a base from which to turn the rest of the body.

68)

A. Incorrect. Excusing the student from activities will not help the student build cardiovascular fitness.

B. **Correct.** Here, the FITT principle is used. It should guide each student's fitness plan.

C. Incorrect. Most third-grade students will already have established some body awareness in their ability to know their body's capabilities.

D. Incorrect. Motor skills are not necessarily related to endurance or cardiovascular fitness.

69)

A. **Correct.** Brushing teeth is an important and developmentally appropriate topic for a kindergarten class.

B. Incorrect. Most kindergartners do not use deodorant.

C. Incorrect. It would be quite hard to effectively demonstrate applying hair conditioner in the classroom.

D. Incorrect. Trimming nails is a somewhat advanced skill and would also be hard to demonstrate effectively in the classroom.

70)

A. Incorrect. Secondary colors are made by mixing equal parts of primary colors. In this case, unequal parts are mixed.

B. **Correct.** Tertiary colors are made by mixing one primary color with half the saturation of a second primary color.

C. Incorrect. Complementary colors are colors that appear opposite each other on the color wheel.

D. Incorrect. While red and blue are primary colors, this activity is more concerned with mixing them to create a tertiary color.

71)

A. Incorrect. Having Mila complete a different activity would likely make her feel excluded.

B. **Correct.** Giving Mila a different tool is a modification that will allow her to participate and feel successful.

C. Incorrect. Instructing Mila to finger paint significantly changes the activity and will not necessarily help her develop the fine motor skills she needs to use a paintbrush skillfully.

D. Incorrect. Likely all of the paintings will be abstract in kindergarten.

72)

A. Incorrect. Timbre refers to the quality of sounds among different instruments.

B. Incorrect. Pitch is the highness or lowness of sound.

C. **Correct.** Rhythm refers to the tempo or time pattern in music. Egg shakers can be used to help students shake the eggs in the same rhythm as the music.

D. Incorrect. Tone refers to the quality and frequency of a sound as compared to itself.

73)

A. Incorrect. Observational notes might provide some data, but the pieces that children create are also important records of their progress.

B. **Correct.** Portfolios create an excellent way for teachers to track student progress over time in visual arts, as artifacts will likely reflect increasing proficiency.

C. Incorrect. Art should be assessed over time, not in one summative assessment at the end of the year or unit.

D. Incorrect. An oral assessment will likely not provide any useful data on student progress.

74)

A. Incorrect. Secondary colors are made by mixing two primary colors together.

B. Incorrect. The students are examining color combinations, not art.

C. Incorrect. Some colors may provide contrast to one another, but this is likely not the lesson's aim.

D. **Correct.** Colors opposite one another on the color wheel are complementary colors that look good together.

75)

C. **Correct.** This is an appropriate activity for a prekindergarten class. The other activities are too advanced.

Follow the link below to take your second GACE Early Childhood practice test and to access other online study resources:

www.cirrustestprep.com/gace-early-childhood-education-online-resources

Made in the USA
Columbia, SC
18 May 2023

16988218R00150